English Journey

Jubilee Edition

English Journey

J. B. PRIESTLEY

Jubilee Edition
With Eighty Illustrations

UNIVERSITY OF CHICAGO PRESS

University of Chicago Press, Chicago 60637
William Heinemann Limited, London W1X 9PA

Printed in Great Britain by
BAS Printers Limited, Over Wallop, Hampshire

92 91 90 89 88 87 86 85 84   1 2 3 4 5

LCN 83-40619
ISBN 0-226-68212-9

To JANE

who has shared so much of this England with me,

and to THOMAS

whose England this is, for better or worse,

with the author's love.

Publisher's Note

This book was first published in March 1934, recording a journey made by the author through England in 1933. It had a vast influence on public opinion, paving the way, amongst other developments, for the Mass Observation movement of the later 'thirties, and ultimately for Mr. Priestley's memorable radio 'Postscripts' during the Second World War. One immediate consequence of its publication was to send several brilliant young photographers to Lancashire and the North of England to make sociological records of scenes that the fashionable photographers had hitherto ignored.

ENGLISH JOURNEY has continued to be in demand through the years, and although it has now acquired a certain 'period' interest many of the author's observations are as apt and valid today as they were fifty years ago.

In publishing a Jubilee edition it was decided to illustrate the book with a series of eighty photographs, all of them dating from the nineteen-thirties. They not only represent outstanding work by such original artists as Bill Brandt, Humphrey Spender, Edwin Smith and Reece Winstone, but they also show scenes in towns like Coventry and Southampton before they were wiped out by enemy action, of cities such as Birmingham whose centres were totally altered after the War, and areas in the Black Country and the North which have been transformed by vast slum clearances since Mr. Priestley made his journey.

At the author's suggestion a few minor cuts in the original edition have been made by his friend, John Hadfield, who has also been responsible for gathering the illustrations and designing the book.

The frontispiece, by an unknown photographer, is of Six-Foot Road, Netherton, Dudley, c. 1930. It was demolished in 1956.

Contents

Chapter 1 To Southampton *Page* 9

2 To Bristol 23

3 To the Cotswolds 39

4 To Coventry 55

5 To Birmingham 64

6 To the Black Country 85

7 To Leicester and Nottingham 91

8 To the West Riding 117

9 To the Potteries 160

10 To Liverpool and Manchester 177

11 To Blackpool and Blackburn 198

12 To the Tyne 218

13 To East Durham 244

14 To Lincoln and Norfolk 262

15 To the End 295

Notes on the Illustrations 312

Index 318

THE GREAT WEST ROAD, 1933   *Topical Press*

To Southampton

[1]

I will begin, I said, where a man might well first land, at Southampton. There was a motor coach going to Southampton—there seems to be a motor coach going anywhere in this island—and I caught it. I caught it with the minimum of clothes, a portable typewriter, the usual paraphernalia of pipes, note-books, rubbers, paper fasteners, razor blades, pencils, Muirhead's *Blue Guide to England*, Stamp and Beaver's *Geographic and Economic Survey*, and, for reading in bed, the tiny thin paper edition of the *Oxford Book of English Prose*. This was the first motor coach I had ever travelled in, and I was astonished at its speed and comfort. I never wish to go any faster. And as for comfort, I doubt if even the most expensive private motors—those gigantic, three-thousand-pound machines—are as determinedly and ruthlessly comfortable as these new motor coaches. They are voluptuous, sybaritic, of doubtful morality. This is how the ancient Persian monarchs would have travelled, had they known the trick of it. If I favoured violent revolution, the sudden overthrowing and destruction of a sneering favoured class, I should be bitterly opposed to the wide use of these vehicles. They offer luxury to all but the most poverty-stricken. They have annihilated the old distinction between rich and poor travellers. No longer can the wealthy go splashing past in their private conveyances, driving the humble pedestrian against the wall, leaving him to shake his fist and curse the proud pampered crew. The children of these fist-shakers now go thundering by in their own huge coaches and loll in velvet as they go. Perhaps it is significant that you get the same sort of over-done comfort, the same sinking away into a deep sea of plush, in the vast new picture theatres. If the proletariat has money in its pocket now, it can lead the life of a satrap. And it does. It is the decaying landed country folk, with their rattling old cars, their draughty country houses, their antique bathrooms and cold tubs, who are the Spartans of our time. But who and where are our Athenians? Perhaps this journey will tell me.

After the familiar muddle of West London, the Great West Road looked very odd. Being new, it did not look English. We might have suddenly rolled into California. Or, for that matter, into one of the main avenues of the old exhibitions, like the Franco-British Exhibition of my boyhood. It was the line of new factories on each side that suggested the exhibition, for years in the West Riding have fixed for ever my idea of what a proper factory looks like: a grim blackened rectangle with a tall chimney at one corner. These decorative little buildings, all glass and concrete and chromium plate, seem to my barbaric mind to be merely playing at being factories. You could go up to any one of the charming little fellows, I feel, and safely order an ice-cream or select a few picture postcards. But as for industry, real industry with double entry and bills of lading, I cannot believe them capable of it. That is my private view. Actually, I know, they are tangible evidence, most cunningly arranged to take the eye, to prove that the new industries have moved south. They also prove that there are new enterprises to move south. You notice them decorating all the western borders of London. At night they look as exciting as Blackpool. But while these new industries look so much prettier than the old, which I remember only too well, they also look far less substantial. Potato crisps, scent, tooth pastes, bathing costumes, fire extinguishers; those are the concerns behind these pleasing façades; and they seem to belong to an England of little luxury trades, the England of Shaw's *Apple Cart*. But if we could all get a living out of them, what a pleasanter country this would be, like a permanent exhibition ground, all glass and chromium plate and nice painted signs and coloured lights. I feel there's a catch in it somewhere. Perhaps I am on my way, at a good fifty miles an hour, to find that catch.

Just before we went through Camberley I made an acquaintance in the coach. I was lighting my pipe when a man who had been sitting on the seat across the gangway came over and begged for a light. Actually he had matches of his own in his pocket, for I noticed him using them afterwards; what he wanted was talk. He had kept silent all the way from London and could bear it no longer. He was a thinnish fellow, somewhere in his forties, and he had a sharp nose, a neat moustache, rimless eyeglasses, and one of those enormous foreheads, roomy enough for an Einstein, that so often do not seem to mean anything. The rimless eyeglasses gave him that very keen look which also often means nothing; and at first he suggested those men who are drawn or photographed for advertisements of American Insurance companies. He looked capable of rationalising huge muddled industries. It was a face with which you could have rescued the cotton trade in Lancashire. But, as so often happens, the man behind the face was quite different. He was neither strong nor silent, but a very ordinary human being, one of us, uncertain, weakish, garrulous, always vaguely hoping that a miracle would be worked for him. Like so many men in business, he was at heart a pure romantic. The type has always been

THE FACTORY FACE OF THE 'THIRTIES, 1933 *Herbert Felton*

with us, and more or less fantastic specimens of it have found their way into literature as Micawber or Mr. Polly. He was the kind of man who comes into a few hundred pounds in his early twenties, begins to lose money steadily, but contrives to marry another few hundreds, then begins to lose them, but is rescued by the death of an aunt who leaves him another few hundreds. Throughout his career he is enthusiastic and energetic, seems knowledgeable and sensible, and yet he never makes anything pay but watches his capital dwindle. Even in these days, there are still a few thousand like him up and down the country, especially in growing towns and new suburbs. At the end of one venture they begin another passionate search 'for an opening'. This man was looking for an opening now.

'That's no good,' he told me, after a minute or two's talk about nothing.

'What isn't?'

'Tea rooms.' And he pointed at one that we were passing. 'I tried it once. The wife was keen. In Kent. Good position too, on a main road. We'd everything very nice, very nice indeed. We called it the Chaucer Pilgrims—you know, Chaucer. Old style—Tudor, you know—black beams and everything. Couldn't make it pay. I wouldn't have bothered, but the wife was keen. If you ask me what let us down, I'd say it was the slump in America. It was on the road to Canterbury, you see—Chaucer Pilgrims—but we weren't getting the American tourists. I wouldn't touch a tea room again, not if you gave me one.'

Camberley came and went. He stared at it, no doubt looking for an inspiration.

'That's a wonderful business if you can get the right opening,' he said wistfully. 'Hairdressing. Ladies, of course. Nothing in men's. But a good ladies' hairdressing—with permanent waves, manicure, and everything—it's a gold mine. Even now it is, if you're in the right place—a gold mine. I could have picked one up two years ago, but I didn't know the business and thought I'd better not risk it.'

'Yes,' I said. 'I suppose now that women have cut most of their hair off—to save time and trouble, as they say—they have to spend hours at the hairdressers every week.'

'That's right. And they won't miss either, any of them. They've all got something to spend on their hair. I believe they're better spenders than men are these days. Are you going to Southampton?' I said 'Yes.'

'So am I. Just to look round. I've heard of one or two possibilities there. Should be a good opening in Southampton. What do you think of electric light fittings?'

I told him that I knew nothing about them.

'Friend of mine swears by them. All this electricity they're putting in, d'you see? Villages, all over, they're getting electric light. And they've got to have fittings, haven't they? Good profit on them too, they tell me. I'm going to look into that. Run wireless too as a side-line.'

'Do you understand wireless sets?'

'Oh yes. I was in the wireless trade one time, about six years ago, in Birmingham. But mind you, wireless then and wireless now—oh!' and he gave a short laugh—'different thing altogether. Look at the developments. Look at the way prices have come down and quality's gone up. Wonderful business now, in the right district. If I could find a good shop in a growing good-class neighbourhood, I wouldn't mind going back to the wireless trade to-morrow, with gramophones and records as a side-line. The wife's against it, but she doesn't understand how things have changed in that business. What do you think of this pipe?'

I had already noticed his pipe, which was of an odd and peculiarly hideous shape and gave off a reek of hot varnish. 'Looks a bit unusual,' I told him, cautiously.

'New patent,' he announced, rather proudly. 'Just on the market. As a matter of fact, it isn't really on the market yet. Bowl's not made of wood at all. Made of a new composition, and it all takes to pieces, d'you see? Every time you've had a smoke, you change one of the pieces—they give you spares— and so it's always nice and clean and cool. Clever, isn't it?'

I admitted that it was ingenious. Actually, it looked and smelt horrible and dirty and hot: a loathsome little pipe.

'Clever, and very cheap. I could get a big agency for this to-morrow. I've only to say the word. But I thought I'd give it a good trial first. I started last night, and the wife said she didn't like the smell of it, but I told her it was new and would have to be broken in a bit. Know Newcastle at all?'

'I've not been in Newcastle since the war.'

'Fine town, Newcastle, though it's not doing the business it did. I was up there three years ago. Cheap raincoats. Looked a wonderful opening. Last man had had a stroke and died quite suddenly. Good position and big stock. Had a bright idea there—you know how you get these ideas, come in a flash. At least mine do. I might be sitting at home, reading the evening paper, you know, or listening to the wireless, and suddenly I've got the idea. Like that— bang! The wife laughs at me. Well, I'd two good big windows up there in Newcastle, and I had one of 'em fitted up with a water-sprinkling device and put three dummies—father, mother and the kiddie—in the window all in raincoats and waterproof hats. Attracted a lot of attention. There was a bit about it in one of the local papers—making a joke of it, you know, but of course I didn't mind that. Well, for three months I did very well, never done better. Splendid turnover. Got rid of the old stock and was ordering a lot of new stuff—all cheap lines but value for money. And then suddenly it went like that—like *that*. Nobody in Newcastle seemed to want a raincoat. It wasn't very fine weather or anything. There hadn't been a sudden slump in the local trade. No reason at all. But the business suddenly went as flat as a pancake. Nobody wanted a raincoat. How do you explain that?'

I couldn't explain it.

'It's always been a mystery to me,' he continued ruefully. 'But that's business all over. You can't force people to buy raincoats, can you? It's all right talking about salesmanship—I believe in salesmanship—but if you can't get 'em inside the shop, what are you to do? Advertising won't do it. Window displays won't do it. Clearance sales won't do it. Do you know anything about the cheap fur trade?'

I didn't, except that it was generally supposed to be in the hands of Jews.

'Friend of mine, who's in the wholesale winter coat trade, says there are some wonderful openings in the cheap fur business if you only know the ropes. But I don't know the ropes. It's the same with shoes. You'd think anybody could be in the shoe trade, wouldn't you? But they can't. It's very tricky.'

We stared at the charred patches of heath we were passing. I began to think about my Kitchener's Army days, in 1914, when we used to advance and take cover, a very uncomfortable prickly cover it was too, on these very heaths. I don't know what my companion was thinking about; perhaps the trickiness of the shoe trade. But he was thinking hard about something, and he puffed away so vigorously at his foul patent pipe that he stank like a paint factory on fire. Together we rolled along over the pleasant empty countryside of Hampshire, which, once your eyes have left the road, has a timeless quality. The Saxons, wandering over their Wessex, must have seen much of what we saw that morning. The landscape might have been designed to impress upon returning travellers, on the boat train out of Southampton, that they were indeed back in England again. I said as much to my acquaintance, who agreed and then added that he had often wondered if South Africa was any good.

'Not that I want to leave England, you know,' he continued. 'But you can't help noticing all these advertisements. We all know what trade's like here. There isn't the money about there was—and it's no good pretending there is—and it's chiefly the big concerns that are getting it nowadays. And I could tell you something about some of those big concerns. I've had experience of

them. Cut you out—clean out—like *that*. No mercy, no mercy at all. I *know*.
And I wouldn't work for one of 'em—I've had my chances too—and I don't
care what they offered me. There's a lot to be said yet for a man running
his own business in his own way. Personal service. It's simply a matter of
finding the right opening, that's all.'

I don't know what he saw in Winchester, what Pisgah sight revealed itself,
but I do know that he suddenly decided to break his journey there and catch
a later bus to Southampton. I never saw him in Southampton, and perhaps
he never arrived there. Perhaps he is still in Winchester, with the right opening,
or back in London, or up in Newcastle with a fresh supply of raincoats, or
trying the wireless trade again in Birmingham. But wherever he is and whatever
he is doing, I am sure he is looking keen, sensible and energetic, and steadily
losing money, and beginning to think about another opening. Sooner or later,
he will find himself in the bankruptcy court; and after that his wife, who will
have managed to save a little from the wreck, will run a boarding house, where
he will dream about openings over the boots in the back basement.

I had left him there, a decayed but not hopeless figure of an optimist, before
the coach had seen the last of Winchester, which, all along the High Street,
had looked very busy and bright and more new than old. I never pass through
these smaller Cathedral cities, on a fine day, without imagining I could spend
a few happy years there, and never find myself compelled to spend a morning
and afternoon in one without wishing the day was over and I was moving
on. We climbed again into the country so empty and lovely, so apparently
incapable of earning its exquisite living, that people ought to pay just to have
a glimpse of it, as one of the few last luxuries in the world for the ranging
eye. And now the road straightened and made inexorably for Southampton.

[2]

I had been to Southampton before, many times, but always to or from a
ship. The last time I sailed for France during the war was from there, in 1918,
when half a dozen of us found ourselves the only English officers in a tall
crazy American ship bursting with doughboys, whose bands played ragtime
on the top deck. Since then I had sailed for the Mediterranean and New York
from Southampton, and had arrived there from Quebec. But it had no existence in my mind as a real town, where you could buy and sell and bring
up children; it existed only as a muddle of railway sidings, level crossings,
customs houses and dock sheds: something to have done with as soon as possible. The place I rolled into down the London Road was quite different, a

real town. This is a fine approach, very gradual and artful in its progression from country to town. You are still staring at the pleasant Hampshire country-side when you notice that it is beginning to put itself into some order, and then the next minute you find that it is Southampton Common and that the townsfolk can be seen walking there; and, the minute after, the road is cutting between West Park and East Park, and on either side the smaller children of absent pursers and chief stewards are running from sunlight to shadow, and there are pretty frocks glimmering among the trees; and now, in another minute, the town itself is all around you, offering you hats and hams and acro-bats at the Palace Theatre. It would be impossible to say where Southampton itself really began, though I should like to believe that the true boundary is that corner of East Park where there is a memorial to the lost engineers of the *Titanic*, to prove that there are dangerous trades here too. Further down, the London Road changes into Above Bar Street; then the traffic swirls about the Bar Gate itself, which is very old but has so many newly-painted armorial decorations that it looks as gaudy as the proscenium of a toy theatre; and then once through or round Bar Gate, you are in High Street. Another quarter of a mile or so, at the bottom of High Street, you must go carefully; otherwise you may lose England altogether and find yourself looking at the Woolworth building or table mountain. One could write a story of a man who walked down this long straight street, on a dark winter's day, and kept on and on until at last he saw that he had walked into a panelled smoke room, where he settled down for a pipe, only to discover soon that Southampton had quietly moved away from him and that his smoke room was plunging about in the Channel. For, you see, you can catch the *Berengaria* or the *Empress of Britain* at the end of this High Street.

This one road, which begins as if it had been lately cut out of the New Forest and ends in the shadow of the great liners, is Southampton's main artery. You walk up and down it, shop in it, eat and drink and entertain your-self in it. We hear a good deal about Southampton's comparative prosperity; and this main street is the symbol of it. When I looked at it, the sun was shining and the day was as crisp as a good biscuit. The pavement on each side was crowded with neat smiling people, mostly women, and the mile of shops seemed to be doing a brisk trade. Here at last was a town that had not fallen under the evil spell of our times. Its figures, I knew, were up, not down. It had recently opened the largest graving dock in the world, big enough for

HIGH STREET, SOUTHAMPTON, c.1933   *Photographer Unknown*

the monsters that have as yet only been planned and not built. The town was making money. At first I felt like a man who had walked into a fairy tale of commerce. The people who jostled me did not look as if they had just stepped out of an earthly paradise; there was no Utopian bloom upon them; but nevertheless they all seemed well-fed, decently clothed, cheerful, almost gay. The sun beamed upon them, and so did I. Their long street was very pleasant. I noticed that it shared the taste of Fleet Street and the Strand for wine bars. I went into one of these; and it had a surprising succession of Ye Olde panelled rooms, in one of which I drank a shilling glass of moderate sherry. Though it was only the middle of the day, there were plenty of people drinking in these rooms, though few of them were taking wine. There was a fair sprinkling of respectable women, mostly having a glass with their men. I had lunch in another of these places, and the food was reasonably good.

When you are nearing the end of this street, with Southampton water sparkling in the middle distance, you notice that the shops dwindle and become more nautical, until at last you can turn in at almost any doorway and buy a flag or two, charts, ropes and all the yachtsman's paraphernalia. I turned to the right at the bottom and followed the old town wall. There I saw the memorial marking the place from which the Pilgrim Fathers first set sail, in a ship about as big as the cocktail bar in which some of their descendants now sail back to this shore. I saw the old West Gate, through which the troops marched when they were on their way to Crécy and Agincourt. In short, I saw historical Southampton whose population, that day, consisted of a few old men, sitting and spitting. I soon left it to return to the Town Quay. Here the present was dominating the past, just as these giant liners themselves were dominating not only the sheds and wharves that tried to enclose them but the very town itself. Against a porcelain sky of palest blue, their black-and-crimson and buff funnels were enormous, dazzling. It did one's heart good to see them. I longed to go aboard. They seemed to me, as indeed they have always seemed to me, these giant liners, to be things not only of formidable size and power but also of real beauty, genuine creations of man the artist. Let us have our laugh, as I have had mine both in and out of print, at the nonsense inside them, their *Louis Quinze* drawing-rooms and Tudor smoke-rooms, but let us also ask ourselves what we have built to compare with them in majesty since the medieval cathedrals. Their very names have an epic roll, suggesting an ample and noble life. (If another Gibbon describes our decline and fall, what play he will make with these names!) Unlike the cathedrals, these ships have not been built to glorify God; they are of this world; they were not even designed to glorify the commonwealth but only to earn divi-

THE AQUITANIA OFF THE ROYAL PIER, 1935 *Ruskin Graphics*

dends; but having arrived at a time when men have a passion—perhaps the purest of their passions—for machines, these ships are creations of power and beauty. I am glad to have lived in their age, to have seen them grow in strength and comeliness, these strange towns of painted steel that glide up to and away from this other town of motionless brick. They would not be here at all, nor would the High Street look so prosperous nor all the women dart in and out of the shops, if there were not an odd narrowing of the English Channel between Portland Bill and Cap de la Hague near Cherbourg. It is this bottling of the water that gives Southampton its double high tides, practically three hours of high water, which is time and tide enough for the manœuvring of these enormous ships. They ought to empty a glass now and again in the wine bars to Portland Bill and Cap de la Hague.

THE MAURETANIA'S LAST VOYAGE, 1934   *Ruskin Graphics*

But the steward I met in High Street did not share my enthusiasm for the great liners. He was in mufti, standing at a bus stop, grinning at me. I knew the face. 'We've met somewhere, haven't we?' I said.

'Yes, sir. Smoke-room steward on the——' And he mentioned a ship I had travelled in. I remembered him at once then, a very smart, obliging youngster, a pattern of smoke-room stewards; and smoke-room stewards, you must remember, are generally the pick of the steward kind. He was on leave, it seemed. But there was a chance, just a chance, of a shore job that he discussed eagerly.

Remembering the snug atmosphere of the smoke-room, the jokes and friendliness, the tips we had given him, I told him that I was surprised he should bother about this job ashore. Wouldn't he be better off at sea?

'Not me.' He was very emphatic. 'I've had enough of it. A steward's life's no good.'

'Not even a smoke-room steward's, in a first-class ship?'

'No, sir. I dare say it looks all right from the passengers' point of view, but it's a rotten life. Bad quarters. Working all hours. And no proper food and nowhere to eat it. If you're a steward, you've got to stand up and snatch a bite when you can. Even with the tips, it's no good. I've had enough of it, sir, I can tell you.' He went on to talk very bitterly about the conditions of service in these ships, with their *Louis Quinze* drawing-rooms and Tudor smoke-rooms. Their owners would do well to make a few less elaborate plans for our comfort and a few more for the comfort of their staffs. It is not pleasant, to say the least of it, to remember that the poor devil who is waiting upon you may have been washed out of his quarters the night before and has not sat down to a decent square meal since the voyage began. Most of us would be willing to give up a little space in the ship and a few items from the menu if we knew that the people waiting upon us were being allowed to lead a civilised life. 'Well, if it's as bad as that,' I concluded, 'I hope you get your shore job.'

His face brightened at once. 'I hope I shall, sir. I'm going to have a good try.'

It may have been that steward or it may simply have been further acquaintance with the town and a sharper vision, but whatever it was, the fact remains that Southampton did not look quite so bright and prosperous when I came to look at it again. Once off that long High Street, I found myself in some very poor quarters. The only thing to be said in favour of these squalid little side-streets of Southampton is that they did not seem as devastatingly dismal as the slums of the big industrial towns. There was still a sea sparkle in these people's lives. They were noisy and cheerful, not crushed. Perhaps it is impossible to live a completely colourless existence on the edge of such blue water. There were brown faces to be seen. The air in the narrow brick gullies, thickened as it was by the reek of over-crowded rooms, bad food, piles of old junk, had not entirely lost its salt and savour. Gramophones were scratching out those tunes concocted by Polish Jews fifteen storeys above Broadway. Cheap food and drink and tobacco and gossip were to be had; the men could guffaw round the entrance to the old junk yards; the girls knew how to powder their noses; the children could always wander to the water's edge. It might have been much worse. But it could be—and at first I thought it was—much better.

The small shop flourishes in this quarter, as it does in all such quarters. Even after you have given yourself the strongest dose of individualistic sentiment, it is hard to look at these small shops with anything but disgust or to find good reasons why they should not be promptly abolished. They are slovenly, dirty, and inefficient. They only spoil the goods they offer for sale, especially if those goods, as they usually are, happen to be food-stuffs. One large clean shed, a decent warehouse, would be better than these pitiful establishments with their fly-blown windows and dark reeking interiors and blowsy proprietors. And these remarks, of course, do not apply merely to Southampton but to every town of any size in this kingdom, where, down every poor side-street, you will find these dirty little shops.

Even the long High Street, now busier than ever, did not look so grand and prosperous after a second and closer examination. The money that was being freely spent was going mostly on cheap things, and there seemed no end of threepenny and sixpenny stores and the brittle spoils of Czecho-Slovakia and Japan. I talked to one shopkeeper, not in the threepenny and sixpenny line, and he said that business was not as good as it was supposed to be and that for the last three years, in spite of comforting statistics, money had been tight in the town. But then he did not know other and less fortunate towns, and was perhaps in the wrong line of business, for he admitted that he had depended a good deal formerly on the custom of people of some means living outside the town, and these people, as we all know, cannot spend as they once could, being the victims of a very quiet and slow but quite efficient revolution. I noticed too quite a number of blatant cut-price shops, their windows crammed with goods, mostly inferior and dubious, and loud with placards so exclamatory that they made one's eyes jump. From one to the other, cut-price to sixpenny store, went the wives of distant third-engineers and stewards, spending their grass-widowhood in cheap shopping before going to the pictures.

Not a bad town, this. That fine approach and the heartening spread of common and park; the long bright bustling street; the genial air of the place, with its hint of a festive Jack's-in-port life; the gigantic new graving dock: here was a town that had not let the universal depression master it and that was contriving to enjoy its unique situation, between forest and heath and deep blue water, a lovely bay window upon the wide world. It was not bad at all. Given a job to do and a bit of money in our pockets, you and I could live there and be reasonably happy. They are rather proud of themselves down there, for though that deep water outside, with London only a couple of hours away, was simply so many fathoms of luck for them, they have had the wit and energy to make the commercial most of it. Nevertheless, Southampton has not been able, just as their very owners have not been able, to live up to those great ships it harbours. They are the soul of the place. Their coming and going light it up. The citizens are knowledgeable about and proud of these visiting giants, but they have not succeeded yet in building a town or planning a life worthy of such majestic company. What a Southampton that would be!

CHAPTER TWO

To Bristol

[1]

There are two or three motor coaches that run between Southampton and Bristol; and I chose the earliest one. But I was before my proper time and the bus was very late, so I had a long hour to spend at the starting place, a large yard with waiting rooms, booking offices, a refreshment bar and a newspaper kiosk in it. All this was new to me. I had never realised before how highly organised this road travel is, with its inspectors and enquiry offices and waiting-rooms and what not.

The most conspicuous object in my neighbourhood, as I sat there, tea in hand, waiting, was a gigantic map poster in blue and green that said, 'You are now only 12 miles from the lovely Isle of Wight'; and so I spent some time thinking about the island, on which I had stayed for the first time that very summer. Certainly a lovely island, at least when you leave the Cowes, Osborne, Ryde area, which has little charm. The rest of it is the English south country at its best in miniature—Lilliputian downs and all—with an island quality added, a lightening of the horizon in whichever direction you look. Tennyson is its poet, Victoria its queen. The little towns on the east coast still seem a little dazed by the passing of the Prince Consort. That Victoria herself should have died there is so right and proper that you could use the fact in a teleological argument. The island population—excluding the summer yachtsmen and all the deck hands and stewards and other men who have to play with yachtsmen—consists chiefly of an amiable and slow peasantry not to be hustled but said to be good in a crisis, and elderly gentlefolk tucked away in charming old manor houses or converted farms. These gentlefolk watch the decay of their incomes and keep open house for young male relatives on leave from the East. If you wish to study the English countryside of the more genteel novelists, you can have it neatly arranged and spread out for you on the Isle of Wight. There is not much bad poverty there, even now, and a good deal of homely enchantment: the Downs high above the Channel; the sub-tropical Undercliff, well away from Farringford but very close to the landscape of Tennyson's poetry; sunsets and the Needles; rooks in the old elms; and the spring, bright with daffodils, that has always haunted English poetry. There are also Cowes and its Royal Yacht Squadron and the less exclusive Parkhurst Prison, to which, if ever I am given a few years, I hope to be condemned. The island would make a superb national park of the American kind, but then I suppose that if you compare it with the real England of our time, it already is one.

Smoothly, powerfully, the coach went down a long straight road that led from Southampton to Romsey. I had not troubled to have a look at it before; quite rightly too, for this road, with its new lock-up shops, its picture theatres, its red-brick little villas, might have been anywhere: it is the standard new suburban road of our time, and there are hundreds of them everywhere, all alike. Moreover, they only differ in a few minor details from a few thousand such roads in the United States, where the same tooth-pastes and soaps and gramophone records are being sold, the very same films are being shown. The sun was now breaking through a fine spread of cloud. Over on the left, mile after mile, went the line of the New Forest, and its sombre crest of foliage had the same solid, heavily shadowed look that you notice in the work of the old landscape artists. It lay there, half in gloom, half smiling, this forest I had never entered, like a piece of time that no clock of ours could tick away; very close to my imagination, which had played with its name and associations, but as remote from the ordinary busy self of me as the jungles of the Orinoco. I believe most of my pleasure in looking at a countryside comes from its more vague associations. Clamping the past on to the present, turning history and art into exact topography, makes no appeal to me; I do not care where the battle was fought or the queen slept, nor out of what window the poet looked; but a landscape rich in these vague associations—some of them without a name—gives me a deep pleasure, and I could cry out at the lovely thickness of life, as different now from ordinary existence as plum pudding is from porridge. It is the absence of these associations, these troupes of pleasant ghosts from history and art, that makes a new country in which nothing has happened, like some great tracts in America, appear so empty and melancholy, so that a man has to get drunk there to feel his imagination stirring and rising. The Hampshire whose gilded fields and deep blue shadows were all about me that morning had this power of quickening and enriching the mind with associations, now reminding me of the old landscape artists, now of Hazlitt, now of the medieval England that must have looked like this through county after county; and so the journey turned into a most pleasant and satisfying experience. It reached its peak when we crossed the spur of the Downs, looked into the distant vale and saw, far away in the autumnal haze, the spire of Salisbury Cathedral like a pointed finger, faintly luminous. This is a noble

SALISBURY CATHEDRAL, 1935 *A. F. Kersting*

view of England, and Constable himself could not have contrived a better light for it. You have before you a Shakespearean landscape, with shreds of Arden all about, glimpses of parks of Navarre, and Illyrian distances. So we descended upon Salisbury. Once in the city, I could not see the cathedral; but I saw the Labour Exchange and, outside it, as pitiful a little crowd of unemployed as ever I have seen. No building cathedrals for them, poor devils: they would think themselves lucky if they were given a job helping to build rabbit-hutches. We ran into the big square, into which coaches like ours were coming from all quarters, and anchored off Oatmeal Row.

Here we changed passengers. The new lot consisted of five mousy women of various ages, of the kind who never speak but in whispers when travelling and always compress their lips and narrow their shoulders as if to make themselves as small as possible and so elude some imaginary pursuer. I now sat on the front seat and looked at the road through a window as big as the plate-glass front of most small shops. But the enchanted landscape had gone; here was ordinary countryside. We passed a brigade of artillery on the march, and I noticed once again that none but a few older officers and warrant officers had war medals, though it still seems only yesterday that I walked through the demobilisation camp. How innocent the field guns looked, all polished and muzzled and in their best clothes! As we passed gun after gun, and dozens of foolish red young faces, I was asking myself when these things would next fire at an enemy and for what fantastic cause. At the next town we made a halt of quarter of an hour or so, 'for refreshments' the conductor told us, as he almost bundled us into the little coffee shop where we had stopped. The five mousy women crept in, whispering, and I followed them, and we were all served with coffee and biscuits by a young woman whose face was far too spotty. Another passenger joined us, a woman in black who looked as if she were busy hating somebody, and we started again.

We nosed our way ponderously through Bradford-on-Avon, which is very different from the other Bradford where I was born and nurtured. Bradford-on-Avon is all quaint, whereas in the other Bradford there is nothing quaint, except perhaps the entire population. Then Bath spread herself before us, like a beautiful dowager giving a reception. Bath, like Edinburgh, has the rare trick of surprising you all over again. You know very well it is like that, yet somehow your memory must have diminished the wonder of it, for there it is, taking your breath away again. There is a further mystery about Bath— which Edinburgh does not share—for I have never been able to imagine who lives in those rows and rows of houses really intended for Sheridan and Jane Austen characters. They all seem to be occupied; life is busy behind those perfect façades; but who are the people, where do they come from, what do they do? As our stay there, on this journey, only lasted for about two minutes, I did nothing to settle this question, though my mind played with it again as we rolled away from these Palladian heights. After that the road was a muddle until at last we came to a place where trams and coasting steamers seemed in danger of a collision and I realised that I had been deposited neatly in the very heart of Bristol.

[2]

At one period during the war I was stationed in South Devon and when I got week-end leave from there I usually travelled at night to save time, and so it happened that I frequently found myself changing trains at Temple Meads Station, Bristol, always in the middle of the night and always with a two or three hours wait. Sometimes I hung about the station or wandered out into the dismal streets outside, and sometimes I went across to the hotel across the way and tipped the night porter so that I could have a nap in front of the dying fire in the smoke-room. And this is all I ever knew of Bristol: Temple Meads Station in the dark hours, Victoria Street, and the deserted smoke-room of the hotel there. The natural result was that I carried with me for years a vague impression that this was an unpleasant city, and until I made this journey I never troubled to go and see what it really was like. Now I know better, a great deal better. Bristol is a fine city. They are right to be proud of it.

There is another reason why Bristol surprised me so pleasantly. I was brought up in a city that was largely the product of nineteenth-century industrialism, a place lacking age, traditions, history; and nearly every other town I saw in my youth was of the same kind: groups of factories and warehouses with quarters for working people, more comfortable quarters for cashiers and managers, a few big houses for the manufacturers and merchants themselves, and the usual sprinkling of shops and pubs, with a town hall and an art gallery in sham Gothic and wondering what on earth they were doing there. That was the sort of provincial city I knew as a child, with the result that it remains my idea of a provincial city. I was not surprised when I found that places like Oxford and Cambridge or York and Canterbury were quite different, because I expected them to be different, knowing that they were all famous museum pieces of township; but I was surprised—and still am surprised— when I find that a provincial city, comparable in size and wealth to the ones I used to know best, is not a dirty nineteenth-century hotch-potch, not merely an extended factory and warehouse, but a real city with a charm and a dignity of its own. I never get over it. I stand gaping, like the barbarian I am. Bristol is not as big as Leeds, for example, but it looks ten times the place that Leeds looks. It is a genuine city, an ancient metropolis. And as you walk about in it, you can wonder and admire. The place has an air.

I knew about Bristol, of course. I knew that the Cabots had set sail from there to discover the mainland of America; that Hakluyt had been one of its deans and Burke one of its Members; that it has associations with all manner of literary folk: Chatterton, Savage, Hannah More, Coleridge and

THE CHATTERTON MEMORIAL, 1935   *Reece Winstone*

Southey. I knew it was a famous old port—or, if you like, a vintage port—and had its cathedral and its St. Mary Redcliffe Church and its Merchant Venturers' Hall and other fine old buildings. I knew that for centuries it had been the great city of the West. I knew all this and a lot more guidebook stuff. Nevertheless, knowing too that Bristol is an English provincial city, somewhere in size between Leeds and Bradford, I had expected to see the usual vast dingy dormitory. What I did see, of course, was something that would not have astonished me at all in Germany, France or Italy, and ought not to have astonished me in England: I saw a real old city, an ancient capital in miniature.

What is especially admirable about Bristol is that it is both old and alive, and not one of your museum pieces, living on tourists and the sale of bogus antiques. It can show you all the crypts and gables and half-timbering you want to see; offers you fantastic little old thoroughfares like Mary-Le-Port Street and Narrow Wine Street; has a fine display of the antique, the historical, the picturesque; but yet has not gone 'quaint' but is a real lively bustling city, earning its living and spending its own money. The Merchant Venturers have vanished; the slave trade, on whose evil proceeds this city flourished once, is now only a reminder of man's cruelty to man; the port, depending on the shallow twisting Avon, is only a shadow of its old self; but Bristol lives on, indeed arrives at a new prosperity, by selling us Gold Flake and Fry's chocolate and soap and clothes and a hundred other things. And the smoke from a million Gold Flakes solidifies into a new Gothic Tower for the university; and the chocolate melts away only to leave behind it all the fine big shops down Park Street, the pleasant villas out at Clifton, and an occasional glass of Harvey's Bristol Milk for nearly everybody. The docks may not be what they were (though I believe you can still hop off a tram here and straightway board a ship for America), but then Bristol has now pushed itself out to sea at Avonmouth, where the bananas come pouring in from the West Indies. It was the original West Indian trade that made this city a great port, and even now its more important industries—such as the manufacture of tobacco and chocolate—have still a West Indian flavour.

Indeed, all the older part of the city, that grand muddle not far from the docks, still has a West Indian flavour. Even the pubs down there have a suggestion of Spanish Main richness about them. There seems to be more colour than usual in the bottles stacked behind the bar; and here are counters on which guineas have gone ringing. This appears, on a first impression, to be a city after my own heart. True, it is having everything in its favour: the weather is glorious, very bright but not too warm; I believe I have just staved off a cold and so am ready to be pleased (a few sneezes and the whole place might look black); I am at the beginning of my journey, not tired yet, still sanguine. Possibly, for these reasons, I may be flattering the place. But, I repeat, so far it seems a city after my own heart. It is old but not living in the past; it is lively and picturesque and comparatively prosperous; the place has dignity, and the people, I imagine, high spirits. It has kept its civic pride. It rejoices in a spirit of independence, of which more later. It may be the fine weather or my own optimism, but my impression of the folk here—especially the working folk—is that the females are above the average in good looks and that the men are above the average in breadth of shoulder and stockiness. There is plenty of good old West Country blood about. You could pick a splendid revue chorus or a sound rugger side out of the nearest street. I feel that the working people here enjoy life. There is not that terrible dreariness which is probably the chief curse of our provincial towns. The people are hearty creatures who like to eat and drink well, and enjoy themselves. In all that old central part of the city, whose pavements seem to be crowded all day, there is a robust life. The pubs open early; the shops are doing a brisk trade; the wireless and gramophone establishments are grinding out tunes; food of the cheaper sort seems plentiful; and the crowded scene has a hearty eighteenth-century quality, reminding you that this is Fielding's country. This would be no place to pick a quarrel in; anybody who asked for trouble, I imagine, could soon have it from these red-faced, thick-set fellows. (But the only creature I saw in bad trouble was a rat in a cage, at the entrance to an alley in Old Market Street, where a small crowd gathered to see a big fat publican bring his terrier to chase the rat down the alley, which it did to everybody's satisfaction. I should not be surprised to learn that there was still cock-fighting somewhere at the end of one of these alleys.) In the old days Bristol was notoriously tough, with a reputation not unlike that of Chicago in our time. And during the Reform riots of 1831 the Bristol crowd burned down the Mansion House, custom-house, the bishop's palace, and the gaol.

If I had stayed longer, I might have seen some trouble, for one night I attended a fascist meeting near the docks. Neither of the black-shirted young men, who looked as fierce as Mussolini himself, could make himself heard for more than half a minute at a time, because most of the audience consisted of communists, who stolidly sang their dreary hymn, the *International*. (I think it was that. I heard something about 'the rising of the masses'. And why is it always 'the masses'? Who cares about masses? I wouldn't raise a finger for 'the masses'. Men, women and children—but not masses.) And a fat little Italian kept lifting his yellow moonface, to scream derisively. 'There are only

BRISTOL SHERRY IN TRANSIT, 1938   *Reece Winstone*

four of us here to-night,' the black-shirt roared, white with anger, 'but you wait until Thursday. Just try it on Thursday, that's all.' And I am still wondering whether they did try it on Thursday. I do not imagine, however, that either of these parties will make many converts in Bristol.

There may be far less unemployed here than in the cities further north, but there are plenty of men out of work, and one morning I attended a meeting of them in a Labour Hall in Old Market Street. The room itself, a fair-sized one used for dancing, was almost full. The men were mostly sturdy, decent-looking fellows, who did more smoking than applauding and cheering. The speaker was an oldish man with very short legs, a droll face and an enormous voice. He was obviously a practised orator and his only fault was a certain irritating trick he had of slowing up and over-emphasising unimportant remarks, probably when he was giving himself time to think. At first his audience seemed apathetic, but then he roared, 'The class to which I belong—and you belong—*our* class—is nothing but a set of damnable silly donkeys.' Everybody laughed and cheered at this. The hall woke up. He then went on to describe some local and rather pettifogging attempts at welfare work, which included a scheme for giving out tiny strips of land and for breeding—to his great joy and ours, of all things—rabbits. He made very artful play with this. 'Radicalism,' he bellowed. 'Talk about radicalism. I remember it fifty years ago—yes, fifty years ago. And they were real Radicals then. Jesse Collings. He wanted three acres for every man—and a cow. Now they've cut the three acres down to inches, and instead of a cow—it's rabbits.' At which we all roared. 'Good old Jack,' some of them shouted. Evidently the speaker was known, respected and delighted in—as a character, and if there is one thing that the English people love it is a character, who, once he has thoroughly established himself as such, may abuse them as much as he pleases. And this the little man did, with all the power of his admirable lungs. Twenty-five thousand members of his class, here in the city, could attend a football match and pay their shilling each, but when collectors and collections were wanted for the Unemployed Fund there were only a few helpers and shillings to hand. 'I've got no hope for the present generation of the working class,' the indomitable little old Radical shouted at us, 'no hope at all. They're a lot of silly mugs. We can only work now for the boys and girls who'll make the next generation. And I hope to God they'll have more sense than the fathers that begot 'em.' And he grinned at us sardonically through the smoke, then suddenly sat down. He was all right. The large Irishman who followed, and who spoke in a soft whine, was such an anti-climax that half the meeting departed and I went out with it.

The middle class here seems to model itself on the civic motto, Virtue and Industry. They are fortunately situated, for the city's prosperity never collapsed and its benefactors—particularly the Wills family—have never locked away their purses; they have Clifton to live in; and they have Clifton Down and the grand gorge of the Avon to play about on or in, with such places as Bath, Wells, Cheddar, Chepstow, only round the corner. No wonder they all live on in Bristol. If they were suddenly dumped into Newcastle or Manchester, life would immediately begin to look a much grimmer business. They are naturally a conservative lot, apt to frown upon an occasional bit of frankness in the local Little Theatre, which was relying upon *Mary Rose* when I visited it. Everybody told me that these Bristol people 'take a lot of knowing', though I seem to have heard as much said of all the people in every provincial city or rural district. But it may be truer here than elsewhere. What is certainly true—and admirable—is that these people are proud of their city, and do not see it, as some north-country people see their towns, as a place in which to make money and then to sneak out of, thinly disguised as English gentlemen. The Bristol merchant remains a Bristol merchant, and for this he may be forgiven a few stupidities and timidities.

Here is one example of the Bristol spirit in action. A few years ago the city had four newspapers: two morning and two evening papers, all owned and run by local people. This would not do. Bristol became one of the campaigning grounds of the warring national newspaper syndicates. After various manœuvres and parleys and armistices, Bristol found that it had lost its chief morning paper and both its old local evening papers. But the Press magnates, who felt that everything had been satisfactorily arranged, forgot that the spirit of independence still exists in Bristol. The city saw no reason why it should be treated as if it were somebody else's back-garden. The citizens decided to start an evening paper of their own. Various prominent persons canvassed for promises of capital, formed a body of directors, and then appealed to the local public for necessary money. All manner of sums, from the workman's pound upwards, were immediately subscribed; the staff, chiefly composed of men who had been thrown out of work by the recent manœuvres and parleys, was soon found; and a new evening paper was launched and at once reached a circulation of seventy thousand. I understand that it has not yet touched its reserve capital and has already paid a dividend to its shareholders and a bonus to its staff. This is more than a piece of local history. It is really of national significance. It is good that the old and honoured city should defend itself so sturdily. It is good that Bristol should have its own paper, a genuine local enterprise, and not merely some mass publication thrown at it like a bone to a dog. It is good that there should be a real independent provincial Press. People ought to read national newspapers, but they also ought to read local newspapers too, for England, even now, is still the country of local government, local politics, strong local interest, and only the newspaper written and published in the immediate neighbourhood can deal adequately with such government, politics, and interests. It is important that people should read that Alderman Smith said this and Councillor Robinson did that. It is important that they should realise what is happening in their own district. Gossip and chatter from Fleet Street is a poor substitute for such information about and criticism of local affairs. Any decent provincial newspaper ought to be able to give its reader a much saner picture of the world than the popular national papers, with their hysteria and stunts and comic antics. Where an evening paper is concerned, publication must of course be always local, but nevertheless there is a wide difference between an evening paper published in the provinces by a Fleet Street combine and an evening paper produced by the people of the district. The citizens of Bristol had the sense to see this and the necessary enterprise to act for themselves. For this I honour them. The inhabitants of provincial towns, these days, are losing the habit of acting for themselves; they grumble but do nothing. They should go to Bristol.

Among the best examples of people actuated by this civic pride are the members of the Wills family, who might easily—following the example of most provincial magnates—have taken themselves and their gigantic fortunes out of the city. But they have chosen to remain in Bristol, the city that has made their fortunes for them, and they have spent enormous sums of money in the place, especially on the University. I spent an afternoon going round the largest of the Wills factories, which is not far from the centre of the city and is an immense building. The inspection was so thorough that I feel I know all about the manufacture of cigarettes and pipe tobacco now. What surprised me was the amount of work still done by hand. There were of course the most ingenious machines in almost every department. One of them has only to be fed regularly with cut tobacco, mile-long reels of paper, printing ink, and paste, to turn out cigarettes by the million. They can even make cigars, of the cheaper kind, by machinery, though it looks hard enough to put a cigar together using a pair of skilled hands. But the human element remains, and indeed dominates the work of the factory. Girls perform most of the tasks, whether feeding the machines or doing some completely manual act, such as stripping the leaf; and this great factory is a warren of girls, in green, pink, brown, blue overalls, every department having a different colour. Some of the tasks are desperately monotonous, requiring the ceaseless performance of one quick little action.

THE SWAN INN, MARY-LE-PORT STREET, 1934 *Reece Winstone*

But the girls on such work do not do it continuously: they change jobs every hour, sometimes even every half-hour. They begin work at half-past seven and end at five, with twenty minutes for breakfast and an hour for dinner. There is a dining-room that will seat 2,400 persons, and the menu, which I examined, is varied and cheap. There is not only a medical clinic in the factory but also a dental one. The welfare work is obviously excellent. Wages are comparatively good; and there are bonus and superannuation schemes. I have no affection for the tobacco combine, and I rarely smoke its products, but I must say that the Wills family have proved themselves admirable large-scale employers. They have made their millions, but not out of anybody's tears and blood. Their policy as employers has been humane and wise, with the result that their people work well and never wish to leave, even at times when other jobs are more plentiful than they are at present. There must be always something inhuman, terrifying, about mass production on a really gigantic scale to a person like myself, who only catches sight of it now and then and hardly understands what is happening among the strange machines (though I found myself having quite an affectionate regard for the busy little gadget that slipped two tiny playing cards into every packet of cigarettes: it always looked as if it were going to be too late, but it never was); but I must confess that the final impression that this giant factory left with me was not one of miserable slavery, not even of grim soulless industry. But perhaps the kindly influence of Nicotina herself was at work here. If we must have factories of this size—and it seems we must—then let them be run in this fashion, no matter whether it is the lucky Wills family or the State itself that does the running.

Not many travellers for pleasure find their way to Bristol, which is a pity, for there is much to be seen in the city and it makes an excellent centre for excursions. My hotel was filled, and almost full up, with commercial travellers of the more prosperous sort, and I spent my last evening there exchanging beer and whisky with three of them in the lounge. Through them I learned how things were progressing in the fancy goods, scent and fur-coat trades respectively. They were good fellows and when the hour was late and we had given and consumed several orders, they took leave of the more sordid views of commerce, with which they had entertained me earlier, and developed the wide vision and the noble sentiment of typical commercial Englishmen who are drinking late. 'Trust,' said one of them, the one who preferred bottled beer. 'That's what you've got to have in our business. Trust. Must have trust. My people give me a certain territory, send me out to represent them, and they've got to trust me and I've got to trust them. The same with my customers.' The other two agreed at once. 'I don't want to unload stuff on them

THE CITY DOCKS, BRISTOL, 1935   *Reece Winstone*

they can't sell,' he continued, a righteous man. 'I'm not like these fellows who go round once—and only once—and unload anything on 'em. No. Must have trust. They've got to trust me. Trust's everything in our business.' We told him he was quite right. 'But,' said another, the one who had had such a marvellous piece of ham for breakfast at Malvern the previous morning, 'that's not all. In my opinion, you've got to have sentiment too. Yes, sentiment. Business is nothing without sentiment. I don't like doing a piece of business unless there's sentiment in it.' Which was to me a new and somewhat mysterious view, though it was certainly expressed at the appropriate time. It is odd that though there must be excellent material in the lives of these commercial travellers—and why shouldn't I mention my own trade for once?—you rarely meet them in novels or plays or films. Yet they would make admirable subjects for all three, for there must be frequent drama in both their business and their personal lives; their minds must be always clouded with hope and fear; and like so many of the most satisfying figures of fiction, whether Ulysses or Don Quixote, Tom Jones or Mr. Pickwick, they are for ever on the move. If ever

COLLEGE GREEN, BRISTOL, 1934 *Reece Winstone*

I write another *picaresque* tale, I will fill it with commercial travellers. But my chambermaid at this hotel had no opinion of them. She got two pounds a month for looking after fifteen rooms, and did not average ten shillings a week in tips, and so regretted that she had ever left the seaside hydro and its invalids for commercial gentlemen in the city. But even she thought the city a fine place.

And that, I conclude, is the note of Bristol; if you like, its signature tune. A civic pride, a vocal civic pride, so rare in these days as to be almost startling. Like most places with a mixed trade, it has been fortunate in avoiding the lower levels of depression. A sharper bout of insolvency and unemployment might possibly have changed its tune. As it is, it remains a city that was strong yesterday and still lively to-day, a city that is old, dignified, historic, and at the same time a bustling modern commercial centre. And its citizens, even if they pile up huge fortunes, do not desert it, and are prepared to stake something on its independence. I was glad to have seen it, if only because it helped to restore my faith in provincial England; and as my taxi gave me a last glimpse of pleasant College Green and that odd conglomeration of ships and trams near Broad Quay and Bristol Bridge, I hoped soon to renew the acquaintance.

CHAPTER THREE

To the Cotswolds

[1]

Then I thought I would make for the Cotswolds, the most English and the least spoiled of all our countrysides. I went by road to Burford, the Eastern gate of the Cotswolds. It was a day typical of that country: damp and heavy, the sky a sagging grey roof, with shreds and tatters of mist among the copses and in the low meadows. You seemed to catch glimpses of a mysterious hollow land. You saw hardly a soul between the villages. Burford, an old acquaintance, looked rather more self-conscious than it used to do, as if too many people had been buying picture postcards in it. The hotel was almost full; most of the guests were middle-aged women—English and comfortably off— and the kind who are for ever writing letters in a corner of the lounge. Having seen my bags deposited in a bedroom carefully decorated and furnished in the very worst taste, I went off in a car to have another look at certain villages that I remembered with particular pleasure. One of them was Bourton-on-the-Water, which has a broad shallow stream running through it and over this stream a number of exquisite old stone bridges. I have long thought of it and talked of it as the most enchanting village in England, but either my memory had been at fault or the place is not what it was, for no longer did it seem the best of its kind anywhere. It is still beautiful, especially when you survey it from one of its delicious bridges, but there are too many poor buildings in it, clean out of the Cotswold tradition, and it is becoming very conscious of itself. I had tea in a studio café, an amusing little high room decorated with antique knick-knacks. Once, I imagine, it had some concern with agriculture or industry; then it was turned into a studio; and now it is a picturesque tea-room: a sequence of some significance. But the tea I had there was excellent. Cheered by it, I explored the valley of the Slaughters.

I thought these two villages, Lower Slaughter and Upper Slaughter, beautiful before, and think them so still. They should be preserved for ever as they are now. A man bringing a single red tile or yard of corrugated iron into these two symphonies of grey stone should be scourged out of the district. I call this stone grey, but the truth is that it has no colour that can be described. Even when the sun is obscured and the light is cold, as it was that evening,

these walls are still faintly warm and luminous, as if they knew the trick of keeping the lost sunlight of centuries glimmering about them. This lovely trick is at the very heart of the Cotswold mystery. It is this, and not the green hills, the noble woods, the perfect flowering of architecture, that makes these villages so notable an enchantment. If it were not for this, they would be beautiful but cold and heavy, for Cotswold weather is often sullen. But not a sunny morning since the Wars of the Roses has passed here without conjuring a little of its golden warmth into these stones. Villages, manor houses, farmsteads, built of such magical material, do not merely keep on existing but live like noble lines of verse, lighting up the mind that perceives them. How long will these two Slaughters remain unspoiled? I am probably hastening their ruin now by writing this. Cursed be the hands that defile them.

After dinner in the hotel, back in Burford, a fellow-guest introduced himself to me. He was an ex-officer of the Regular Army whose first serious novel I had once reviewed and praised heartily. We settled down to talk. He had just returned from taking his boy, an only and adored child, to his public school. This boy wanted to be a farmer, a fact that my acquaintance announced with pleasure and pride. His family, he told me, had been on the land, either as farmers or owners, for eight hundred years. He himself had no land now, had indeed been forced off it, to soldiering and authorship and such-like dubious pursuits, and saw in his boy's decision the satisfactory working of some deep hereditary principle. There was nothing, he declared, like being close to the land. I told him that I was a child of the streets, of the hotch-potch urban and industrial life he despised, and therefore knew little about the land. He was all in favour, he told me, of the peasantry—'a bold peasantry, their country's pride'—and thought its re-establishment would be one cure for our ills. To this I replied, rather lightly, that though the theory always seemed attractive, I found myself mistrusting it because on the few occasions when I had come into contact with peasants I had not greatly liked them; nor did they seem to be much admired by the more eager spirits in the very countries that cherished their peasantries. A peasant on paper, a romantic literary man's peasant, I hinted, was all very well, but always seemed a very different sort of creature from the actual ignorant, stupid, mean peasant of reality. So we wrangled, in a friendly fashion, until it was time for bed. I mention this talk because it seemed to sound a sort of *leitmotif* that was to accompany me throughout this visit to the Cotswolds. Yet my acquaintance,

Opposite: LOWER SLAUGHTER, c.1931   *G. F. Allen*

like me, was merely passing through, there in the hotel only for this one night, and there was no obvious reason why he should have started this topic. But there it was, the *leitmotif*. I have noticed this happening before, and every time it does happen one feels that a pattern has suddenly, momentarily, been imposed on the chaos of encounters and arguments and chatter.

The next morning I went from one entrance to the Cotswolds to another, from the Eastern gate to the Northern, for my destination was Chipping Campden, where these Wolds narrow to a fine edge. The day was just right. There were shifting and broken mists below, and, somewhere above, a strong sun, which meant that the country was never seen in one blank light. It was one of those autumn mornings when every bush glitters with dewy gossamer. One moved mysteriously through a world of wet gold. Nothing had boundaries or real continuity. Roads climbed and vanished into dripping space. A beech copse was the near end of an impenetrable forest. The little valleys were as remote as Avalon. The villages arrived like news from another planet. As we went, we would startle and scatter hosts of little birds, linnets and finches and even goldfinches, which flashed marvellously about us for a second and then were gone before we could really believe they were there. The trees, especially the great elms, still had indigo night tangled in their branches, but they would jump suddenly into sunlight and show us their patches of dead yellow leaves. And sometimes the mist would retreat dramatically from one bit of ground, perhaps an orchard, and we would see a bough bright with ripe apples. We might have been journeying through the England of the poets, a country made out of men's visions. At the end of our road was Chipping Campden, with not a wisp of mist about it, full and fair in the sunlight.

[2]

Chipping Campden has a population of about 1,500, but it is a town and no village. It used to be a very prosperous town, the centre of the Cotswold wool trade and, later, of its silk manufacture. The whole of this region, though it seems now so Arcadian, is actually a depressed industrial area. It was once famous for its textiles. It had the wool, just as it has to-day; it had water power and plenty of soft water for dyeing; it had a good local supply of fuller's earth in the hillsides; and it was not far from the port of Bristol. The Western area of the Cotswolds made broadcloth, which our grandfathers recognised as the best of all clothing fabrics. The other districts had their own specialities. To this day the best blankets come from Witney, just off the eastern edge of the Cotswolds. Even as late as 1801 a map of England showing the density

CHIPPING CAMPDEN, WOOL HALL, c.1940   *E. W. Tattersall*

of population includes this region in its most heavily shaded areas, with an average density of more than a hundred to the square mile. A similar map of modern England shows the bigger part of the region in its most lightly shaded division, with an average density of less than 128 persons to the square mile. There must be a great many districts that actually had far more people living in them in the Middle Ages than they have to-day, though now, when the road is rapidly triumphing over its former conqueror, the railway, many of those districts are beginning to fill up again. It was steam power, with its large-scale plants and reliance upon coal, that packed people together, herding them into hundreds of narrow streets. If there had been a few thick seams of coal between Gloucester, Evesham and Cirencester, the Cotswolds would have been torn up and blackened and built over with brick horrors, and would now be enjoying an industrial depression far worse than anything it knew when steam power arrived to rob it of its ancient trade. As it is, the Cotswolds is singularly remote even from the railway, for only one line finds its way across these hills. It had its depression before the railway came, and no doubt had its painful problems too, with one little mill after another, one merchant after another, going out of business. But all that now is like an old bad dream. And there is Chipping Campden, not at all the important town it was when William Grevel built his house in the High Street, but exquisite in the sunlight, with no tall brick chimneys, no rows of hovels, no crowds of workless men. It went out of business at the right time and so escaped the grand uglification. That it has also escaped the new uglifying processes, which belong to our age, is not an accident. The credit must be given to one or two of its citizens, notably Mr. F. L. Griggs, the artist, who has spent time, energy and money for the last twenty-five years, keeping the place beautiful. Now, after a hard fight, the people themselves are ready to protect their town, which fortunately is still a real little town and not simply a show place and glorified tea establishment for tourists. There is no Ye Olde Chipping Campden nonsense about it.

When you look at the curved wide main street, you feel that such an unusual and exquisite harmony of line and colour in architecture could only have come from one particular period, almost from one particular mind. The secret, however, is that these Cotswold towns and villages and manor houses are the products of a definite tradition. They were not all built at one time. Some buildings are hundreds of years older than their neighbours. But the tradition persisted. Houses were always built of certain material in a certain way. If you told a Cotswold man to build you a house, this is how he built it. He knew—thank God—no other way of building houses. This tradition has lasted until our own time. There are still some old Cotswold masons who work in that tradition and could work in no other. In their hands the stone flowers naturally into those mullions. They can see Cotswold houses already stirring in the very quarries. I say these men still exist, but there are not many of them and they grow old and feeble.

I was introduced to old George, a Cotswold mason. He is in his seventies but still at it. When I met him he was engaged in the almost lost art of drywalling, pulling down some ramshackle old walls and converting their materials into smooth solid ramparts. He was a little man, with a dusty puckered face and an immense upper lip so that he looked like a wise old monkey; and he had spent all his long life among stones. There were bits of stone all over him. He handled the stones about him, some of which he showed to us, at once easily and lovingly, as women handled their babies. He was like a being that had been created out of stone, a quarry gnome. He was a pious man, this old George, and when he was not talking about stone and walls, he talked in a very quiet though evangelical strain about his religious beliefs, which were old and simple. Being a real craftsman, knowing that he could do something better than you or I could do it, he obviously enjoyed his work, which was not so much toil exchanged for so many shillings but the full expression of himself, his sign that he was Old George the mason and still at it. Bad walls, not of his building, were coming down, and good walls were going up. The stones in them fitted squarely and smoothly and were a delight to the eye and a great contentment to the mind, so weary of shoddy and rubbish. I have never done anything in my life so thoroughly and truly as that old mason did his building. If I could write this book, or any other book, as well as he can build walls, honest dry walls, I should be the proudest and happiest man alive. Old George has always been a mason, and his father and grandfather were masons before him; they were all masons, these Georges; they built the whole Cotswolds: men of their hands, men with a trade, craftsmen. I do not know for what pittances they worked, or how narrow and frugal their lives must have been, but I do know that they were not unhappy men; they knew what they could do and they were allowed to do it; they were not taught algebra and chemistry and then flung into a world that did not even want their casual labour; they were not robbed of all the dignity and sweetness of real work; they did not find themselves lost and hopeless in a world that neither they nor anyone else could understand; they did not feel themselves to be tiny cogs in a vast machine that was running down; they had a good trade in their fingers, solid work to do, and when it was done—and there it was, with no mistake about it, ready to outlast whole dynasties—they could take their wages and go home and be content. I am glad I met old George and saw him at work. And if ever we do build Jerusalem in this green and pleasant land, I hope he will be there, doing the dry-walling.

There are some grand old folk in these parts. By the famous old church at Campden are some almshouses, ancient and mellowed. There, sunning himself at his door, I found Old Bennett, well in his eighties and a fine big figure of a man yet. It is no use your suggesting to Old Bennett that Chipping Campden cannot have changed much. He knows better. It has changed a lot, he says grimly. They don't bake their own bread any more there. They used to have three flour mills in the town, but now they have gone. The home-made bread was fine stuff. Old Bennett is not the oldest there. Old Polly is over ninety and can still dance when she has a mind to it. A film company came round and took some shots of these almshouses and their old folk. They wanted Old Polly to dance, but she wouldn't, not, that is, until they'd gone, and then she danced like mad. But they made a great fuss of her, put her in the middle and asked her to say something. This sudden film stardom had the usual results. 'Her wouldn't talk to us for the next two or three weeks,' said Old Bennett grimly. He told us that they had been given for their posing 'a ten-shilling paper', which I suppose is what you may expect from a man who has spent most of a long life among solid metal coins. He does not call them ten-shilling notes, not he: a 'ten-shilling paper', that is his verdict.

I went out one evening to a typical Cotswold farmhouse, whose owner is a large genial fellow. In his parlour, which was like a farmhouse parlour anywhere in this island, he did his bit of grumbling, but when I pressed him, he had to confess that he was not so badly off. He kept sheep on his high ground, raised crops in the valley, and had between sixty and eighty cows. (Though most of his butter came from New Zealand.) He had two grown-up sons with him, and about a dozen men. He objected to the compulsory minimum wages, on the ground that there was a vast difference between a good willing man and a slack one, and while he had no objection to paying a good man more than the minimum, he begrudged paying a poor hand even the minimum. He told me that the Cotswolds he knew best were returning more and more to general farming, except on the hills, where sheep farming was still the rule. The young men were quite glad now to stay on the land and earn their six-and-thirty shillings a week. He got his weather now from the wireless, but added that it did not seem any more accurate than the prophecies of his oldest shepherd, who was very cunning in these matters. When he had given me a whisky and himself a gin, he told me about the old Cotswold games they used to have at Whitsun on the neighbouring hill. One of them was a shin-kicking contest. The competitors, who must have been hardy fellows, placed their hands on each other's shoulders and then, at a signal from the referee, hacked away at each other's shins. And there was cudgel play at these games, up to a fairly late date. Probably Shakespeare walked from Stratford to see them. 'How does your fallow greyhound, sir?' Justice Shallow's cousin Slender asked Master Page; 'I heard he was outrun on Cotsall.' There was mighty sport on Cotsall for centuries. And if there was anything in that way now, my farmer would be the man for it. Once he had had his bit of grumbling, he livened up wonderfully and was the best of company. I told him that he was safer than anybody in the world, these days, for if the worst came to the worst, he and his family could still sit there snugly, a good old roof over their heads, living on their own produce and live-stock. The farm was his own; he was in nobody's debt; the land was there, working for him; and he did not live, like the rest of us, in a world of paper. In the end he was asking me to find a neighbouring manor house to live in. 'You'll like it,' he assured me earnestly. 'They do tell me it's a very pretty bit of country we've got round here.' He spoke as if he had never seen any other countryside but this. And where indeed would he find better country, so long as he did not mind the spells of sullen weather?

I did not look for a manor house for myself, but I visited several charming old houses, in each of which was a Cotswold enthusiast, ready if need be to serve on protection committees and even to spend money in defence of the district's amenities. The odd thing was that not one of these was a Cotswold man. Some of them had come from afar. Thus, one of them was a New Englander. Another was a rich man from Lancashire, who, having once deserted the blackened bricks of Oldham or Burnley, treated his Cotswold village as if it were a collection of precious objects, which indeed it is. With these men, it was not the usual social snobbery that set these wheels of interest and charity in motion. They had all genuinely succumbed to the Cotswold charm. The green hills, the strangely remote little valleys, the luminous old stone, had claimed them for their own. The spell was upon them and would be until they died. When I was there, I heard much talk round the open log fires of haunted woods and spectral appearances in the lanes—and indeed this is a ghostly region—but what fascinated me was the magic that had touched these solid middle-aged men and kept them in thrall. They were lost for ever among these Gloucestershire hills, dream-drowned in these green valleys. Consider how artful the guardian spirits of this region have been. They would not allow it to be drawn into the ugly scramble for quick profits, and so have kept its charm intact, its beauty unravaged; but when they have found it needing money, they have laid their spell upon rich men from the black holes of industry and, by showing them a manor house lacking a tenant, a village wanting a patron, have conjured the money out of them; so that many a prospect here is unspoiled and exquisite because of the muck and sweat of Birmingham and Manchester. There's the real magic for you, and I watched it at work.

Perhaps it was the guardian spirits of the region who lured me into paying that visit on the last day, a visit that still haunts me and retains a certain magical quality of its own. A friend asked me if I cared to see yet another manor house, owned by a very charming but rather eccentric gentleman. The proposal did not excite me, but as I had arranged nothing else, I agreed and off we went. We had to pass through Broadway, now, I suppose, the best-known of all the Cotswold villages. The guardian spirits have left this place to its own de-

SNOWSHILL MANOR (*See page 313*), c.1930   *Photographer Unknown*

vices, and those devices are not very pleasing. In short, Broadway is at Ye Olde game. The morning we passed through, it was loud with bright young people who had just arrived from town and *The Tatler* in gamboge and vermilion sports cars. I noticed that one of Ye Olde Shoppes proudly announced that it had been established in the Nineties. Even the other Broadway, which sends so many visitors here, could do better than that. However, this anything-but-deserted village was soon left behind, and then we crept into one of those green little valleys that at once make you feel so oddly remote, miles and miles from anywhere, clean out of the world. It is easy enough to feel remote in wild mountainous country, but the Cotswolds are not wild and mountainous. Yet you have only to take a turn or two from a main road there, into one of these enchanted little valleys, these misty cups of verdure and grey walls, and you are gone and lost, somewhere at the end of space and dubiously situated even in time, with all four dimensions wrecked behind you. The map may tell you that you are only so many miles from Broadway or Cheltenham, but you do not need the elaborate dubieties of the mathematicians and astronomers to tell you that the map is a mere convention and not the fantastic truth. This, then, was one of these valleys, and one of the best of them, looking as if it had decided to detach itself from the rest of England about the time of the Civil War. The day was brilliant above, but below there was a very faint haze over everything, so that hillsides and trees and walls had that gauzy gleaming look which belongs to the unreality and enchantment of the theatre. In this valley was a hamlet, and old church, and the manor house that was our destination, all of them clustered together in a lovely huddle of ancient tiled roofs. The moment we were inside the gate and could see that manor house, I knew that anything might happen now, that we were trembling on the very edge of common reality, that life might turn into a beautiful daft fairy tale under our very noses.

The house itself had a Gothic craziness. There was no sense, though an infinite antique charm, in its assembled oddity of roofs, gables, windows, doorways. It might have been plucked straight out of one of Hoffmann's tales. You caught glimpses of such houses in the old silent films of the *Ufa* company, when it allowed its producers to be as romantic and symbolical as they pleased. There was a tiny courtyard between the house proper and a large outhouse, which had on its wall a painted wooden knight whose hand was waiting to strike a big bell. In this courtyard were a score or so of white pigeons that rose and fluttered at our approach, so that for a second there seemed to be a blizzard raging. When the last pigeon had gone creaking to the roof, the courtyard and the manor house, the whole valley, sank again into deep quiet. Not a mouse stirred. Round the walls were coats-of-arms and painted inscriptions. Beyond the outhouse were descending squares of garden, where a stream wandered from one clear carp pond to another, slipping past clumps of miniature box, marjoram and rue and thyme, and the shadow of the yews. Olivia and Malvolio would have been at home anywhere in this garden. We could not find its contemporary owner, of whom the gardener at the gate had only the vaguest news. I began to fancy that there was no such person or that at the best he would turn out to be a ghost. And when at last we did meet him, though he spoke and behaved like a very courteous and charming English gentleman of leisure, I could not rid myself of this fancy, which was sustained by the fact that his clothes and general appearance were not the clothes and general appearance of a contemporary person. He was, in fact, one of the last of a famous company, the eccentric English country gentry, the odd and delightful fellows who have lived just as they pleased, who have built Follies, held fantastic beliefs, and laid mad wagers. But why English? Was there not Don Quixote? You could have settled *him* into this house in a jiffy. I half expected to meet him.

The owner then, in the most charming fashion, conducted us over his house. He did not live there, but in the outhouse. The manor itself he now used as a sort of museum. The inside was as crazy as the outside, and as beautiful in its own way. We looked into ancient dim panelled rooms, in which were collections of spinning wheels, sedan chairs, model waggons, weapons, old musical instruments (you ought to have seen the black wooden Serpents), and blazing lacquer from Peking. One room was filled with old costumes, cupboard after cupboard of gowns, crinolines, uniform coats, bonnets, beaver hats, cockades. You could have dressed whole opera companies out of that room. I have never seen such a collection outside a public museum. He then took us over the outhouse, where he had his bachelor living-room and workshop. They looked at a first glance like the early illustrations to *The Old Curiosity Shop*. It is only those Dickens illustrations that can give you any idea of the amazing litter of things in these queer ramshackle rooms. There were tools and implements of every kind, coats-of-arms, skulls, black letter folios, painted saints, colossal tomes of plain song, swords and daggers, wooden platters and I know not what else. Neither in one house nor the other did I catch the smallest glimpse of a modern book or a newspaper or anything else that belongs to our own age. The twentieth century was nowhere in evidence and the nineteenth had only just dawned there.

But the owner no longer spent his time collecting these relics of the past; his hobby now was the construction of a whole miniature old-fashioned seaport; boys' play on a smashing adult scale, defying all common sense but glorious in its absorption in the exquisitely useless. This miniature seaport, which must be on a scale of about an inch to a foot, for most of its houses were about two feet high, has a proper harbour in one of the ponds in the garden. It has its quay, its fleet of ships, its lighthouse, its railway system, with station, sidings and all, its inn, main street and side streets, thatched cottages, and actual living woods, made up of the dwarf trees in the garden. The owner, who has had some architectural training, has designed, built and painted the whole village himself. It is portable, except for the harbour works, and is brought out and erected in the garden in summer and then taken into the house in winter. Its creator has now decided that it should have a castle, and he showed us an excellent preliminary drawing of this imposing building, which will be several feet long and will easily dominate the place. I hope there will be no trouble in the village with the two-inch lord of this castle, for by

SNOWSHILL'S OWNER, c.1930   *Photographer Unknown*

this time the place may have settled down to an easy democratic existence and it may resent this sudden descent into the feudal system. This Lilliputian seaport, which has a name, is still so real in my mind that I could easily write a novel about it. I know that, if I have a chance, I shall have to go there again and see what is happening to it, in the shadow of that castle, above which I shall be able to tower gigantically, like Gulliver himself. And if I have no opportunity of seeing it again, I am glad to have seen it once. It crowned the day for me. Most excursions of this kind, which begin with such promise, offering you some remote valley, some village or house drowned in lost time, so many signposts to what will be supremely odd and romantic, have a bad trick of fizzling out; but not this one, which became curiouser and curiouser until at last, at the other side of the moon, we landed at the seaport that was two feet high, in a harbour where the goldfish, fat fellows of nine inches or so, came glittering in like whales of red gold.

So much for fancifulness and fine writing. But I am here, in a time of stress, to look at the face of England, however blank or bleak that face may chance to appear, and to report truthfully what I see there. I know there is deep distress in the country. I have seen some of it, just had a glimpse of it, already, and I know there is far, far more ahead of me. We need a rational economic system, not altogether removed from austerity. Without such a system, we shall soon perish. All hands must be on deck. My eccentric but charming friend of the fantastic manor house, who lives an antique dream of life supported by an unearned income, cannot possibly be counted as a hand on deck. Would there be any justification for such an existence in any rational economic system? The answer is obviously: none whatever. It would be very easy to dismiss this leisured gentleman and all his toys in a few sentences. But I cannot bring myself to do it. The system, however rational it may be, must somehow be stretched to fit him in, manor house, museum, hotch-potch, toy village and all. I am glad he is at play under those crazy roofs, in that green cup among the hills, and would not have him sent to clerk in the gasworks or draw plans for communal garages. It is not such as he, who bring their own charm and poetic play to life, however withdrawn and eccentric they may be, that I would dub anachronisms and promptly extinguish. After all, he makes no noise, does not lust for power, is no braggart or bully. Moreover, he does not live a herd life, but shows us what we are beginning to need being shown, that is, an original experiment in living. We may not want to live it ourselves (a month in that manor house would be more than enough for me; after that I should be ready for the gasworks or the communal garages), but we are glad to know that such experiments are still being made, that all the eccentrics are not dead and gone. And I suspect that the system that rigidly excludes him will prove to be too narrow for the good life, which would not be good if it banned the mild dreamer and his antique trifles and his toy villages. I know; because that day was a good day; I feel its heartening quality yet; the light it left in my mind was a little dim and Will-o'-the-wispish, but it has since seen me through some dark places.

I dined that night with a friend, a good artist and a Cotswold enthusiast, and we soon fell to arguing when the table had been cleared and our smoke clouded the candlelight. He is a Catholic, a medievalist, a craftsman who would have all men craftsmen, a thorough hater of everything modern. (He has no telephone, of course, but does not scruple to use the one across the way. Detests motor cars, but jumps into one readily enough to show you his beloved Cotswolds.) Living where he does, he has some foundation for his opinions. He has lived in the Cotswolds for thirty years, ever since he ceased to be an art student, and during that time he has watched the decay of the old craftsmen who were educated in their trade and in no other way, men like Old George the mason, men who were not only superb workmen, who would scorn to do a bad job, but also solid lumps of character, with an earthy humour and sagacity about them; and he has seen their places taken by young men who have not a tenth of the skill or the character, who were half-hearted about their work or play, mass children of a machine age. All our labour troubles, he declared, did not come from a quarrel about the distribution of the profits but from a deeper cause, the crushing of the workman's self-respect by mechanical labour in which he could not find himself. He would have everything made by hand again, restore the craftsman and banish the machine, replace the Trade Union by the Guild, with its insistence upon a high standard of workmanship; and if that meant doing without a lot of things, then we must do without them. (He himself had built his own house, and was doing without a great many little comforts and conveniences, presumably because he had not yet been able to have them made by hand.) It was a point of view I could respect and understand. If I had been an artist and craftsman, living as he has done in those Cotswolds, I should have held such views. As it was, of course, I opposed him, pointing out that comely objects in a museum or a rich man's house gave one a very faulty notion of the actual life of the past, when most people had to do without nearly everything and were far less merrie than he appeared to suppose, that machines, rightly used, simply did away with a horrible dead weight of miserable toil and that anyhow a machine was not the bogey thing he seemed to think it but really an elaborate tool, and that our business now was not to sentimentalise the Middle Ages but to take the whole roaring machine-ridden world as it is and make a civilised job of it, using mechanical power when it suited us—and the change-over from steam to electrical power gives us far more freedom—and then our hands (though not mine, God help them!) when the work or our inclination called for them. The machine itself, I said, was not at fault, being merely our dumb slave, but the shoddy, greedy, profit-grabbing, joint-stock-company industrial system we had allowed to dominate us, there was the real villain. We had to civilise it. This could not be done, in his opinion. He disliked all our ways. He asked me to share his contempt for the new urban mob, the products of industrial towns and free education at council schools and cheap books and so on and so forth; but as I consider myself one of these very people, I had to decline. He remembered seeing, some time about the end of the war, a battalion of Sherwood Foresters arrive at some place in Southern Ireland where he was staying, and he said that, compared with the Irish peasants, these city-bred troops looked, and behaved, like a lot of monkeys. To this I replied that I had fought with such troops in the war, and was willing to bet that they had more courage, intelligence, eagerness, chivalry, humour, irony, than any peasants, Irish or otherwise. There came a moment then when it looked as if we were about to quarrel; but we laughed at the right second, drank to the Cotswolds, and parted better friends than ever.

There is not, I imagine, much distress anywhere in this region. The men on the land are not well paid, but they can live on their wages. People looked comfortable there. The children were noticeably in good shape. The towns are without those very squalid patches you often find in country towns. The average standard of life in these parts must be fairly high. It would be interesting to know how much money from outside has been spent in the Cotswolds, partly to preserve the unique charm of their domestic architecture. In no other part of the country do we see so large a tract of the beautiful old England still unspoilt. What will happen to it? At the moment, especially in the Northern half, it is probably in less danger of being spoiled than it has been at any time during these past twenty years, thanks to the ceaseless vigilance of certain persons, mostly settlers from outside. But one never knows when danger may threaten again, and once the Cotswolds are ruined now, they are ruined for ever. A few spaces, such as Dovers Hill, have been acquired by the National Trust; but this is not enough. We ought to take the whole of that exquisite countryside and lay it on our consciences. It could be turned into a sort of national park, and by that, of course, I do not mean a playground or mere picnicking place—for the mere size of the region makes any such proposal absurd—but a district that, regarded as a national heritage of great value, is controlled by the commonwealth and, so far as it is possible, acquired by the nation itself, which would not, however, turn away the people who work the land. It would be really a question of control and responsibility. The beauty of the Cotswolds belongs to England; and we must see that nobody is allowed to carve and tinker and daub away at these hills and their enchanting villages. I for one should like to see a good many people like my ferocious friend, the artist, making their homes in this region, as guardians of its traditions and, if necessary, as experimenters in a mode of life governed by those traditions. After all, we need such experiments in life rather badly now, when everything and everybody is being rushed down and swept into one dusty arterial road of cheap mass production and standardised living. It may be necessary to banish from these hills the grimmer realities of our economic life, to make it artificially secure in its fairy tale of grey old stones and misty valleys. There will remain a countryside that will be able to give both body and spirit a holiday, and that may yet offer our minds material out of which we can conjure for our grandchildren a way of life better than the dirty hotch-potch of to-day.

CHAPTER FOUR

To Coventry

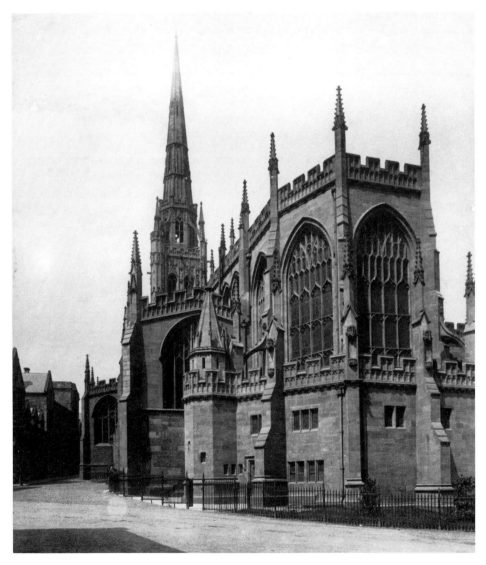

CATHEDRAL CHURCH, COVENTRY, 1933 *Photographer Unknown*

BABLAKE HOSPITAL, COVENTRY, 1937 *Sir John Summerson*

My plan was to go from the Cotswolds to the Black Country, but I decided to make a little detour and first visit Coventry, a city I did not know at all. The weather was all wrong. As I left the glorious pastures of the Cotswolds and turned my face towards the Black Country, the sky should have darkened. As it was, I had a brilliant morning for my little cross-country journey; and the nearer I drew to Coventry the better it became. When I actually arrived there, late in the morning, there was not a single shred of cloud in the sky, an exquisite luminous azure. Everything was crystal-clear. Not an outline anywhere had the faintest blur. The brick walls, full in the sun, might have been newly painted by Vermeer. Distant factories, rigidly defined in three dimensions, had a Canaletto quality. Things near at hand, a passing bus, a big yellow poster, dazzled and hurt the eyes. Coventry itself, ancient steeples and motor-car factories and all, was stated so emphatically against the green hollow and the silken sky that to see it gave one a sharp jolt of pleasure. There was the famous old city of the three steeples, and the equally famous new city of bicycles and motor cars and wireless sets, and all so clear that it might have been transported into Italy. This was all wrong. I had been prepared for a dull day and gloomy vistas and was ready to overhaul my stock of sombre adjectives. I felt I could not cope with this unexpected brightness. The bedroom they gave me at the hotel was true to form, being the usual inhuman little box lined with stained wallpaper and containing no running water. The window looked out on to a blank brick wall. But the brick wall was fiery-hued and the water-pipe running down it had just been painted a bright green, and so the effect was that of a bold picture by some modern. I had a mind then to dodge the town, to say not a word about having been there. Honesty won, however, though the victory will not prove a spectacular one.

Coventry is one of those towns that have often changed their trades and have had many vicissitudes, but, unlike nearly all the rest, it has managed to come out on top. In the thirteenth century, it was making cutlery: in the fourteenth, cloth; in the fifteenth, gloves; in the sixteenth, buttons; in the seventeenth, clocks; in the eighteenth, ribbons; in the nineteenth, sewing machines and bicycles; and now, in the twentieth, motor cars, electrical gadgets, machine tools, and wireless apparatus. You may judge how artfully it has backed its fancy by the following figures: in 1901 its population was 69,978; and its estimated population for this year is no less than 182,000; figures that suggest that the city has got lost in time and imagines that the Industrial Revolution is in full force. In the centre of the city I found ample remains of the cutlery, cloth, button, clock and ribbon periods scattered about, now oddly mixed up with Lyons, cheap tailors, Ronald Colman, cut-price shops, berets, and loud speakers. It is genuinely picturesque: the cathedral church of St. Michael, St. Mary's Hall, Ford's and Bablake Hospitals, Butcher Row, and the old Palace Yard. You peep round a corner and see half-timbered and gabled houses that would do for the second act of the *Meistersinger*. In fact, you could stage the *Meistersinger*—or film it—in Coventry. I knew it was an old place—for wasn't there Lady Godiva?—but I was surprised to find how much of the past, in soaring stone and carved wood, still remained in the city. Though even here, in the centre, the two buildings that dominate the rest are new and enormous bank offices, very massive and Corinthian and designed to suggest that there is nothing wrong with our financial system. If you do not understand why our banks give so little interest on our loans to them and demand so much more interest on their loans to us, or why they are encouraged, for private profit, to exchange mere credit for solid buildings and machinery and businesses at work, you should go and have a look at those colossal white stone pillars of theirs in Coventry. Perhaps they will reassure you; that is what they are there to do.

The picturesque remains of the old Coventry are besieged by an army of nuts, bolts, hammers, spanners, gauges, drills, and machine lathes, for in a thick ring round this ancient centre are the motor-car and cycle factories, the machine tool makers, the magneto manufacturers, and the electrical companies. Beyond them again are whole new quarters where the mechanics and fitters and turners and furnace men live in neat brick rows, and drink their beer in gigantic new public houses and take their wives to gigantic new picture theatres. Tennyson, in his poem about Godiva that begins, so uncharacteristically, *I waited for the train at Coventry*, must have foreseen all this, for does he not mention there, 'New men that in the flying of a wheel, Cry down the past. . .' Here are the new men and the flying wheels. Coventry seems to have acquired the trick of keeping up with the times, a trick that many of our industrial cities find hard to learn. It made bicycles when everybody was cycling, cars when everybody wanted a motor, and now it is also busy with aeroplanes, wireless sets, and various electrical contrivances, including the apparatus used by the Talkies. There are still plenty of unemployed here, about twelve thousand, I believe. But as I write, the place has passed its worst period of decline and unless this country reels back into a bottomless pit of trade depression, Coventry should be all right. Factories that were working on short time a year or two ago are now in some instances back on double shifts. I saw their lights and heard the deep roar of their machinery, late that night.

My own car, a Daimler, was made in this city, and so after lunch I went out to see how they did it. I climbed a hill and there, just over the summit, were the Daimler works, like a young town of long brick sheds. I was given a guide, an intelligent young engineer who took me first to the laboratory where a number of young men were enjoying themselves testing the various samples of metal. I took a hand myself in testing the hardness of a small metal part with a diamond point, which was connected with an indicator showing the degree of resistance in exact figures. In other rooms there were bubbling test-tubes and enlarged microscopic slides of sections of metal. In the manufacturing of motor cars the metal's the thing, and it seems they are very scientific about it now. I was then taken through various huge sheds in which hundreds and hundreds of mechanics were at work making and testing parts. (There are about four thousand men employed here.) All these sheds were the same: a long vista of blue electric-light shades, a misty perspective of flywheels above and brown overalled men below. They were all hard at it and most of them were having a smoke too, for they are allowed to smoke for three-quarters of an hour in the morning and in the afternoon: a wise rule. Every man in these departments was limited to one job, but there was a certain amount of variety inside the job. This was not strictly mass production: there was

BUTCHER ROW, COVENTRY, c.1933   *F. Smyth*

no endless moving chain; there were no men restricted to putting on a bolt there, a nut here; it was highly organised large-scale jobbing production. Its size, my guide told me, was in its favour, because parts were put through tests that would be impossible in a tiny workshop. A manufacturer in a small way could not afford to use the various machines necessary for these tests, such as the machine, one I watched with interest, which tested the exact balance of the flywheels and showed exactly where there was still a fraction too much metal on some segment. One had an impression of the most rigorous testing everywhere. The idea now is to cut down the preliminary trials of the finished car outside the factory, so the various parts—engine, gears, crankshafts, axles—are ferociously tried out before they are assembled. The modern motor car represents an astonishing feat of human ingenuity. Consider the number of them out on the roads and the extraordinarily few accidents due to any fault in the vehicle itself. If we were one half as clever in the matters that lie far outside machinery as we are about machinery itself, what people we should be and what a world we should leave our children! If life were only an internal combustion engine! The skill and the care that are lavished on these cylinders and pistons and gears! I have no doubt that boys and girls in Coventry are comparatively well looked after, but nobody has attended to them as their fathers are attending to the proud young Double-Six Daimlers.

There is a bus department in these works. I was allowed to see the giant steel entrails of these creatures. Two very fine specimens had just been completed, and my guide and I explored them, inside, top deck, and the driver's seat, where you suddenly feel very powerful. One of these grand new fellows, immensely powerful and roomy and ready to take you anywhere with its forty horses, costs between fifteen hundred and two thousand pounds. It would be a good idea, I said, to have one as a private car. It would be a better idea, I continued, to buy one and then rig it up as a caravan. As usual, I was not being original. The thing had already been done. An ingenious sportsman had commissioned a caravan bus, with sitting-room, two bedrooms, kitchen and bath. I envy him. I ought to have one for this journey, and then I could travel amusingly and comfortably and be free of these beastly hotels. The only trouble is, I imagine, that a great many roads must be closed to buses this size, which are at once very high and very heavy. But I have no doubt that you could travel fairly easily in one—at about nine miles to the gallon—with your family or some friends aboard, from Land's End to John o' Groats. I commend

ASSEMBLING DAIMLER CARS, c.1933   *Photographer Unknown* the notion to anybody who has a couple of thousand pounds to play with and thinks he could drive a bus. And the young man from the Daimler works, who had driven everything, assured me that once you are familiar with the enormous length of a bus—and at first it must seem like turning a row of cottages round a corner—it is easier to drive than an ordinary car.

Notwithstanding the great size of these works and the extraordinary variety of tasks performed in them, I noticed, as I had done before in such places, the strange absence of any obvious supervision. An elaborate plan of work was first laid down—they have a special planning department here—and then the thousand-and-one jobs were distributed and the huge machine of production was set in motion. After that, the works almost ran themselves. Everybody knew what to do; you took something over from Bill, did your own job on it, then passed it on to Jack over there; and thus motor cars seemed to flower out of cast iron, steel, aluminium, as naturally as dandelions flower in a field. Once the plan was put into action, the machinery set going, the very minimum of supervision was necessary. I said something to this effect to the young man who was showing me round, and he agreed, rather ruefully, that it was true. He was rueful because this method of production means that men of his kind, not mechanics but educated engineers, find fewer and fewer avenues of promotion open to them. He himself had learned the practical side of his trade as an apprentice and the theoretical side at a university—he was an Oxford graduate—but nevertheless, though he was now thirty years of age, he was still only earning about four pounds a week. He was not condemning the firm, for which he seemed to have almost an affection. It was simply that these new methods of production demanded fewer and fewer intermediaries between the two or three managers and their planning department, on the one side, and the thousands of artisans on the other side. The technical man with his university degree, unless he was lucky and found an opening or had one made for him, was worse off now than the workmen themselves. At this very moment there are probably thousands of parents preparing to make heavy sacrifices in order that their boys should be turned into square pegs, when unfortunately industry itself is arranging that there shall be only more and more round holes.

The Daimler young man, who took me back to my hotel, was not a Coventry man and did not like the place. Here he was in entire agreement with the head porter of my hotel, also not a Coventry man—perhaps there are no Coventry men—who answered my questions about a possible evening's amusement with the most sardonic negatives. It was the wrong night (it always is) to see them enjoying themselves; and anyhow they didn't enjoy themselves much. 'You go into one of these pubs,' he said bitterly. 'All right. What do you hear?

All about gears and magnetos and suchlike. Honest. That's right. They can't talk about anything else here. Got motor-cars on the brain, they have. I hardly ever go into a pub. I go home and have a read.' I went to an ugly café, full of bamboo and wet tables, and drank tea while a large gramophone thundered *Carmen* and *Tales of Hoffmann* at me. Then I returned to my little box of a bedroom, which was cold and had no fireplace, and there put sheets of paper, ripe for a masterpiece, into my portable typewriter and then, after depths of vexation, savagely tore them out again. When this had gone on long enough, I washed myself in the chipped basin, and went downstairs and had a gin and bitters in a small room off the bar, where a barmaid with an enormous bust and a wig was busy exchanging badinage with four friends, two Bass (male) and two Guinness (female): 'He did, didn't he, Joe?' ''S ri',' 'Cor, he didn't ever,' 'Well, you ask Florrie,' 'I don't mean what you mean,' ''S ri',' ''Ere, Joe, you tell'er.' After that, I took myself and my evening paper to a grill room. There I had a poor meal but made a discovery that did something to comfort me. The reason why English cookery was allowed to lapse into barbarism was that gradually only one article of diet was taken seriously. That is Steak. This is venerated and idealised. When an ordinary English waiter mentions any other dish, he is a realist and his very tone of voice tells you what that dish really is—muck. But when he mentions Steak, his voice is low, hushed, reverent. First, it is Steak impersonal, the great noble viand. Then, when you have been converted into giving an order, it is Steak personal, *your* Steak. How will you have your steak, sir? He's just doing your steak, now, sir. Here's your steak, sir. It is as if he were talking about your wife. Name any other item on the menu that is discussed in this fashion, that is even treated with the merest hint of respect. It cannot be done. We live in the empire of the steak. Centuries hence, Central Asian anthropologists will prove to one another that a bleeding steak had some religious significance in the life of this forgotten island people. Incidentally, the steak I had that night in Coventry was much too tough, and I ate far too many fried potatoes with it, so that afterwards I had to walk miles and miles into the night and at last came to a hill from which I had a good view of the old constellations remotely and mildly beaming, and the new Morris works, a tower of steel and glass, flashing above the city of gears and crankshafts.

CHAPTER FIVE

To Birmingham

[1]

I caught the bus that runs between Coventry and Birmingham. It was very full and very uncomfortable. The weather was still fine but colder than it had been, with a sharp nip in the wind. We trundled along at no great pace down pleasant roads, decorated here and there by the presence of huge new gaudy pubs. These pubs are a marked feature of this Midlands landscape. Some of them are admirably designed and built; others have been inspired by the idea of Merrie England, popular in the neighbourhood of Los Angeles. But whether comely or hideous, they must all have cost a pot of money, proving that the brewers—and they seemed to be all owned by brewers—still have great confidence in their products. At every place, however, I noticed that some attempt had been made to enlarge the usual attractions of the beer-house; some had bowling greens, some advertised their food, others their music. No doubt even more ambitious plans for amusement would have been put into force if there had been no opposition from the teetotallers, those people who say they object to public-houses because you can do nothing in them but drink, and at the same time strenuously oppose the publicans who offer to give their customers anything but drink. The trick is—and long has been—to make or keep the beer-house dull or disreputable, and then to point out how dull or disreputable it is. It is rather as if the rest of us should compel teetotallers to wear their hair long and unwashed, and then should write pamphlets complaining of their dirty habits: 'Look at their hair,' we should cry.

In the midst of a russet solitude we came upon a notice board saying, *This is the City of Birmingham*. There was nothing in sight but hedgerows, glittering fields and the mist of the autumn morning. For a moment I entertained a wild hope that this really was the City of Birmingham, that the town had been pulled down and carted away. Not that Birmingham had ever done anything to me. I had never been there; this was my first visit. I knew very little about it. The little I did know, however, was not in its favour. I had always thought of the place, vaguely, as perhaps the most typical product in civic life of nineteenth-century industrialism, as a city of big profits and narrow views, which sent missionaries out of one gate and brass idols and machine guns out of another. It made a great many articles, chiefly in metal, but so far in my life not one of these articles had gained any hold over my affections. I had never said, 'Good old Birmingham!' myself, and never heard anybody else say it. In my limited experience *Made in Birmingham* had been a dubious hallmark. And the Chamberlain family had supplied no heroes of mine. Then there were jokes about a foolish Watch Committee there. On the other hand, any guide-book could offer a great many facts on the credit side. In the eighteenth century Birmingham had a Lunar Society that met every month, and among its members were James Watt, Matthew Boulton, Joseph Priestley, Josiah Wedgwood, Erasmus Darwin, Sir William Herschel, and Samuel Parr: a good all-round team of talents. The number of important inventions, from the steam engine to gas lighting and electro-plating, that either first saw the light or were first brought to perfection in this city, is very impressive. Its commercial success has not been merely a matter of geography and geology, the fact that it has been the centre of a district rich in coal, iron, wood and sand. History comes into play here. Not being a place of any importance in the Middle Ages, Birmingham was not controlled by the guilds and did not suffer from the various restrictions imposed upon the then larger towns. It was not a chartered borough and therefore Nonconformists were free to settle and work there, and as the industrial revolution was largely nonconformist Birmingham was able to take full advantage of it. Thus, when you hear jokes about the Birmingham Watch Committee and chorus girls' stockings, you are really at the end of a very long chain of historical cause and effect. Having allied itself to the black slavery of industry, the city managed to strike one or two stout blows for liberty in other directions, for which it must be given credit. And now it is the second city in England. By the time I had considered these matters, the fields had gone and we were passing houses and shops and factories. Did all this look like the entrance into the second city in England? It did. It looked a dirty muddle.

Where the bus finally stopped, a Birmingham citizen asked me if he could carry my two bags to the hotel. He was a young man, this Birmingham citizen: he was dressed in a ragged brown coat and a pair of patched and torn flannel trousers and the wreck of a pair of boots; his face was swollen and it was so long since he had shaved that he was well on his way towards wearing a matted tow-coloured beard. On our way to the hotel I asked him a good many questions, but many of his replies I cannot give you here because he spoke so badly that I could not catch them. But he was twenty-two, had been out of work since he was sixteen, was not receiving the dole, had a father but no mother, and his father was also out of work. It was a fair step to the hotel, and one of my bags, I knew, was heavy; so I told him to put them down and rest the moment he was tired; but there must have been good blood and bone somewhere in that ruin of a young fellow, for he never stopped or even slowed up but moved on at a good pace until he came within a yard or two of the hotel porter, who looked at him and spoke to him in a fashion that most of us would hesitate to adopt in talking to a mongrel that was snapping at our heels. However, I gave him a florin, which was what he usually made, with luck, in a whole day, and he went off delighted.

There was a sudden access of civic dignity in the place. Here in Colmore Row you could imagine yourself in the second city of England. There is a really fine view at the end, where the huge Council House turns into Victoria Square. You see Hill Street mistily falling away beneath the bridge that the Post Office has thrown high across the road. If there is any better view in Birmingham than this, I never saw it. For a moment, as you stand there, you believe that at last you have found an English provincial city that has the air and dignity that a great city should have, that at last you have escaped from the sad dingy muddle of factories and dormitories that have been allowed to pass for cities in this island, that at last a few citizens who have eyes to see and minds to plan have set to work to bring comeliness into the stony hotch-potch, that Birmingham has had the sense to design itself as well as its screws, steam cocks, and pressure gauges. This is an illusion, and the only way in which to keep it would be to hurry away from that corner in a closed vehicle and see no more of Birmingham.

I could not do that, but I did the next best thing: I entered the Corporation Art Gallery and Museum, of which I had heard a good deal. The Director of the Gallery assured me that Birmingham had always had its craftsmen too and proved it by showing me case after case of local silver ware, some of it of tasteless design but all of it admirably executed. He also showed me some drawings done by young students—one of them a boy of only fifteen—at the local school of art; and these were surprisingly good. He assured me too that Birmingham could be very generous towards its Gallery and Museum. There were two cases of exquisite Chinese porcelain, and he told me that the necessary sum—I think it was between two and three thousand pounds—to buy these objects of art, which are quite useless and will never declare a dividend, had been raised in a few days. Oddly enough, two other cases of Chinese porcelain, equally exquisite, had been lent to the museum by a famous comedian, whose jests about Birmingham's prudery I still remember. The Picture Gallery is famous for its wealth of examples from two English schools, the old water-colourists and the Pre-Raphaelites. I did not spend much time with the Pre-

Raphaelite collection, which is particularly rich in drawings, because I get very little pleasure these days from the work of Burne-Jones and his friends. I was fascinated, as I always am, by Ford Madox Brown, who was not really a Pre-Raphaelite, and whose best work always seems to me to have an odd magical quality of its own. Perhaps the secret lies in its queer mixture of realism and the fantastic. You stare at his emigrants and workmen until it all grows eerie and you begin to feel that somebody, probably Ford Madox Brown himself, is looking at you through the canvas. Actually, if he were, he would be better off than you in this gallery, which is spaciously contrived and well built but badly lit, with more honest daylight falling on the floor than ever reaches the walls. It is probably good and proper that Birmingham should accumulate Pre-Raphaelite works of art, which are so entirely different from itself that their very presence together is sufficient to prove the rich breadth of this world. But for my part, I like life and art to be neither Birmingham nor Burne-Jones, but to travel on the honest roads that march between the deacons in counting houses, on the one side, and the drooping maidens in hot-houses on the other. In fact I like life and art to have much more in common with that other school of painting so well represented here, that of the good old English water-colourists, who, whatever their private lives may have been, always impress me as being about the happiest set of men who ever lived in this country. They wandered about while the countryside was still unspoilt; they saw everything worth seeing; and what they saw they turned into enchanting bits of drawing and water-colour painting. They are the equivalent in visual art of our lyric poets. God created them, while there was yet time, to catch the lovely old England in line and wash, to open some little windows on to it for ever. Their very names, Turner, Girtin, Cotman, Cox, Varley, Bonington, are like the names of villages and apples. They have more of Cox's water-colours here in Birmingham than you can find anywhere else; they are not all good, for nearly all these industrious fellows were very unequal; but the best of them would make a man shout for pleasure if he were not in a picture gallery, which I take to be a place where we never raise our voices. It is the great weakness of visual art that it must be largely sought for in these inhuman institutions, where you cannot lounge and smoke and argue, and where you unconsciously begin to tiptoe until very soon your feet and legs ache. I had the luck, however, to get into a part of the gallery temporarily closed to the general public, and there a friendly curator fished out some lovely specimens of Girtin and Cotman and De Wint. They have there a little *Harvest Scene* by De Wint—a tiny wagon or two, then a glorious melting distance of rolling country and sky—that I should dearly like somebody to steal for me. It lit up my morning. All the years between Peter De Wint and myself were annihilated in a flash; he pointed and I saw, he spoke and I heard; and his mood, felt on that autumn day long ago, was mine. Whatever cloud of gloom covers Birmingham in my memory, I have only to recollect that corner of its gallery, to recall that stipple and wash of paint on a bit of board, and my memory is touched with colour, warmth, vivid life. How many people have already felt that about one little picture there, and how many people have still to have the experience? And how many pounds were paid for that water-colour? There's a nice little sum waiting to be worked out by some ingenious person. The result, I think, would prove that Birmingham—or any other city with a decent art gallery—can disburse enchantment at less than a penny a head. At the entrance to this art gallery and museum they put up the daily returns of visitors. The recent average was about eight hundred a day on week-days, with a sudden leap into thousands on Sundays. This is not, I was told, because Birmingham has a passion for art on Sunday afternoon, but because then all the young people promenade up and down the galleries, not looking at pictures but at one another. Apollo has to serve Venus. But what of it? The boys and girls have to begin mating somewhere, and they could obviously begin their acquaintance in much worse places. And you never know. Venus may be a strict taskmistress, but no doubt Apollo is allowed a word now and then. A picture will occasionally catch an eye, then hold it; and so the old leaven of art will start working. There may be new masterpieces presented to this gallery in twenty years' time because a boy and girl were promenading and 'clicking' there last Sunday afternoon. The director, a wise man, is of the same opinion. No doubt there are protests in Birmingham as there are elsewhere; and probably from those people—who must hate the whole commerce of the sexes—who protest with equal vehemence against the youngsters going anywhere else on Sundays, and when they have finally driven them out into the streets, protest against their being there too. They forget, these protesters, that both cities and the Sabbath were made for man. If the social arrangements do not fit in with the time-old desires of ordinary decent human nature, it is the social arrangements that should be changed.

So long as you keep within a very narrow limit in the centre, Colmore Row, New Street, Corporation Street, Birmingham has quite a metropolitan air, and on the fine afternoon I first explored them these streets had quite metropolitan crowds in them too, looking at the windows of the big shops and hurrying in and out of cafés and picture theatres. The city has a passion for arcades, and I never remember seeing more. It also has a passion for bridging streets, usually by joining two tall buildings somewhere on the third or fourth storey.

When you get to the end of New Street, you can cross into Paradise Street and then arrive in Easy Row. There you find the white Hall of Memory, built to commemorate the 14,000 Birmingham men who were killed in the great war, some of them possibly with bits of Birmingham metal. Behind this Hall of Memory is Baskerville Place, called after the great printer, John Baskerville; and I should like to think there was something symbolical and fateful in the conjunction of this war memorial and the famous printing press. Among the many statues in this part of the city there is one to Joseph Priestley, whose house was sacked and burned down by the mob not long before he himself was compelled to leave the country altogether. It is a pity that some of the charred remains of his library and laboratory were not kept to be exhibited by the side of the statue.

Tired of walking round, I climbed to the top of a tram. I did not know where it was going, and when the conductor came for his fare, I said I would go as far as the tram went, and took a threepenny ticket. As if it knew what was about to happen, the sun immediately went out. This treachery did not leave us in a kindly dusk—it was too early for that—but only in the middle of quite a different day, lowering and sullen. Then followed one of the most depressing little journeys I ever remember making. No doubt I was tired. And then again the electric tram offers the least exhilarating mode of progress possible. It is all very well for the Irish poet 'AE' to call them 'those high-built glittering galleons of the streets'; but no man inside a tram, no matter how he strains his fancy, really feels that he is inside a glittering galleon. The people show a sound instinct when they desert the tramway for any other and newer kind of conveyance. There is something depressing about the way in which a tram lumbers and groans and grinds along. But it was Birmingham itself that did most of the mischief. In two minutes, its civic dignity, its metropolitan airs, had vanished; and all it offered me, mile after mile, was a parade of mean dinginess. I do not say that this was a worse tram-ride than one would have had in Manchester, Liverpool, Glasgow, any of our larger cities, or smaller ones either for that matter; I am not making comparisons between cities now. I only know that during the half-hour or so I sat staring through the top windows of that tram, I saw nothing, not one single tiny thing, that could possibly raise a man's spirits. Possibly what I was seeing was not Birmingham but our urban and industrial civilisation. The fact remains that it was beastly. It was so many miles of ugliness, squalor, and the wrong kind of vulgarity, the decayed anæmic kind. It was not, you understand, a slum. That would not have been so bad; nobody likes slums; and the slum hits you in the eye and you have only to make an effort to get it pulled down. This was, I suppose, the common stuff out of which most of our big industrial towns are made. And those of us who have not got to live or go shopping or amuse ourselves in such a thoroughfare as this probably do not notice it at ordinary times; we are on our way somewhere else, and we let it slip past us, outside the motor or the tram-car, without ever having a good look at it. But I was there, on that tram, to have a look at it, and if I was tired and perhaps a little low-spirited when I began, I was still more tired and far lower-spirited before I had done. For there was nothing, I repeat, to light up a man's mind for one single instant. I loathed the whole long array of shops, with their nasty bits of meat, their cough mixtures, their *Racing Specials*, their sticky cheap furniture, their shoddy clothes, their fly-blown pastry, their coupons and sales and lies and dreariness and ugliness. I asked myself if this really represented the level reached by all those people down there on the pavements. I am too near them myself, not being one of the sensitive plants of contemporary authorship, to believe that it does represent their level. They have passed it. They have gone on and it is not catching up. Why were the newest and largest buildings all along this route either picture theatres or pubs? Because both of them offer an escape: they are bolt-holes and safety-valves. Probably not one person out of a thousand along that road would roundly declare, 'All this is a nasty mess, and I'm sick of it.' But it is my belief that at least six hundred of them out of that thousand entertain an unspoken conviction that is constantly troubling them inside and that calls for either the confectionery drama of the films or for a few quick drinks. I think I caught a glimpse then of what may seem to future historians one of the dreadful ironies of this time of ours: when there never were more men doing nothing and there never was before so much to be done.

The conductor announced the terminus. I had arrived. I got out, to find that we had climbed to the top of a hill and that a cold wind was blowing over it, bringing dust and grit and filthy bits of paper. On one side was a stretch of high brick wall, which some posters told me was a sports ground. On the other side were some patches of waste ground and some decayed allotments, where the last green rags of gardening were shivering. Further along was a yard filled with rusted parts of motors and scrap-iron. I walked to the end of the brick wall and saw below and afar the vast smoky hollow of the city, with innumerable tall chimneys thrusting out of the murk. The wind dropped, and all along the edge of the pavement the filthy bits of paper settled for a moment before beginning to rustle uneasily again. A tram came making its ponderous moan, and I signalled it like a man on a raft seeing a sail. On the way down I looked at nothing, but some little things caught my eye. One

VICTORIA SQUARE, BIRMINGHAM, 1931 *George Bott*

of them was a notice outside a grimy tabernacle: *Get the Brotherhood Spirit.*
What would happen, I wondered, if we did. Surely the result would startle
those mild folk who put up that notice, for there would first be such a burning
down and blowing up and wholesale destruction. Or so, in that depressed hour,
it seemed to me.

Having some work to do, I stayed in my room and tried to collect my
thoughts and some words for them. It was late when I went down to dinner,
and much later when I wandered out into Colmore Row for a breath of air
before bed. It was not quite eleven o'clock, however, and the look of these
Birmingham main streets was very queer, for they were all blazing with light
and yet almost empty. Victoria Square was like another Place de la Concorde.
Never have I seen such brilliant illumination in a provincial city. But the old
habits had prevailed; the theatres and picture palaces had closed; the crowd
had gone home to bed; and central Birmingham emptily sparkled and shone
as if it expected the arrival of a new and more nocturnal set of citizens. No
doubt they are already on their way.

[2]

I spent the next day, which was fine and warm, at Bournville. There were several good reasons for doing this. To begin with, I was interested in the manufacture of chocolate, having bought and eaten in my time great quantities of the stuff, and having several times, when I was about ten, tried unsuccessfully to make it myself. Then I wanted to see another highly organised giant works, and Cadbury's was one of the biggest in the country. Again, Cadbury Bros. were renowned as employers of the benevolent and paternal kind, and I wanted to see what it was they did. And then again, there was Bournville itself, the village. So out I went, through dignified Birmingham, messy Birmingham, to planned Birmingham, which had put on its autumnal colouring and was looking charming.

There are a good many things to be said about Bournville, the village. The first is that it has nothing whatever to do with the firm of Cadbury Bros., Ltd. This came as a surprise to me—as I imagine it will to many people—for I had always thought that the firm built the village for its work-people, on a sort of patriarchal employers' scheme. Nothing of the kind. Here are the facts as they are set out in one of the Bournville publications:

The Bournville Estate was founded by the late George Cadbury in 1895. In 1879, he and his brother Richard, who were partners in business as Cocoa and Chocolate manufacturers, moved their works from the centre of industrial Birmingham to what was then an entirely rural area, four miles from the city. The removal gave George Cadbury an opportunity to put into practice ideas he had long in mind, the result of his contact with working men as a teacher in Early Morning Adult Schools, with which he was connected for over fifty years. He had been led to the conclusion that the root of most social evils lay in the bad housing conditions in which all too many had to live. He was himself fond of country life, and knew its material and spiritual advantages over life in crowded industrial areas, and when the factory was thoroughly established in its new environment he began to see ways and means of giving more and more people the opportunity to enjoy it. He did not, however, contemplate a scheme only for the benefit of his own workpeople; rather, his idea was to make what he called 'a small contribution to the solution of a great problem'—the problem of housing as affecting large industrial towns.

He bought land in the neighbourhood of the factory, and in 1895 began to build Bournville village. Five years later—in 1900—the estate covered 330 acres, and 300 houses had been built. At that time, in order to secure the perpetuation of his ideas, he handed over the whole property to a body of Trustees—the Bournville Village Trust—on behalf of the nation. He thus gave up entirely his financial interest in it, and secured that all profits—for it was set up on a sound commercial basis—should never accrue to any private individual or body, but be devoted to the development of the Bournville Estate, and to the promotion of housing reform elsewhere.

These then are the facts. It is worth noticing that this Quaker manufacturer, fifty years ago, talked about something that the newspapers and the government are just beginning to talk about now, namely, bad housing. And he not only talked, but he did something. And what he did has proved very successful. His Trust Deed was really a housing plan that could be legally enforced. Thus, he laid down that each house was not to occupy more than a quarter of its own site, that factories were not to take up more than a fifteenth part of any developed area, and that one-tenth of the land, in addition to roads and gardens, should be given up to parks and recreation grounds. Since then, the Trust has really acted like a local authority. It has leased land to Public Utility Housing Societies, which are on a co-partnership basis. These societies—and there are four of them—build houses and then rent or sell them to their members. Some experimental bungalows—each made of different material—have been built, as a test of costs and durability. There are some tiny bungalows, for single persons. There is also a residential club for business women. Some of the owners and tenants work for Cadbury Bros., others come from Birmingham, and are clerks, artisans, teachers, and so forth. The vital statistics in the booklet I have before me are of some importance. They are taken from an average of the seven years ending 1931. Death-rate per 1,000: England and Wales 12.1; Birmingham 11.6; Bournville 6.5. Infantile mortality per 1,000 live births: England and Wales, 69, Birmingham 72; Bournville 56. Some years ago, the heights and weights, age for age, of Bournville children and children from one of the bad areas in Birmingham were compared, and the Bournville children were from two to four inches taller and between four and nine pounds heavier. And the Estate is flourishing.

I saw the whole of the village; if it can still be called a village, for now it has the size and population of a small town. Its tree-lined roads, pleasant spaces, villas and gardens are not, of course, the eye-opener they must have been thirty years ago. Nevertheless, they are still infinitely superior to and more sensible than most of the huge new workmen's and artisans' quarters that have recently been built on the edge of many large towns in the Midlands. For example, in many of these estates, no provision whatever has been made for recreation, whereas in Bournville you see everywhere recreation grounds and halls. Model yachting is very popular in this district, and it was decided to make another small lake in one of the recently developed areas. A gang of unemployed was brought out from Birmingham to do the digging and drain-

WITHERFORD WAY, BOURNVILLE, 1933 *Roy Dixon*

ing, and most of these men were not professional navvies at all. For the first day or two they worked with raw and bleeding hands; but they stuck it, and out of the whole fifty or sixty, only one dropped out. And now the little lake is there; I saw it myself, ready for whole fleets of model yachts. (I mention this for the benefit of those people—and there are still plenty of them—who think that most unemployed men are unemployable, or, if not that, at least not very willing to go very far out of their way to find work. I should like to set some of these people on a long digging job in heavy clay.) The village would look prettier if it did not consist almost entirely of detached and semi-detached small villas. I would prefer houses arranged in small courts and squares. I do not understand this passion for being detached or semi-detached, for you can have gardens just the same if the houses are built in little rows. The most charming houses in England, excluding manors and the like, are built in rows and not detached. (And so, of course, are the least charming, all the horrors.) There is something at once fussy and monotonous about a long road on which tiny villas have been sprinkled, as if out of a pepper-pot. I am sorry Bournville has not been able to experiment more with rows, courts, quadrangles; but I was assured by those who know that their tenants greatly prefer to be semi-detached. Within these limits, Bournville has done its work very well. If it has rather too many public halls of religion and too few frivolous meeting places for my taste, after all I am not one of its tenants. And its real importance is as an example of what can be done by some careful planning and an absence of the jerry-builder's motives. It is neither a great firm's private dormitory nor a rich man's toy, but a public enterprise that pays its way. It is one of the small outposts of civilisation, still ringed round with barbarism.

This is the age, among other things, of chocolate. Think of the number of chocolate shops you see in a day's journey. A very large proportion of this chocolate is made in the Cadbury factory at Bournville. I seem to have spent hours and hours being rushed from one part of this colossal works to another. It is really a small town engaged in the manufacture of cocoa and chocolate. I was shown a warehouse in which more than a hundred thousand bags of cocoa beans can be stored. These bags are mechanically hoisted to the top of a building, and then their contents pass from floor to floor, are shelled, winnowed, baked, crushed, refined, pressed, and finally pack themselves neatly into tins, which tins have been made by some busy little machines in a neighbouring room. Everywhere is the sickly sweet smell of cocoa and chocolate. I was told that an old foreman, who had spent fifty years in this atmosphere, still had his two cups of cocoa every night. The manufacture of chocolate is a much more elaborate process, and though I could make a shot at describing it, I see no reason why I should. But there were miles of it, and thousands of men and girls, very spruce in overalls, looking after the hundred-and-one machines that pounded and churned and cooled and weighed and packed the chocolate, that covered the various bits of confectionery with chocolate, that printed labels and wrappers and cut them up and stuck them on and then packed everything into boxes that some other machine had made. The most impressive room I have ever seen in a factory was that in which the cardboard boxes were made and the labels, in that shiny purple or crimson paper, were being printed: there is a kind of gangway running down the length of it, perhaps twenty feet from the floor, and from this you had a most astonishing view of hundreds of white-capped girls seeing that the greedy machines were properly fed with coloured paper and ink and cardboard. In some smaller rooms there was hardly any machinery. In one of them I saw a lot of girls neatly cutting up green and brown cakes of marzipan into pretty little pieces;

DECORATING EASTER EGGS, c.1930   *Photographer Unknown*

and they all seemed to be enjoying themselves; though I was told that actually
they preferred to do something monotonous with the machines. I know now
the life history of an almond whirl. There is a little mechanical device that
makes that whirl on the top, as deft as you please. I saw thousands of marshmallows hurrying on an endless moving band of silvered paper to the slow
cascade of chocolate that swallowed them for a moment and then turned them
out on the other side, to be cooled, as genuine chocolate marshmallows. It
is part of the fantastic quality of our time that what seem trifling bits of frivolity
to most of us are of terrific importance to some people. I saw departments
where solemn specialists sit in conference over a bit of coconut dipped in chocolate or whatever the trifle may be. Men with learned degrees, men with
charts, engineers from all quarters of the world, have to be called in to decide
the fate of that bit of chocolaty stuff. When you buy a box of these things,
you have also bought the services of a whole army of people. It is all very

strange, rather frightening. You have to shut your imagination off or you might go mad. Even I will never feel quite the same now about a box of chocolates.

There was a girl whose duty it was, for forty-two hours a week, to watch those marshmallows hurrying towards their chocolate Niagara. 'Wouldn't that girl be furious,' I said to the director who was showing me round, 'if she found that her Christmas present was a box of chocolate marshmallows?' But he was not at all sure. 'We consider our staff among our best customers,' he told me. Other people there told me the same thing. Such is the passion now for chocolate that though you spend all your days helping to make it, though you smell and breathe it from morning until night, you must munch away like the rest of the world. This says a good deal for the purity of the processes, which seemed to me exemplary, but what it says for human nature, I cannot tell.

As it is human nature and not the manufacture of chocolate that really interests me, I will take leave now of Messrs. Cadbury as ingenious organisers and consider them as employers. They have of course long been in the top class of the school of benevolent and paternal employers. Their workpeople are provided with magnificent recreation grounds and sports pavilions, with a large concert hall in the factory itself, where midday concerts are given, with dining-rooms, recreation rooms, and facilities for singing, acting, and I know not what, with continuation schools, with medical attention, with works councils, with pensions. The factory is almost as busy in the evenings as it is in the daytime. Games, music, drama, lectures, classes, hobbies, conferences, all keep the place in full swing. Once you have joined the staff of this firm, you need never wander out of its shadow. I saw a club-room, fitted up with billiards tables and draughts-boards and the like, where old employees who have been pensioned off come to spend their leisure, playing while their younger comrades are working all round them. The membership of the various clubs and societies is about seven thousand. No form of self-improvement, except those that have their base in some extreme form of economic revolution, is denied a person here. No pastime, except the ancient one of getting drunk, is impossible. Here, in a factory, run for private profit, are nearly all the facilities for leading a full and happy life. What progressive people all over the world are demanding for humanity, these workers have here. Those in charge insist that the firm uses no compulsion whatever and never moves to provide anything until it knows that a real demand exists. It simply offers facilities, they say. And here let me add my conviction that whether all this is right or wrong, the employers themselves have acted in good faith, and genuinely prefer spending a good part of their money on their factory and its employees instead of on racing stables and yachts and Monte Carlo.

Is it right or wrong? This is a very pretty problem. It is easy for some academic person, who has never spent an hour in a factory and does not really know how people live, to condemn it on philosophical grounds, but this may possibly be the result of turning off one's imaginative sympathy and not turning it on. We will assume now that our goal is other people's happiness, that what we want is that the mass of people should have a chance of leading the sort of life we lead—or should like to lead—ourselves. Now there is no getting away from the fact that here, owing to this system of paternal employment, are factory workers who have better conditions, more security, and infinitely better chances of leading a decent and happy life, than nearly all such factory workers elsewhere. They have, at least in part, what we should like everybody to have. Thanks to good management and an ever-increasing public passion for chocolate, a goal of some sort has been reached. It is easy, when you are sitting in a pleasant study and you know that it is unlikely that you will ever have to apply for work in a factory, to say that all this will not do; but could you honestly say as much if you found yourself a factory hand, and a factory hand who worked in bad conditions, who had no security, and whose employers did not care a rap if their people did nothing but drink themselves silly in their leisure? If you strike a balance of ordinary human happiness, in a class that has had all too few chances of it, then here is a definite and enormous gain. The Russians, in their plans for a proletarian millennium, are only taking aim at such a goal as this. What has been promised in Russia—in such matters as hours of work, food, housing, education, amusement—has been actually performed here. No factory workers in Europe have ever been better off than these people. And I doubt if America, even during its very prosperous years, could show us workers of the same kind who had such opportunities for a full, active, healthy life. On any sensible short view, the experiment must be praised.

It is when one takes a longer view that doubts begin to creep in. Is it good for people to see the factory as the centre of their lives even if that factory offers them so much, and so much that is genuinely significant? Does this system of paternal employment suggest (as Hilaire Belloc pointed out, years ago, in his *Servile State*) the decay of genuine democracy? I believe that this very firm, when it opened a branch factory in Australia, tried to pursue the same policy there but met with a decided rebuff from the Australians, who, whatever their faults, are at least in practice the thorough-going democrats they pretend to be. 'No,' said these Australian employees, in effect, 'we don't

want your recreation grounds and concert halls, for if you can afford to give
us these things, you can afford to pay us higher wages, and we'll take the
wages.' I do not say that this leaves the paternal employer without a retort,
for he can reply: 'Very well, if you don't want my welfare schemes, you needn't
have them. I will follow the example of other firms and not give you any recreation grounds or concert halls. But neither will I give you any higher wages.
I'll put what I've saved in my pocket.' But though he may be worse off in
other respects, it is clear that the Australian employee as a political being is
occupying the sounder position. He is selling his labour, and nothing else.
He is not acknowledging that his employer is a superior creature, whose bene-
volence may fall upon him like the rays of the life-giving sun. A workman
whose whole life is centred in his factory has put all his eggs into one basket.
He may enjoy many unusual luxuries, but there is obviously one luxury he
cannot enjoy and that is—a spirit of independence. Moreover, he is in danger
of believing what his employers are anxious for him to believe and what, in
all sincerity, they may believe themselves, namely, that the particular work
of that factory is the most urgent and the grandest of human activities, that
cocoa is not made for man, but man for cocoa. Pensions and bonuses, works
councils, factory publications, entertainments and dinners and garden parties
and outings organised by the firm, these are all very well, but they can easily
create an atmosphere that is injurious to the growth of men as intellectual
and spiritual beings, for they can give what is, when all is said and done, a
trading concern for private profit a falsely mystical aura, can drape its secular
form with sacramental cloths, and completely wreck the proper scale of values.
Very soon, when this atmosphere has been created, you begin to hear talk
of 'loyalties' that soar high above the common and reasonable fidelity of a
decent man trying to do the job for which he is paid. Business cant swells
into business mysticism, as it did in the United States before the slump, when
there was no end of rubbishy talk about 'service' and 'loyalty,' the kind of
talk we get here chiefly from advertising men in their windy conventions. And
no institution is fit to dominate men's lives unless it is solemnly dedicated
either to God or the commonwealth; and by the commonwealth I do not mean
the State, which may be simply a number of elected persons or a dictator and
his friends who happen to have collared the army and the police force. If one
of these paternal factories were taken over by the State tomorrow, only one
weakness of the system would disappear, the fact that the whole organisation
is there for private profit; all the other weaknesses and dangers would remain,
for the individual workman would still be compelled to look only in one direction for all the benefits of his life, would run the same risk of losing his indepen-

dence, could still believe that he was made for his factory and not his factory for him, could confuse and mislay all his values, even though the directors had now to report to a public ministry instead of to a body of shareholders. (Many people easily avoid the pitfalls of business worship or mystical commerce only to fall into the trap of the mystical State, which makes them imagine that a group of institutions and a rough-and-ready organisation for political and economic purposes—let us say a combination of the British Museum, the Metropolitan Water Board, and New Scotland Yard—are somehow more important, of deeper significance to the wide universe, than the sum total of the human beings concerned. And I take this to be the most fashionable and potent illusion of our time; perhaps the father of those warring children, Communism and Fascism.) We must return, however, to the paternal factory system as it is working here and now.

I would say then, in a desperate attempt to conclude the matter and continue my journey, that workers in such places as Bournville have so many solid benefits conferred on them, benefits that must inevitably raise their status, both physical and mental, that, in spite of the obvious dangers of the system, they are better placed, as citizens of to-day or to-morrow, than the ordinary factory worker, who is probably not so content either at work or play. (Though I cannot help wondering whether a girl or boy, put to some monotonous characterless task, then exercised, amused, and educated, will want to continue working at that monotonous characterless task. In short, the system may be sowing the seeds of its own destruction.) On the other hand, I for one would infinitely prefer to see workers combining to provide these benefits, or a reasonable proportion of them, for themselves, to see them forming associations far removed from the factory, to see them using their leisure, and demanding its increase, not as favoured employees but as citizens, free men and women.

And now, back in Birmingham in the dusk, I must offer a score of apologies to Messrs. Cadbury and their busy ten thousand, good hosts all of them and benefactors of the sweet tooth, for using them all as pegs when they had used me as a man and a brother.

[3]

On Saturday night I attended a public whist drive. Bear in mind that card games, like almost everything else in this land of social hierarchies, are not without their class distinctions. Whist was once the favourite card game of the upper classes. Now that those people play bridge, auction or contract, whist has found its devotees in a very different set of people, chiefly the small shop-keeping, artisan, and working classes. Why don't these people play bridge, which is, after all, a much better game? We can only guess. Some of them think bridge much too complicated for them. On the other hand, many of them play a good game of solo whist, which demands considerable initiative and skill. (I have often thought that some of its devices—such as the *misère* call, the contract to lose tricks instead of making them—might have been profitably adapted to bridge.) Probably a second and weightier reason is that many of these people do not play bridge because they shrink from imitating the wealthier classes and do not want their friends and neighbours to think they are suddenly 'trying to be posh'. After all, there is more than one kind of snobbery. We hear a lot about the man who dresses for dinner in Central Africa; but that must not make us forget the existence of a much larger number of men who would die of shame if they were discovered by their acquaintances conveying soup to their mouths above a stiff white shirt. But whatever the reason may be, the fact remains that whist is still the favourite card game of the mass of the English people. The whist drive I attended, one of several advertised in the evening paper, was not a private social function, the equivalent of a bridge party, but a public affair, a combined entertainment and gamble, run by some astute person for profit. (And a very nice thing he must make out of it, too.) It seemed from the advertisement to be the largest and most swaggering. You paid two shillings to compete, but there were money prizes amounting to twenty-three pounds. I concluded, rightly as it turned out, that a man who promises to part with so much prize-money must be fairly certain of getting a great many patrons at two shillings a head. The whist drive, one of a tri-weekly series, was held in a certain public hall and began at eight-fifteen. So I raced through my dinner and hurried on to it.

The hall was large, austere in colouring and decoration, and lighted in the most uncompromising fashion by unshaded bulbs of high voltage. It had about as much intimate charm as the average big railway station. I guessed at once that we were in for a formidably business-like evening. Suspended from the ceiling, about a third of the way down the room, was a large indicator, showing the four suits. The remaining two-thirds of the hall, beyond this indicator, were filled with very small chairs ranged round very small tables, most of them not proper card tables but mysterious objects covered with what seemed then, and afterwards, squares of rather dirty blanket material. When you paid your two shillings, you were given a scoring card, either black or red. (Mine was black.) On this card were the rules, the number of your first table, and then spaces for the numbers of your succeeding tables, the tricks you made, and your totals. There were several hundred people there, and most of them seemed to be regular patrons and to know one another. They were mostly middle-aged decent working folk, with only a sprinkling of younger men and women. Nearly all the men smoked, and a fair proportion of the women; but there were no ash-trays. I knocked my pipe out on my heel. What the cigarette smokers did, I do not know. After about ten minutes a man shouted at us through a megaphone and we all went to our tables. The indicator told us what were trumps by lighting up a gigantic ace of clubs. We started. There followed what seemed to me one of the most strenuous hours I have ever spent. To begin with, the games were played at a tremendous speed, aces being banged on kings without a moment's hesitation. Then there was so much to do. You had to fill in your card and to initial the card on each table. If you were the losing man arriving at a new table—and I nearly always was—you had to shuffle the cards before the cut for deal. And three times out of four it seemed to be my fate to deal, and as the packs at each successive table appeared to be older and older and greasier and greasier, so that they were about four inches thick when they were stacked ready to be cut, dealing was an unpleasant business. Never in my life, not even in the trenches, have I ever seen dirtier and older packs of cards. It was not pleasant to hold them, even when they showed you a smudge of aces and kings; and it was a downright penance to be continually shuffling and dealing them. So what with shuffling, cutting, dealing, playing, gathering tricks up on those bits of blanket, clerkly work with the table card and your own card, changing tables, pushing past enormous fat women, I was kept so busy that after about half an hour of it I was fairly perspiring. And there was never a minute to lose. The whistle blew, as a signal to change tables, the indicator lit up its new suit of trumps, and if you had not finished your game, there were people waiting and looking very cross about it. There was practically no time for conversation, hardly time to smile. What conversation there was about the game, if for once it finished before the whistle blew, I could not understand. Three times my various partners said to me, 'I'd a good back hand,' and I could only assent feebly, for I did not know then and do not know now what a good back hand is. As I have not played whist, which is a very different game from bridge, for twenty years, and as all these games were run off at such a colossal speed, I cannot tell you whether these people played well or badly. I suspect that most of it must have been very perfunctory play, with no nonsense about finessing in it. All my partners were either very big fat women, who bulged over their chairs and the tables, and sweated good-humouredly, or else little witch-like females with sharp noses, tucked-in mouths, and iron spectacles, who held their cards very close to the brooches they wore, hardly ever spoke, and looked very cross, though I do not actually think they were. There were two distinct types among the men: the solid hearty chaps who sat bolt upright, puffing out clouds of smoke and banged each card down, as if sheer force might win the trick; and the little thin cunning fellows who sank down and down and half-closed their eyes as they played, like so many Nibelungs. When the whistle blew after the twelfth game everybody made a rush for the top end of the hall, and reappeared a few minutes afterwards, eating fruits, tarts and slabs of cake.

This was the interval and by this time I had had quite enough whist-driving, but it seemed to me that if one player disappeared the whole elaborate organisation would be flung into disorder. So I stayed on and played another twelve games, nearly always losing and so going from table to table and shuffling packs of cards greasier than any I had ever seen before, cards that ought to have been thrown into the dustbin months ago; and I found myself in a far corner where the tables were almost touching one another and enormous women were unable to extricate themselves, and it was sweatier and hotter and smokier than ever. My total score was one hundred and fifty-five, which was some thirty or forty below the best. But there was still a chance that I might win a prize for a 'mystery number,' which was drawn by the promoter, after he had given the prizes for the winning scores. There was no excitement at the end, no cheering, no applause. It was all as brisk and business-like as the whole evening had been. When the last prize had been awarded, everybody cleared off, rather as if they were leaving a factory than making an end of a night's pleasure. I supposed they enjoyed it—which was more than I did—otherwise they would not regularly attend these functions, as they undoubtedly do, but anything superficially less like a night's pleasure I never did see. Considering that many of them must be engaged all day in work that must be at once bustling and boring, it is surprising that they should choose this method of passing the evening. I do not believe that it is card-playing that attracts them there, for nobody could enjoy playing cards at such a speed. The secret is the gamble, the chance of winning two or three pounds for your two shillings. The purely social side of the whist drive was negligible; or at least so it seemed to me, though of course I was a stranger and may have missed some quiet fun. At the end, two impressions remained with me. It is difficult to find words for them here without appearing unpleasantly patronising; but I must take that risk. First, I was struck by the extraordinary ugliness of most of the people there. Nobody has ever called me handsome, and I do not ask for a very high standard of good looks in other people. It is not that these people lacked regular features, fine figures, bright eyes, and so forth. They were, for the most

BIRMINGHAM TRAMSCAPE, c.1930   *H. J. Whitlock*

part, downright ugly, really unpleasing to look at closely. The women were either much too fat or far too thin. The men looked like lop-sided oafs, gnomes, hobgoblins. Nearly all looked as if life had knocked them into odd shapes, taken the bloom out of their faces, twisted their features and dulled their eyes.

The second impression that remained was of a different character. These people might be ugly to look at but they were not ugly to be with; in other words, they were surprisingly good-mannered and good-humoured. I never saw one exhibition of bad temper all the evening. Some were obviously much better players than others, and there was money at stake, but nevertheless there was never an embarrassing moment. Even the witch-like, iron-spectacled little women were never actually rude to anybody. They were all patient, decent, good-tempered folk, and they compared extremely favourably, startlingly, with the well-nurtured people I have often seen giving a show of bad manners and egoism at bridge tables, not merely in private but also in functions such as this. The sharp contrast between appearance and manner was very curious.

CHAPTER SIX

To the Black Country

From Birmingham I went to have a look at the Black Country, which lies to the north and west of the city. This notorious region was strange to me. Now I have seen it, but of course it is still strange to me. You have to live some time in these places to understand their peculiar qualities. All I can do is to offer a few sketches, probably not at all accurate nor free from a certain subjective colouring, for in retrospect it is difficult to disengage the scene from the mood. But perhaps that does not matter: the record of a journey of this kind may be more important if it chronicles a succession of moods than if it captures a succession of scenes. Here, I think, I ought to say a little more about myself. It happens that during the last few years I have been away from industrial districts and have spent most of my time in far pleasanter places. But the first nineteen years of my life were passed in the industrial West Riding, in the shadow of the tall chimneys; and even now I am not unduly fastidious about my surroundings. So you may take it that throughout this book I am not adopting some absurdly high standard that would make life in half of England impossible. I am not shocked because an iron foundry or a wool-combing mill has little in common with an author's drawing-room or study: I have long known what kind of places men have to labour in. My standard may be rough and ready and somewhat uncertain, but you can assume it is a reasonable one. If I declare that Coketown is a horrible hole, I do not merely mean that it cannot be fitted in to some private fairy-tale Merrie England of my own: I mean that it is a damned horrible hole. And I hope you will take my word for it.

I spent the better part of two days staring at this Black Country. The first day was fine and fairly bright. I went from Birmingham through Smethwick and Oldbury to Dudley, which seemed to me a fantastic place. You climb a hill, past innumerable grim works and unpleasant brick dwellings, and then suddenly a ridiculous terra-cotta music-hall comes into sight, perched on the steep roadside as if a giant had plucked it out of one of the neighbouring valleys and carelessly left it there; and above this music-hall (its attraction that week was *Parisian Follies*) were the ruins of Dudley Castle. I climbed a steep little hillside, and then smoked a pipe or two sitting by the remains of the Keep. The view from there is colossal. On the Dudley side, you look

GAS WORKS, TIPTON, c.1931   *Photographer Unknown*

down and across at roofs and steeply mounting streets and pointing factory
chimneys. It looked as if a great slab of Birmingham had been torn away and
then tilted up there at an angle of about forty-five degrees. The view from
the other side, roughly, I suppose, to the north-east, was even more impressive.
There was the Black Country unrolled before you like a smouldering carpet.
You looked into an immense hollow of smoke and blurred buildings and factory chimneys. There seemed to be no end to it. In the vague middle, dominating everything, was an enormous round white tower, which I afterwards
learned was a new gasometer. It looked bigger than anything else in sight,
and as nothing had dimension that could be measured it was any size you
like to imagine it. You could think of it, without unduly straining your fancy,
as the temple of some horrible new religion. The only sounds that arrived
from this misty immensity below came from the tangle of railway lines that
gleamed in the foreground of the scene, and these noises were so clear that
they might have been picked out and then amplified. There was the scream
of a locomotive; there was the clanking of the bumped wagons; there was
the long pu-u-ushing of a train gathering speed. I never remember hearing

these railway sounds so clearly. Nothing else came from that enormous hollow. You could easily believe that there were no people down there, that a goods locomotive was probably the most playful inhabitant of the region. I was glad that I did not know the names of the towns down there in the smoke; I felt that I was not looking at this place and that, but at the metallic Midlands themselves, at a relief map of a heavy industry, at another and greater exhibition of the 'fifties. No doubt at all that the region had a sombre beauty of its own. I thought so then, and I thought so later, when I had seen far more of its iron face lit with hell fire. But it was a beauty you could appreciate chiefly because you were not condemned to live there. If I could do what I liked with the whole country, I would keep a good tract of this region as it is now, to be stared and wondered at; but I would find it difficult to ask any but a few curators to live in it.

I descended into the vast smoky hollow and watched it turn itself into so many workshops, grimy rows of houses, pubs and picture theatres, yards filled with rusted metal, and great patches of waste ground. There was a cynical abundance of these patches of waste ground, which were as shocking as raw sores and open wounds. In my own West Riding, industry of the grimmest and most uncompromising kind has long been allowed to work its will on the countryside. There, however, the countryside itself is grim and uncompromising. Sometimes the mills, the rows of little houses, the cobbled streets, all seem like natural outcroppings of the Pennine rock. Huddersfield and Rochdale, Keighley and Nelson, may look grim, but the high lands that still separate them look even grimmer. But here in these Midlands, the countryside is mild and friendly. It is on the border of Arden itself. Industry has ravished it; drunken storm troops have passed this way; there are signs of atrocities everywhere; the earth has been left gaping and bleeding; and what were once bright fields have been rummaged and raped into these dreadful patches of waste ground. And nothing I saw there, not even the slums, impressed me more painfully.

The places I saw had names, but these names were merely so much alliteration: Wolverhampton, Wednesbury, Wednesfield, Willenhall and Walsall. You could call them all wilderness, and have done with it. I never knew where one ended and another began. I remember noticing in Wolverhampton, after half an hour of dingy higgledy-piggledy, the new building of the Midland Counties Dairy, white and trim and with immense windows, and thinking how alien it looked there, like the outpost of a new civilisation. I remember arriving at the very end of the earth, where the land appeared to have been uprooted by a giant pig and where there were cottages so small and odd that they must

have been built for gnomes, and this end of the earth was called Gornal, and there the women, returning home from the brickworks, wore caps and shawls. The shawls were like those that the weavers used to wear in my own town, but our women had worn their shawls over their heads. Here, however, they wore caps as well, and looked as outlandish as the place they lived in. Afterwards I ran right through the Black Country and came out at the other end, almost within sight of the Potteries. On the way back, somewhere between Stafford and Rugeley, I came to a bit of heath country, glowing with autumn, that was as pleasant as you could wish. There the sun went down. It was dark long before I got back to Birmingham; the ravished waste ground, the miserable houses, the muddle of dirty brick, the whole battlefield of industry, sank down and disappeared, and in their places appeared mysterious red gleams of fire and a pretty tracery of lights, so that I was happier staring about me than I had been all day.

My second day there was a Sunday, and in foul weather. Sometimes the raw fog dripped; sometimes the cold rain steamed; but throughout it was thick and wet and chilled. I lunched in one of the smaller towns with a man in the metal trade. There were several Black Country business men there, large hearty fellows, sturdy eaters and drinkers. There had been a sudden flurry of business in the metal trade, and my friend was going back to his office and warehouse in West Bromwich after lunch. I went with him, and on the way was shown, among other things, the last dairy farm in the district. It stood there surrounded for miles by the grim paraphernalia of industrialism; I had only a glimpse of it, a solitary surviving farmhouse in the wet fog, with a few ghostly fields on either side. My friend's warehouse was in—shall we say?—'Rusty Lane,' West Bromwich. He keeps sheets of steel there, and no doubt any place is good enough to keep sheets of steel in; but I do not think I could let even a sheet of steel stay long in Rusty Lane. I have never seen such a picture of grimy desolation as that street offered me. If you put it, brick for brick, into a novel, people would not accept it, would condemn you as a caricaturist and talk about Dickens. The whole neighbourhood is mean and squalid, but this particular street seemed the worst of all. It would not matter very much— though it would matter—if only metal were kept there; but it happens that people live there, children are born there and grow up there. I saw some of them. I was being shown one of the warehouses, where steel plates were stacked in the chill gloom, and we heard a bang and rattle on the roof. The boys,

PHOENIX PASSAGE, DUDLEY, c.1930   *Photographer Unknown*

BLACK COUNTRY VISTA, 1934   *Photographer Unknown*

it seems, were throwing stones again. They were always throwing stones on that roof. We went out to find them, but only found three frightened little girls, who looked at us with round eyes in wet smudgy faces. No, they hadn't done it, the boys had done it, and the boys had just run away. Where they could run to, I cannot imagine. They need not have run away from me, because I could not blame them if they threw stones and stones and smashed every pane of glass for miles. Nobody can blame them if they grow up to smash everything that can be smashed. There ought to be no more of those lunches and dinners, at which political and financial and industrial gentlemen congratulate one another, until something is done about Rusty Lane and West Bromwich. While they still exist in their present foul shape, it is idle to congratulate ourselves about anything. They make the whole pomp of government here a miserable farce. The Crown, Lords and Commons are the Crown, Lords and Commons of Rusty Lane, West Bromwich. In the heart of the great empire on which the sun never sets, in the land of hope and glory, Mother of the Free, is Rusty Lane, West Bromwich. What do they know of England who only England know? The answer must be Rusty Lane, West Bromwich. And if there is another economic conference, let it meet there, in one of the warehouses, and be fed with bread and margarine and slabs of brawn. The delegates have seen one England, Mayfair in the season. Let them see another England next time, West Bromwich out of the season. Out of all seasons except the winter of our discontent.

CHAPTER SEVEN

To Leicester and Nottingham

[1]

The sun was warming the famous hunting country—the very heart of 'the Shires'—as I passed through it. I did not break my journey to have another look at Market Harborough. Hunting country and hunting people have their own literature, and I have no wish to add to it. I have only now and again met hunting people and I do not understand them. Men and women whose whole lives are organised in order that they may ride in pursuit of stray foxes two or three days a week, who risk their necks for a vermin's brush, who will deny themselves this and that to spend money on packs of hounds, who spare no pains to turn themselves into twelfth-century oafs, are past my comprehension. All I ask is that they should not pretend to be solemnly doing their duty when in reality they are indulging and enjoying themselves. The fox-hunter who begins mumbling excuses, who tells you that he hunts to rid the countryside of foxes, that hunting is valuable because it improves the breed of horses (i.e. hunters), is a contemptible fellow. But I am prepared to respect the hunting man who looks you straight in the eye and declares in downright fashion: 'I hunt because I like it. Hunting's the most glorious sport in the world, and I live for it. It may be extravagant, cruel, antisocial, anything you like, but I don't give a damn. And as long as society allows me to hunt, I shall hunt. Halloo!' But I have not met him yet. There is a fair chance that I shall, however, because people tell me that the sport is taking on a new lease of life, in spite of the shortage of money. More and more people are hunting or wanting to hunt, just as more and more people are beginning to ride again. The horse as a mere beast of burden may be at the end of his days, but as a sporting companion he is starting life all over again. It will be some time yet before these little rolling hills of Leicestershire forget the pounding of hoofs.

The sun had not set when I came into Leicester itself, which looked quite bright and new. Actually it is very old and offers you a very rum mixed list of historical associations: for example, King Lear and his daughters lived here, if they ever lived anywhere; it is Simon de Montfort's town; the broken Cardinal Wolsey came here to die, and has now acquired a new immortality by having his name stamped on thousands of bales of stockings and underclothes;

John Bunyan saw the siege here during the Civil War; and among its nine-teenth-century citizens was the original Thomas Cook, who ran his first little excursion out of Leicester station. But somehow you do not believe in all these goings on. The town seems to have no atmosphere of its own. I felt I was quite ready to praise it, but was glad to think I did not live in it. There are many worse places I would rather live in. It seemed to me to lack character, to be busy and cheerful and industrial and built of red brick, and to be nothing else. Such was my immediate impression.

I spent my first evening there walking about the centre of the town, which is neither dignified nor very extensive, indeed hardly worthy of the excellent residential quarters outside it. I wanted some travelling slippers. The first shop I went into had none at all, and the second could only offer me three pairs to choose from; yet Leicester itself is in the boot and shoe trade. There was a large open market, well lighted with electricity, but though it was doing good business in everything from tablecloths to cough mixtures, it was not amusing. Indeed I found nothing amusing in these streets. (It would not be difficult to invent something amusing for them, but I am here to tell the truth.) Possibly I may not have been in the right frame of mind to discover anything amusing, but I suspect it was chiefly the town's fault. I returned to my hotel for dinner. Outside, this hotel looked like a large go-ahead Congregational chapel *circa* 1900, and its entrance compared unfavourably with that of most Underground stations. But inside, in parts, it was better. The basement was very gay and modern with a grill room (food not bad) and a cocktail bar com-plete with white-coated barmen, salted almonds, and price lists shaped like cocktail shakers. There was quite a brisk demand for cocktails, mostly double ones too, while I was there, and not from guests in the hotel but mostly, I imagine, from young business men and their wives and girl friends. I have noticed before that the more dashing persons of both sexes in provincial towns have a passion for cocktails and seem to be ready to drink them at any time. The cocktail is no longer an *apéritif*, which is what it was designed to be, but a drink for all hours. The taverns offer you cocktails in bottles of all sizes. Perhaps very soon, as the wave of fashion slowly travels outward and enlarges itself, all the landlords of country alehouses and the farmers will be hard at it rattling cocktail shakers and adding dashes of absinthe and spearing olives; by which time the tide of sherry will have reached the larger provincial towns from London. These waves of fashion, rising in Berkeley Square and then slowly travelling out until at last they ebb and dwindle into demi-detached villas outside Newcastle and farmhouses in Devonshire, are very curious and instructive, and are particularly noticeable in the matter of furniture and decoration. Now fashionable persons collect glass ornaments of the mid-Victorian period—the very ornaments that the smarter housewives in the provinces were banishing to the lumber room when I was a small boy. We have gone round the full circle. Somebody ought to write a *Cavalcade* of these travelling fashions.

During dinner I examined the two local papers to see how I could spend my evening. A Leicester man had boasted to me that the town was now the chief sporting centre of the provinces, being able to offer you good examples of every sport, and notably boxing; but on this particular evening it had no sport to offer. So I asked the waiter, who was a Leicester lad born and bred, but who had somehow contrived to give himself a foreign look (he will probably go far, that boy), where I could go to see Leicester enjoying itself of an evening, and he suggested a certain dance-hall, which was having one of its 'popular nights'. So there I went, paying one and sixpence to go in and threepence to leave my hat and overcoat in the cloak-room. The hall itself, which had a balcony all round it, a large floor and a lighting equipment superior to that of most of the London hotels and supper-dancing places, was quite good; it could have comfortably entertained six times as many dancers as were there. Most of the patrons were young and there were nearly as many boys there as girls. They seemed to me to dance very well—fox-trots, quick-steps, rumbas, waltzes—and in a much more reserved and dignified fashion than their social superiors in the West End. They were, I imagine, mostly factory hands, and apart from an occasional guffawing from a group of lads, they were quiet and serious, as sedately intent on their steps as a conference of dancing teachers. I felt an intruder, and left after a quarter of an hour or so, only to discover that the music hall where I had formerly seen a good robust show was now given up to Constance Bennett. In the whole of Leicester that night there was only one performance being given by living players, in a touring musical comedy. In a town with nearly a quarter of a million people, not without intelligence or money, this is not good enough. Soon we shall be as badly off as America, where I would find myself in large cities that had not a single living actor performing in them, nothing but films, films, films. There a whole generation has grown up that associates entertainment with moving pictures and with nothing else; and I am not sure that as much could not be said of this country. I rather like films, but not in my capacity as an enquiring traveller. They do not offer you any knowledge of the town you are visiting, only an escape from it; once inside a picture theatre, you might be anywhere, from Iowa City to Preston. A theatre or a music-hall not only has real performers but it also has real audiences, and so can tell you something about the local people, who come alive and are not merely deeper shadows in the murk. This is yet another reason for deploring the growing scarcity of proper theatres.

So I walked round the Clock Tower once again, and then went back to the upstairs lounge of my hotel, which was now filling up with commercial travellers, who sat in groups of three and four at little tables, convivial with Worthington and White Horse. At one of the tables were three women, one middle-aged and the other two young—the only women present—and they seemed to be busy talking shop and were apparently commercial travellers too. Or were they buyers of some kind? I ought to have found out exactly what they were—for obviously they were brisk women of business—but I lacked the courage. Somebody ought to write a book about the newer occupations, among which, I take it, female commercial travelling will have a place. Then to bed, where I slept wretchedly, as I generally do the first night in one of these hotels. I have to write about what happens during the day, but what happens during the day is a mere flash, a fleeting gleam of sane daylight, compared with the stifling epics of dark dream and miserable waking and re-awakening that make up one of these bad nights.

[2]

The next morning was bright again, and I came to it like a man creeping out of the grave. The Imperial Typewriter Company, which is a large-scale British organisation in this business, has its headquarters in Leicester, and so I went out to their factory, in one of the suburbs. After all, I have been using typewriters (I am using one now, to write this) for over twenty years; it was high time I saw how they are made. There are some things that you can imagine yourself making in a rough-and-ready fashion, but typewriters are not one of those things. And for twenty years, I had more or less taken them for granted. During that time they had developed amazingly. I can see my first typewriter now. It had the old double keyboard, an entirely different set of keys for capitals and figures, so that the paper seemed a long way off, and the machine itself was as big and solid as a battle cruiser. Typing then was a muscular activity. You could ache after it. If you were not familiar with these vast keyboards, your hand wandered over them like a child lost in a wood. The noise might have been that of a shipyard on the Clyde. You would no more have thought of carrying about one of those grim iron structures than you would have thought of travelling with a piano. Since then I have owned machines of wildly different sizes and shapes and capabilities, and at this very moment possess several neat little portables, the ingenious implements of my trade. Just as some men talk about the motor cars they have driven, so, when I occasionally meet a fellow typewriter-owner of long and rich experience, I talk about the various machines I have hammered at. I had a grand talk of this kind with the general manager that morning, though of course he did most of the talking, out of a very long and rich experience. There is romance, the genuine glinting stuff, in typewriters, and not merely in their development from clumsy giants into agile dwarfs, but in the history of their manufacture, which is filled with raids, battles, lonely pioneers, great gambles, hope, fear, despair, triumph. If some of our novels could be written *by* the typewriters instead of *on* them, how much better they would be.

A typewriter is a very difficult machine to manufacture because it has so many parts, from fifteen hundred to two thousand, mostly tiny; and it must be accurate. Imagine taking a typewriter to pieces, down to the last tiny screw, and then giving yourself the job of manufacturing all these parts and of assembling them accurately afterwards. I went first through the workshops where the separate parts are made. It was rather frightening, like finding yourself inside a typewriter with some colossus hard at work writing on it. There seemed to be an awful lot of power for the space. There were dozens and dozens of small machines, of the lathe kind, turning out springs and screws and nuts. These machines were so close to one another, and there seemed such enormous power harnessed between these narrow aisles, that you felt that if one belt broke you would be torn to pieces. Every machine had a constant thick flow of lubricating oil. But on one machine the pouring liquid was crimson, and it looked for one startling second as if the moving metal were being drenched in blood. But that, I was told, is a new lubricant, strongly antiseptic. There are actually very few accidents here, in spite of my fears. But I was glad to get out of that workshop, though I must say that the mechanics themselves seemed cheerful enough. Across the way the parts were assembled. I now know a great deal about typewriters that I never even guessed before. I know how they are made to look so black and shiny in front, for I saw the frames being sprayed with lacquer and then artificially dried. I know how the pretty gold lettering is put on, for I saw them applying the transfers. I know how the type—and these people made all manner of type—is manufactured, for I was shown how first a drawing is made, fifty times the required size, then how, from that, a steel 'master' is made, ten times the required size, and then how from that a die is made, and how this die stamps out the type, in various busy little machines. I saw the typewriters being assembled, passing from hand to hand and becoming more like my familiar companion of the study at every

'GOOD COMPANION' PORTABLES, 1936   *Photographer Unknown*

fresh move. Every process seemed to me astonishingly ingenious. And *amusing*, that is, amusing to plan and work out and first construct and then to revisit occasionally, but not of course equally amusing to attend to in a dumb mechanical fashion for eight hours a day. They had a clever arrangement of movable coloured pegs in a board that showed how everybody was getting on with everything. This must have been huge fun for the man who first worked it out, but not such fun for the people whose day-long activities are pegged there. In fact, what struck me here, as it did in most of the large-scale factories I saw, was the enthusiasm of the men responsible for all these ingenuities. They it is who are the happy children of our mechanical age. They have been allowed to play with gadgets to their hearts' content. And very well they have played too. Their cunning and resource are wonderful. What an artful creature the modern engineer is. Give him a wheel or two, a pulley and a moving arm, and he can make anything. He ought to be—and, I think, is—the happiest of us all. We must not forget that though machinery has enslaved some people, it has liberated others, who have found themselves in a world they can enjoy. There is an ingenious, machine-minded man, not apt at expressing himself except in terms of mechanics, who comes to his perfect fulfilment in this age. When he is at work, he has machines to think about, and when he is at play, there are motor cars and airplanes and wireless set for him. You find men of this type, square pegs in square holes, in all the executive positions in these factories, and their happy enthusiasm is almost infectious. But there is a big drop from them to the mass of employees, all caught up in monotonous routine work. Nor do bonus and welfare schemes, admirable though they may be, do anything to bridge the gulf between these two classes, the masters of the machines and the servants of the machines. It is not here a question of the capitalists and the proletariat, the bosses and the workers. The men I call the masters of the machines may not have a penny of capital and they are workers too, and workers who are ready to go on working long after the whistle has sounded. It is not a question of economic status at all. In the more old-fashioned enterprises, in which machinery plays a much smaller part, you do not notice this sharp division between the employees who can and must be interested and those who cannot even be expected to have any real personal concern for their work. But I suspect that the more we use machinery, the greater this gulf will be, and I do not see that any change in the economic system will do much to bridge it. If the State ran the factory, the division would still be there. It is of course rapidly becoming a division between sexes, because the interested executives, the masters of the machines, are men, and the routine workers, the servants of the machines, are recruited more and more from girls and young women. (Not in the manufacture of typewriters. I have left that behind now.) Some very big concerns, engaged in highly organised production, employ only a few men, because the men expect permanent jobs, but they take on crowds of girls because it is assumed that most of them will leave to get married when they are in their middle twenties. But if this goes on—and it is going on—all the prospective bridegrooms will be out of work. Here, in short, is a pretty little nest of problems; but for the moment I must leave them. I have been all over the Imperial Typewriter Company's works, have duly admired the enterprise and ingenuity displayed there, and now it is time for lunch.

It was one of the directors of the above concern who entertained me to lunch. He has a house in what seemed to me a very pleasant residential quarter of the town, a quarter with wide streets and detached villas. This particular house was of an excellent design, and when I was told that it had been built forty years before, when houses were rarely designed or executed with any taste, I was curious to learn why my host should have been so fortunate. It seems that Leicester has had for some time, more than forty years, a few citizens who have been first-class designers and craftsmen, and this house had been the creation of one of them. I remembered then that I had heard of these Leicester craftsmen before, and indeed knew one or two good artists who had come from this place.

During lunch, which was both substantial and good, a blue budgerigar flashed about the room, like a handful of June sky. I then discovered that my host was a man with a hobby, the breeding of rare cage birds. After lunch I was taken into the garden and there found a whole aviary; half a dozen wired enclosures, sufficiently spacious, bright with velvety finches, parakeets and macaws, and yellow, emerald and blue budgerigars that turned themselves, when they were disturbed, into a sudden dazzle of colour. There were dozens and dozens of these brilliant little creatures, some of them amusingly tame, and all of them healthy and enjoying life. As he popped in and out of these enclosures, or offered some particular pet its favourite delicacy, my host was a happy man, gloriously riding his hobby-horse, which must have been a fairly expensive steed. There was in all this something delightfully unexpected. You meet a middle-aged business man in a prosaic provincial industrial town; you go with him to his house in a pleasant but tame suburb; and then the next minute you see him among little tropical birds that flash like jewels. When there are no more charming or droll adventures like this for a traveller, England will be England no longer. But this is still the country of gigantic hobby-horses. My host himself seemed to think it wasn't. Men should have hobbies, he declared, but now, in this world of cheap popular amusements, the hobby was not what it was. This, I told him, I doubted. Some of the old interests may have declined; though that was no great matter, as we could well spare them. But when one gets at the facts, they always disprove these head-shaking statements about cheap popular amusements driving this and that out of men's lives. You find on enquiry that men are still mounting hobby-horses as gaily as ever. Many people forget that the patrons of cheap popular amusements, the cinema and the wireless and so on, have largely come from a class of persons that before did nothing in its leisure but gossip and yawn and kick the cat and twiddle its thumbs. Moreover, these people have far more leisure than they ever had before. Very soon, the hobby-horse will be flourishing on a scale beyond the dreams of our fathers. So much I suggested to my host, who, when I asked him whether there was a dwindling interest in his own hobby, was compelled to admit that so many of these coloured birds had been bred of late years that the prices had rapidly dropped. No, the hobby-horse is with us; and I was delighted, on this occasion, to see it grow such emerald wings.

[3]

Leicester has been a hosiery town these last three hundred years. Since the Industrial Revolution it has specialised in worsted hosiery, for which the Leicestershire long wools are very suitable. Recently it has linked itself to other textile industries by its large manufacture of knitted goods. The biggest concern in the hosiery and knitted goods trade is the Wolsey company, which has factories all over the town. I went over three of them, that afternoon. Everywhere, except among the vats of dye where men do the work, there were enormous rooms filled with women and girls, who worked with small machines or at long tables. I saw no big machinery at any of the factories I visited. One has got into the habit of associating mass production with mental pictures of vast machines, into whose oily maws goes the raw material, to be transformed into the finished product somewhere in the interior of the machinery. The reality is quite different. There is still far more hand labour than machine work. The machines that are used are nearly always quite small. In these factories at Leicester you saw long rows of sewing machines worked by electric power but guided by hand. In some rooms there was hardly a revolving wheel to be seen. I cannot describe the numerous processes I was shown. I was left with a dazed impression of miles and miles of stockings, underclothes, knitted dresses and the like, with bright acres of femininity at work on them. I remember a cutting machine that went through a thick soft pile of material for men's pants like a knife going through cheese. But that seemed the most dashing wholesale process on view, for after that an immense amount of hand work, merely eked out with electric power, appeared to be expended on the garments. There were energetic little machines that made buttonholes or sewed on buttons. But the most relentless of the machines had nothing to do with the textile side of the business; it made cardboard boxes and stuck labels on them. Here the girls had to feed the machines at a very brisk pace, with pasted labels and the like, and this looked to me the worst set of jobs, for horrible pace and monotony, in all the rooms I visited. In another place I saw a girl printing—or rather transferring—the firm's name on pairs of socks. She had a pile of socks on one side, a pile of little transfer papers on the other, and a sort of iron in her hand, and the speed with which she put a transfer on a sock and ironed the name in and then removed the used transfer was enough, merely watching her, to make you dizzy. The manager and I stopped to look on. She was a pleasant-looking girl, and quite bright. She explained that she was on piece-work, had to do so many pairs of socks, hundreds and hundreds a day, and was generally able to make between two and three pounds a week. The manager had been telling me that, in his experience, girls preferred purely routine and monotonous jobs because once they had learned the fairly simple necessary movements they could then work all day and think about something else while they were working. Their fingers would be busy with the sewing machines or irons, but their minds could be far away, wondering how Elsie was getting on with Joe or brooding over the film stars, male and female, whose photographs we saw pinned up here and there. I said that it seemed to me impossible that the girl who did the conjuring trick with the socks and the transfers could possibly think about anything else; but she assured us that she could, and though it looked all wrong that she should be performing such a task at such a speed all day, truth compels me to add that she showed no signs of being anything but a cheerful, healthy young woman.

In these factories they are using some elaborate new system of organising and tabulating their production in its various units, with the result that these enormous rooms, some with hundreds of girls at work in them, almost look after themselves. You see hardly a sign of active supervision. The foreman class has been nearly eliminated. The embryo of a sock or pair of woollen pants finds its way into one room, and then goes from floor to floor, perhaps from factory to factory, coming ever nearer to perfection in its kind, until at last it packs itself in a neat box with eleven others; and nobody responsible and authoritative has seen it once on its way, and from first to last there have been no orders, no fuss. Only one or two men in an office know exactly what has happened, from beginning to end. The plan is there, perhaps inside a desk, and the huge building, with its crowded floors of busy work-girls, simply carries out the plan. You never seem to see the dumb secrecy and uncontrolled orderliness of a bee-hive or an ant-hill. It is queer, rather frightening. Moreover, though machinery plays a big part, power being on tap everywhere, these are not places filled with machines, for the human element in labour appears to be still dominant; but the point is that this human element has been woven into a gigantic system of minute subdivision of labour until the whole place is really an enormous machine in which the workers are simply cogs and levers. And now we see again, in a still more marked form, that great distinction between the fortunate few who are outside the machine and are capable of making changes in it, and the great mass of ordinary workpeople, mostly women, who are inside the machine, simply part of it. This distinction is so great that you feel that the two sets of people ought to belong to two different races. It is something too, I feel, that belongs to our own time, with its large-scale methods of production, its scientific systems, its experiments in industrial psychology. Fifty years ago, in industrial life, the difference between these classes *outside* the factory was probably much greater than it is to-day, but it was not so great inside, at work, where you had all manner of people sometimes supervising and sometimes lending a hand with the job. The workpeople in these new factories nearly always have a share in the profits, and of course they are much better paid and looked after than their grandfathers and grandmothers were in their young days; but for all that, I cannot help feeling that they are really much further from the controlling centre of things, the heart and brain of the industry, than their grandparents were, for they cannot know what happened to the material they are working with half an hour before it reached them or what will happen to it half an hour after they have let it go. Their outlook must necessarily be restricted to their one endless tiny task. They are not bullied or even nagged at; their very weaknesses are elaborately taken into account; their comfort is considered; but between the time when they 'clock in' and 'clock out' their central human dignity, which entitles them under our democratic system to a vote as good as anybody else's, has no real existence, except in that dream of life which occupies their minds as their fingers fly to do their one mysterious little task.

When I had seen as much as I wanted to see of this imposing industrial organisation, we lingered at the outer door, three or four of us, and began discussing the mechanical and monotonous work imposed by this mass production. There was no putting back the clock, they said; and I did not remind them that we would all be putting back the clock on the following Saturday night, at the end of summer-time. There was general agreement that we are committed to these industrial methods. The only thing to do now was to keep on cutting down the hours of this monotonous employment. Which meant much more leisure, said one of them, and that meant that this leisure would have to be organised. The whole point about leisure, another objected, is that it should not be organised. A third said that most of the men working under his management did not really want more leisure and did not know what to do with themselves when some accident thrust it on them. The danger is, of course, that this robot employment will alternate with robot leisure, passive amusement as standardised and impersonal as the tasks at the machines. If within these next few years the hours are cut down in these highly organised factories, then the people who work their five or six hours a day in them should be encouraged to be as active and individual and freely creative as possible in their spare time; though I cannot help suspecting that if that encouragement is successful and these people are active and individual and freely creative in their leisure, they will soon want to make a full-time job of being active and individual and may take it into their heads to blow up the factories. The trouble is that a man does not want to work at something he despises in order to enjoy his ample periods of leisure; he would much rather work like blazes at something that expresses him and shows his skill.

And when I say man, I mean not the race but the male. Women undoubtedly take more kindly to these monotonous tasks and grey depths of routine, chiefly I suppose because they expect less from work, have no great urge to individual enterprise, have more patience with passivity and tedium, and know that they can live their real lives either outside the factory or inside their heads. But nine out of every ten of those girls working at the long rows of machines only see their factory life as a busy but dreamy interlude between childhood and marriage. What would happen if you told them that there were no marriages, no homes of their own, waiting for them? Do they realise that the system that enables any number of them to obtain employment is quietly barring the door against the very young men towards whom they are already looking as the future and real wage-earners? For one little piece of knowledge it offers me, this journey seems to uncover half a dozen great pits of ignorance. Already I stare into them in dismay, then leave them gaping behind me.

[3]

The motor bus that took me from Leicester to Nottingham was not one of those superb coaches that I have already handsomely praised in this book. It was a most uncomfortable vehicle. It shook and rattled. When it reached a fair speed it struck terror into my heart, like a French express. At more than forty miles an hour, we seemed to be swaying on the edge of catastrophe. Even when it was going slowly, you could not read print inside it, your eyes being shaken like dice in a box. The back of the seat in front of mine danced a jig all the way. There were only two or three of us out of Leicester, but about half-way the bus suddenly filled up, chiefly with women and children, who were probably on their way to the Goose Fair. The two small boys who sat behind me were only interested in filling stations. 'Oo, there's a petrol shop,' they cried every time. 'I'n't it pretty?' They are lucky, those lads, for if their taste does not improve, they will be able to travel on all the main roads of England in an ecstasy of æsthetic appreciation. We rattled by the famous cricket ground, Trent Bridge, and finally arrived at the bus terminus in Huntingdon Street, which is well contrived for the manœuvring of buses, but has claims to be considered one of the most dismal thoroughfares in Europe.

Having seen Leicester at work, I had come to see Nottingham at play, with its Goose Fair. I know that Nottingham works too, though I imagine that it is not as prosperous as Leicester. It is not only foreign competition but also certain recent developments in popular taste that have struck at Nottingham's chief trade, which is—or was—the manufacture of lace. The town was busily engaged in the lace, hosiery and silk trades even when Arkwright, who had to leave Lancashire because the weavers hated his machines, first settled there. It has been fortunate in not having to depend entirely upon the textile trades. Such big concerns as Player's, the tobacco firm, Boot's the chemists, and the Raleigh Cycle Company, have their headquarters in Nottingham. The town has some very rough quarters still, but it is developing itself sensibly both in the old parts and the new, the housing estates on the outskirts. I saw some photographs of council schools that had just been built on one of these housing estates, and they had obviously been most attractively planned and laid out, with gardens round them and a great playing field; thanks to a most progressive and energetic Director of Education. Whatever else is happening in Nottingham, the children, amply provided with open-air schools, are better off now than they have ever been before. But it was not the Nottingham of such excellent educational work any more than it was the Nottingham of the lace and hosiery trade or the Nottingham of history (the Civil War really began there) that I had gone to see. This was Goose Fair Week, the city's ancient festival, and I proposed to see how Nottingham enjoyed itself, and also to explore one of the biggest of present-day fairs.

It was not unjust that I should single out this particular phase of life in Nottingham, for the city has always had a name for enjoying itself. Among provincial towns it has always passed for the most frivolous. I can remember hearing talk of it when I was a boy, when the annual 'football trips' from the North frequently headed for Nottingham. It was supposed to be a paradise for commercial travellers of the livelier sort. Rumour had it that the place was rich with pretty girls who were anything but prudes. There were goings-on in Nottingham. So ran the legend, which turned the place into a sort of industrial Venusberg. The truth is, I suppose, that in the old days the enormous numbers of girls employed in the lace trade were more independent and fonder of pleasure than most provincial young women; and so the legend began. Certainly, in my tiny experience of it, Nottingham seems gayer, in its own robust Midland fashion, than other provincial towns, though its young women these days do not appear any better-looking than young women elsewhere. They seem to accompany their young men into all the pubs, but I am not prepared to accept that as a mark of easy virtue. There are a great many pubs in the place, and now and then a rough house in one of the vaults down in that old-fashioned quarter, the Poultry; but that does not necessarily indicate an orgiastic life. That it is even now less prim than most industrial towns is probably the result of tradition, for most industrial towns, certainly most of these in the North, grew up in an atmosphere of grim nonconformity, whereas Nottingham was a place of considerable importance long before that period of big profits and little bethels. It is situated, of course, in the very centre of England, and people who do not like it say that its people lack both the solid virtues of the Northern folk and the charm and kindliness of the South. The local accent is noticeable, having the harsh quality of the Northern accent without the leavening and salt of rich dialect: it is, in short, ugly speech.

Goose Fair, that ancient institution, does not mean as much as it did. To begin with, it has been moved out of the market square to the Forest on the edge of the town. And then it is no longer regarded as an excuse for a general holiday. The children are given one half-day holiday for it, but the factories do not close. Still, it was impossible to be there five minutes without knowing that the fair was on, for almost every tram and bus announced *To and From Goose Fair*, and there were everywhere small but distinct signs of a holiday spirit abroad in the town.

In the section on *English Fairs and Markets* in my encyclopædia is the following statement: 'Nottingham has a fair for geese.' I can only add that during my stay in Nottingham for the Goose Fair I never set eyes on a goose and did not even find one on the menu. The Goose Fair I saw was the usual agglomeration of roundabouts, shows and stalls, though no doubt some of these had been designed to attract human geese. Any roots this fair had ever had in commerce had withered long ago. Neither had it any concern now with popular sports and pastimes and competitions. It offered the people no opportunities of amusing one another. And the only fairings they could buy there were little plates of peas or winkles, portions of ice cream, or packets of brandy snap. It was now simply an assembly of devices, chiefly mechanical, contrived to attract the largest number of pennies in the shortest possible time. What was remarkable about it was its size. I am told there are a few fairs that are larger, but this was the largest travelling fair I had ever seen. I spent two evenings there and never saw it all, though of course I could have done if I had really tried to explore it systematically. But with most fairs, you soon come to the end of them, whether you want to or not.

On my first evening, Friday, which was fine and quite warm, the scene was brilliant and the crowd enormous. Long before the fair itself came into view you saw its great roof of lighted sky. It had not been allowed to sprawl but was strictly confined to a large rectangular piece of ground; and within this area not an inch of room was wasted; the roundabouts and shows and stalls were laid out in rows and as close together as possible; the lights and the noise buffeted your senses; you seemed to walk into a square of blazing bedlam. Its narrow avenues were so thickly packed with people that you could only slowly shuffle along, pressed close on every side. In this crushing mass of gaping and sweating humanity were little children, some of them hardly more than babies, who had long ago wearied of all these huge glittering toys, who were worn out by the late hour, the lights, the noise, the crowd, and either tottered along like tiny somnambulists or yawned and whimpered over their parents' shoulders. The brazen voices of the showmen, now made more hideous and gargantuan than ever by the amplifiers and loud speakers, battered our hearing, which could not pluck words out of these terrifying noises. The mechanical organs blared in batteries, so closely ranged that the ear could never detect a single tune: all it heard was the endless grinding symphony. The real patrons of fairs of this kind are youngsters in their teens; and there were thousands of them pushing and cat-calling and screaming in the crowd: the boys, their faces grinning and vacant in the whirl of coloured light, sometimes looking like members of some sub-human race surging up from the interior of the earth; the girls, whose thickly powdered faces were little white masks without lines but daubed with red and black, looked like dolls out of some infernal toyshop; and the appearance of them all was fascinating and frightening. And this was Goose Fair, and Merrie England.

I climbed into the tail of a ruby and emerald fish which, after I had paid it threepence, rushed up and down and round and round, and mixed the whole fair into a spangled porridge. At the other end of my car, in the fish's mouth, were half a dozen adolescents, all jammed together, and at every dip the girls screamed and screamed, like slavering mænads. Now and then, high above the topmost cluster of electric lights, outlining the platform from which the diver would plunge into a tank with a surface of blazing petrol, there came a glimpse of a misty moon, mild and remote as the benediction of some antique priest. I went into a boxing show, where, for the benefit of a roaring crowd, a local middle-weight ('Hit him, Tom,' they cried to him) was battering away at one of the showman's pugs, a thick-set negro with a mere remnant of a face but with a golden-brown torso that wore the bloom on it of ripe fruit. The men were not boxing, they were simply hitting one another, through round after round, and every now and then the negro, who knew his job as a show-man, would stagger about, clutch at the ropes, and even fall, pretending a last extremity. At the end of the agreed ten rounds he miraculously revived, looked fierce and made threatening gestures; and then the referee, amid an uproar of excited half-wits, announced that they would fight another five rounds later, but in the meantime would come round with the hat. It was not boxing; it was not even genuine fighting; but a nasty and artful mixture of slogging and acting, and an insult to any but an audience of bloodthirsty oafs. Having no opportunity of learning the negro's opinion of life, which would have been of more interest than his boxing, I left the show. Close by there were gigantic hoots and screams of laughter coming from a mysterious square building labelled *Over The Falls*. Never had I heard such brassy bellow-ings. I paid my threepence, and then found myself in a heaving darkness inside. There were two or three corners to be turned, and at every turn the darkness heaved more violently, and one might have been deep in the hold of a thou-sand-ton ship in an Atlantic gale. It was then that I realised that the giant laughter, which I could still hear, was not coming from me or from the few others in distress in the dark there, but from a machine. Afterwards I heard several of these machines, hooting and bellowing with satanic mirth. (Probably they are quietly chuckling now, somewhere on the road or at the back of a shed.) When I was finally shot out, on a downward-moving platform, into the gaping crowd, the machine giggled thunderously and then went off into another brazen peal. Even H. G. Wells, in his earlier and wildly imaginative days, never thought of machines that would laugh for us. He can hear them now: not only laughing for us but also, I suspect, laughing at us. I continued my exploration with that laughter still hurting my ears. While circling round in that fish I had caught a glimpse of a show called *The Ghost Train*, which excited my curiosity. When I left the fish, this show had disappeared, but now I suddenly came upon it, with a queue of folk waiting to take their seats in the miniature wooden trains. At last I was given a train, which was immediately pushed through some swing doors and went plunging and bumping into the gloom beyond. It was a perilous journey. Green eyes suddenly glared at me; I rushed to collide with skeletons; hangmen's nooses brushed my forehead in the dark; dreadful screams tore the thick air; the mad little train hurled me straight at an illuminated blank wall that somehow dissolved into dark space again; so that at the end of two or three minutes I felt that I had had a terrific adventure. I should have enjoyed this piece of grim ingenuity much better if while I was waiting I had not seen two tired little children taken into one of these trains by their idiotic parents, who might have guessed that behind

GOOSE FAIR BOXING BOOTH, c.1930   *Photographer Unknown*

those swing doors there was material enough for a hundred nightmares. It is not as if the children were clamouring for these mysteries. The hour had long past when small children clamoured for anything but home and a bed. It is not always fun being a child in Nottingham during Goose Fair.

Suddenly weary of the glare and din, the foolish faces, the hot press of bodies, the whole tawdry paraphernalia of the fair, I walked out of it towards some rising ground, which I discovered to be part of the Forest. I turned at the top of the slope, where the night was fresh and cool again and once more there were stars to be seen, and looked down on the fair. It was all different then. You could not believe in the hundredweights of warm pennies changing hands, the sordid humbug, the syphilitic faces, the children dragged round like sacks, the machines that laughed: it was all transmuted. Between me and the fair-ground was a line of trees, dead black, with their foliage sharply silhouetted against the mist of light that hung above the actual glitter of the roundabouts and shows. The fair itself was coloured radiance. Staring

GOOSE FAIR AT NIGHT, c.1930 *Photographer Unknown*

hard at it, you could just see the tiny jewelled ostriches and whales and dragons curving round the switch-backs. The hooting and the grinding organ tunes dwindled and were blended by distance into a faint symphony of gaiety. Down there, you felt, was enchantment. If I had not been allowed to go any nearer, if I had looked and then been driven away, I would have sworn that I had been robbed of a glorious evening of pleasure. Never have I seen a few hundred yards of darkened space work such a change. This was the fair as it ought to have been, as it really was not, as it probably never had been, the fair that sparkled and sang in the minds of children. It was a superb romantic illusion glittering in the night. Golden Goose Fair. I stayed long enough, still warm from my sweaty progress, to smoke a pipe out as I stared and stared at this bright mirage beyond the black trees, and then I joined the crowd that was hurrying down the road to the trams and buses. Our bus was noisy with a young woman who was drunk, one of the very few I saw that night. The porter in my hotel was extremely slow and very mysterious in his manner, and it was not for some time that I realised that he was quietly drunk too. Some time later I wished I was also drunk, for I spent the next three hours or so listening to the shattering noise of motors being started up in the street outside my bedroom window. It will not be long before quiet is the most luxurious commodity in the world. Even now I doubt if wealth can buy anything better than a little extra privacy and quietness. That night I turned from side to side in my bed, tired out and aching, and I cursed the internal-combusion engine. If my Cotswold friend had asked me then, I would have joined him in a crusade to destroy the whole modern world, which cannot make a movement without rending the air with frightful sounds.

[4]

On the following afternoon, Saturday, I went with two Nottingham friends to see an association football match, for it was the local 'Derby Day,' Notts Forest *versus* Notts County. The weather had changed; the day was hung about with a cold mist that soon melted into a drizzle; but that did not prevent the supporters of Notts Forest and Notts County, two distinct groups of partisans (though on what principle they elect themselves I cannot imagine) from filling the ground to the palings. It is one of the anomalies of professional football partisanship that twenty-two players, collected from almost every corner of this island, can call their sides Notts County and Forest respectively, and divide the sporting allegiance of the city. Near us we had men who looked at one another with eyes shining with happiness when the County scored a goal. There were other men who bit their lips because the Forest seemed in danger. Sitting immediately in front of us was a party of two comfortable middle-aged women and a little elderly man who was like a mouse until some incident in the game roused him, and then he barked fiercely. But the two women were more unusual. Perhaps they were related to one of the players, for they were in possession of Christian names and used them freely in giving advice. 'Nay, Tom,' they would say quietly, as if reproving an erring child, 'don't stand still.' The huge crowd would roar like maniacs, but then in the silence that followed you would hear one of these two women gently remonstrate with a player: 'Nay, Bob, you ought to ha' let 'Erbert 'ave it.' It was as if the two teams had brought their two mothers with them. They were the oddest knowledgeable spectators of a football match I have ever seen. I have known games that displayed the finer points of association football much better than this one, but for all that it was a good match, clean and fast and exciting. Nearly everything possible has been done to spoil this game: the heavy financial interests; the absurd transfer and player-selling system: the lack of any birth or residential qualification for the players; the betting and coupon competitions; the absurd publicity given to every feature of it by the Press; the monstrous partisanship of the crowds (with their idiotic cries of 'Play the game, Ref.' when any decision against their side has been given); but the fact remains that it is not yet spoilt, and it has gone out and conquered the world. It is easy to understand, though some austere persons elaborately refuse to understand, why these crowds in the industrial towns pay shillings they can badly afford to see twenty-two professionals kick a ball about. They are not mere spectators in the sense of being idle and indifferent lookers-on; though only vicariously, yet they run and leap and struggle and sweat, are driven into despair, and raised to triumph; and there is thrust into their lives of monotonous tasks and grey streets an epic hour of colour and strife that is no more a mere matter of other men's boots and a leather ball than a violin concerto is a mere matter of some other man's catgut and rosin. It has yet to be proved to me that these men out of the dingy side-streets ever did anything better with their free time and their shillings. I never see them at a match without disliking their stupid partisanship, their dogmatism that has no foundation in knowledge of the game, the whole catcalling idiocy (though at their worst they are better than the soft fat rich men you see at boxing matches screaming at the pugilists 'to make a fight of it'); but it is still good, when the right side has scored a goal, to see that wave of happiness break over their ranked faces, to see that quick comradeship engendered by the game's sudden disasters and triumphs. I know they do not last, that happiness, that comradeship; I know that religion, art, politics would give them something infinitely truer and more enduring; that comparatively this sport-turned-spectacle is a poor thing; yet if it is a poor thing it is their own, and I am glad they have it, this uproarious Saturday plaything.

The drizzle of the afternoon became a downpour in the early evening, and it was not until after nine that my friends and I, heavily booted and raincoated,

NOTTS COUNTY v. NOTTS FOREST, 1931 *Nottingham Guardian*

set out for the Goose Fair. Rain or no rain, I had to see it on Saturday night, they told me, for this was the fair's last great night. Actually, there were not as many people there as on the evening before; for it was still wet and the fair-ground was now inches deep in mud. Nevertheless, there were still enough people to jostle you down most of the long avenues. The lights, reflected in a million raindrops, seemed brighter than ever; but whatever had seemed tawdry the night before now seemed tawdrier still. This was obviously an evening to visit the shows, of which there were about a dozen, and so keep under cover. Fair shows are usually wretched entertainments, and for one good reason, namely, that however skilful the performers may be—and some of them are not at all bad—they have lost, or have been compelled to exile, that genuine desire to do their best to please which should be the very soul of entertainment. Go to the shabbiest theatre in the country, the most broken-down pier-head performance you can find, and you will yet discover in these places a certain players' pride and a real attempt, no matter how pathetic it may seem, to amuse you—as they say in all their speeches—'to the best of their ability.' But the men and women who perform in fair shows have said good-bye to this pride and this desire to please; they are the cynical outlaws in the performers' kingdom, and all they want is to collect audiences and then get rid of them as soon as possible; they are taking part in a catch-penny process and in nothing else. That is why, even at their best, these shows never please us. Nevertheless they are interesting, if only because they still preserve some of the oldest devices for entertaining, which linger on here long after they have vanished elsewhere. Thus, in the middle of the last century, one very popular form of entertainment was given by the mesmerist and his comic assistants, who under the pretence of being hypnotised would perform all manner of ridiculous antics. Where is the mesmerist now? He has disappeared from the theatres and lecture halls and mechanics' institutes, but he was at the Goose Fair that night, packing his booth at sixpence a head. We saw him, and we also saw the divers, the Texas sharp-shooters, the young lady who by a cunning arrangement of mirrors appeared to have a head and nothing else, the man with dwarf arms who called himself a human seal, and Al Capone's armoured motor car; and though we did not visit the snakes, the African pigmy princess, the Parisian Sisters in their world-renowned guillotine act, and the collection of freak animals, we did see the Ugliest Woman In The World. There was no swindle here; the poor creature was all that she was represented to be. Doctors and keepers of asylums may have seen more unprepossessing mortals—for God knows what Nature the Great Mother can do when she tries—but these eyes have never seen a fellow-creature, certainly no woman, so grotesquely sculptured. She was of ordinary height, though thickly built, but her head, hands and feet were fully three times the common size. She surveyed us with dull eyes, entirely without expression, and there was no movement in that vast yellow leathery face, which after all was perhaps not the ugliest in the world, for it showed no marks of any treachery of the human spirit, only its complete absence, and it had a curious saurian dignity of its own. As I stared, and was ashamed of myself for staring, at this sad wild caricature of a woman, I reflected grimly that this was what can happen to you, not when you have sold your soul to the devil and God is angry, but when some tiny ductless gland, the pineal or the pituitary, has decided that it has worked properly for you long enough and then turns rebellious. And then the whole scene, the tent and the little steaming crowd inside it, the great blank wrinkled face on the platform, the fair outside whose lights and blare and mechanical cachinnation penetrated the wet canvas, became very shadowy indeed, a dream that hovered on the edge of a nightmare. While we had been waiting for those gaudy curtains to be drawn aside, to reveal the Ugliest Woman, we had been a very noisy little audience, with plenty of guffaws from

HELTER-SKELTER, GOOSE FAIR, 1933   *Photographer Unknown*

the boys and screams of laughter from the girls as jokes of a fairly coarse sort were being flung about; but I noticed that we were not so noisily amused when we were given our threepennyworth, and that we did not linger on but went quietly enough. Not, somehow, a good turn, the Ugliest Woman In The World. I still wonder what was going on inside that monstrously carved head of hers, what she thought of her travels (for she had been shown all over the world), of her place in the social scheme, of her gaping audiences. And I shall never know.

Time had stolen away while we had been inside these various tents, not perhaps while we had been actually seeing the performances but certainly while we had been waiting for them to begin. It was getting on for midnight when we left the last one. On the stroke itself the fair would stop, and all its ingenuities and glittering toys and horrors would be packed away, and the whole caravanserai would not see Nottingham again until the next October. There was still a flashing drip of rain, and the mud was deeper than ever. The hideously amplified voices still roared out their invitations, but the people were drifting away. One stall-holder, a wet wisp of humanity, was so drunk that he shouted incoherencies and clung to the props of his stall. In the morning that bit of Forest, where the deer once went and the green-jerkined outlaws went after them, would look as if all the filth of nine counties had been emptied upon it. As we left, tired out, I remembered an argument I had had a little time before with an old-fashioned friend, who had said that his local fair meant nothing to him now that the people themselves did nothing in it but shower their pennies on mechanical amusements. Once, he said, there had been sports, dances, jolly competitions, and the people entertained themselves, really played. Now they merely spent money. To this I replied that a glittering roundabout seemed to me a pleasanter spectacle than the sight of a village oaf grinning through a horse collar or of two louts kicking one another's shins. But now, walking away from Goose Fair, I felt less sure. That a good many people, especially lads and girls in their teens, had enjoyed themselves at the fair, there could be no doubt; yet, thinking over both evenings I had spent there, I could not honestly feel that I had been attending a genuine popular festival. Not even a suggestion of real gaiety remained with me. True, these people, unlike their ancestors, had amusements of various kinds all the year round, and did not need to look to this one week to give them uncontrolled pleasure. On the other hand, none of these new amusements, for the most part so passive and tepid, could be said to take the place of the old roaring saturnalia. Perhaps we no longer need saturnalia. Probably we could not let ourselves go if we tried. It is a pity that we no longer hold great popular carnivals. If we could only agree to devote a few days to the craziest folly, and then let folly alone for the rest of the year, we might be a wiser people. Obviously there should be times and seasons when the high spirits of the populace, checked and damned at ordinary times by hard and monotonous work, burst almost every bond, when everybody can be uproariously gay. But the modern fair, for all its glitter and blare and ingenuities, is no true carnival. There is a great deal of noise and a great many coloured lights, but there is not much fun. It is at heart cheap, nasty, sordid. It offers no grand release from ordinary reality. It does not expand a man. It cannot light the mind in retrospect. It does not suggest a people letting loose their high spirits, but a people trying to keep away low spirits. It has the wrong, catch-penny kind of ingenuity. It blinds, deafens and stuns us into accepting a momentary pretence of pleasure. The brazen or dilapidated men, the hard-eyed women, it brings to town are no true votaries of the carnival spirit: the sight and the sound of them give the sordid game away at once. We have all had far more fun out of a couple of false noses or a few toy instruments or a Punch and Judy show or an impromptu dance in a barn. Let us have, not only for fun but for sweet sanity's sake, some great popular festivals, some days of universal high jinks, as an escape from the growing pressure or monotony of our ordinary lives. But they must be better than any Goose Fair. I do not want to hear any more laughter from machines.

CHESTERFIELD, THE TWISTED SPIRE, 1935 *Reece Winstone*

CHAPTER EIGHT

To the West Riding

[1]

Leaving Nottingham I travelled towards Yorkshire in my own car, being carried there like a precious parcel in a glass case. I used to drive myself, but
have given it up these last few years, not because I think myself too important
to change my own gears but simply because I am a very bad driver.

The early afternoon, sunny but not warm, found us well outside Nottingham
and making for Chesterfield. Somewhere about half-way we passed through
the main street of a very small town, and each side of this street was lined
with folk, old and young, who were all looking in one direction. Possibly there
was a big funeral or perhaps a wedding among the notables, but there was
no sign of either, and the staring crowd gave us no clue. It was very odd and
rather disquietening to see all those faces and not to know what was the matter.
It was as if we were not really there or alternatively as if we had gone rushing
on into some mad England, not on the map. To travel swiftly in a closed car,
as so many of us do nowadays, is of course to cut oneself off from the reality
of the regions one passes through. When people moved slowly in their travel
there was time to establish proper communications with what was strange,
to absorb, to adjust oneself. Now that we are whizzed about the world, there
is no time for absorbing and adjusting. Perhaps it is for this reason that the
world that the traveller knows is beginning to show less and less variety. By
the time we can travel at four hundred miles an hour we shall probably move
over a dead uniformity, so that the bit of reality we left at one end of a journey
is twin to the bit of reality we step into at the other end. Indeed, by that time
there will be movement, but, strictly speaking, no more travel.

The fancy that we might be rushing on into some strange mad England,
inspired by the sight of those staring people, returned to me a little later when
we reached Chesterfield. I have often noticed its famous crooked spire from
the train, but had never been so close to it before. It was startling. To begin
with, it was much bigger than I had imagined it to be; actually it is 230 feet
high. Then again it is most grotesquely warped, twisted, crooked; the oddest,
drollest tower in the country. It dominates the town and its narrow streets,
but only in its own queer fashion, like an enormous antique jest set for ever

in the skies. The people who live in its shadow ought to be folks out of the common. They ought to go careering about like the elvish burghers and peasants in old Breughel's enchanting pictures. They ought to be humorists. Every time the morning papers arrive in Chesterfield roars of laughter ought to ascend to the black barley-sugar stick of a spire. For a moment I thought there was an air of cheerful madness about the whole place, welcomed it, and said to myself that England ought to be filled with such fantastic pieces of architecture, to match its fantastic characters and books. Just as there is a grimly sane England that is really lunatic, so too there ought to be, on a big scale, an apparently mad England, with towers all awry, that is really sane and sweet, like some of Shakespeare's comedies. Probably the old citizens of Chesterfield were annoyed when they saw what happened when you build a lofty spire of wood and lead and do not use properly seasoned timber. But if they are not proud and fond of their spire now, they are poor creatures. Warped minds and hearts, these are our trouble, not warped spires. It does not matter into what twisted folly the architecture breaks so long as we can live merrily and affectionately beneath it. And the more I see of this country the more firmly am I convinced that it is not its cheerful fools but its grimly practical hard-headed men who have always been its chief source of danger. With that mad spire to live under, Chesterfield ought never to have been allowed to enter industry; it should never have passed a dividend, never come within sight of double-entry book-keeping; but ought to have been kept as a Derbyshire stronghold of cheerful English eccentricity, a fortress of pleasant folly, a last refuge for Cousin Silence, My Uncle Toby and Mr. Micawber.

Between Chesterfield and Sheffield, where the fields are preserved in the place-names and hardly anywhere else, the countryside looked very queer. Industrial man and Nature sing a rum sort of duet in those parts. I saw a row of sharply conical little hills that looked like a topographical freak until I came close to them and then realised that they were old slag-heaps now almost entirely covered with grass. Further on we passed a hill that might have been brought from some other planet. It was black where the low rays of the sun were not faintly gilding it, and was everywhere deeply scarred and seamed. Not even passing through mountainous Nevada, where the landscape is only so much geology, have I seen so strange and desolate a hill as this; only of course Nature had not been at work here, for this was really a colossal slag-heap, the biggest I have ever seen. We were now drawing near to Sheffield. There was some fine high country on the left, good Pennine stuff. The sun was low but still shining strongly and, with the increasing smokiness of the air, it made a strange chiaroscuro, as Northern as high tea and the proper

DRY-WALLING NEAR HAWORTH, c.1937　　　*E. W. Tattersall*

short 'a' sound. For one minute Sheffield, far below, looked like the interior of an active volcano. The road ran along a ridge. Down below, on the left, were rows and rows of little houses, acres of slanting and gleaming slates. We ran under the murky canopy and were in Sheffield. The smoke was so thick that it made a foggy twilight in the descending streets, which appeared as if they would end in the steaming bowels of the earth. In the centre of the city was a large new white building that threw into darker relief its older neighbours. We were now in the true North country. One glance at the people, with their stocky figures and broad faces, humorous or pugnacious, told you that. On the road to Barnsley the stone walls began, settling any possible doubts. The North of England is the region of stone walls. They run from the edges of the towns to the highest and wildest places on the moors, firmly binding the landscape, unbroken and continuous from every tram terminus to the last wilderness of bog and cloud. No slope is too steep for them. No place is too remote. They will accurately define pieces of ground that do not even know a rabbit and only hear the cry of the curlews. Who built these walls, why they were ever thought worth building, these are mysteries to me. But when I see them, I know that I am home again; and no landscape looks quite right to me without them. If there are not a few thousand leagues of them framing the bright fields of asphodel, it will be no Elysium for me.

Along this road to Barnsley the sun flared hugely before finally setting. All the western edges of the slag-heaps were glittering. I saw in one place a great cloud of steam that had plumes of gold. In another, we passed under a vast aerial flight of coal trucks, slowly moving, in deep black silhouette, against the sunset. It would not have made a bad symbolical picture of the end of one phase of industrial England. When we looked down upon Barnsley, we saw it for a moment dimly ranged about an ebony pyramid of slag. When we stopped in the town for tea, the sun had gone and the air was nippingly cold. In the café where I ate my toasted tea-cake a young man was being funny to his girl about somebody's bad elocution. (I suspect that the somebody was a local big-wig.) 'He said "lor" for "law", said the young man, 'and "dror" for "draw". Honestly he did. "We will now dror to a conclusion," he said. Yes, really.' And as they were in that stage of courtship in which each finds the other's least remark a miracle of apt speech, they were very happy, two refined but humorous souls in a wilderness of clods. It was almost dark when we left Barnsley for Huddersfield. The hills were now solidly black; their edges very sharp against the last faint silver of the day. They were beginning to take on, for me, that Wordsworthian quality which belongs to the North. The factories might be roaring and steaming in the valleys, their lighted windows glaring at us as we passed, but behind were those high remote skylines, stern enough and yet still suggesting to me a brooding tenderness:

> The silence that is in the starry sky,
> The sleep that is among the lonely hills.

A road well lighted and of immense width led us into Huddersfield, which is not a handsome town but yet is famous in these parts for the intelligence and independence of its citizens. Whether they really deserve this reputation, I have never been able to discover, though I know the place fairly well. We climbed from Huddersfield, on our way to Bradford, to the heights of Shelf. The familiar nocturnal pageant of the West Riding was all round us. This is the region of mountaineering trams; you see them far away at night, climbing the hills, like luminous beetles. You will go through mile after mile of streets, climbing all the time, and then suddenly arrive at a stretch of open country that seems nearly as wild and cold as Greenland. From such heights you look across at hills that are constellated and twinkling with street lamps. If the towns in the West Riding were as brilliantly illuminated as Los Angeles, they would run excursions from London so that people could see these patterned hills at night. Even as it is, the spectacle has a never-failing charm. We ran down from Shelf, which is a place as mysterious to me as it probably is to you, into the centre of Bradford, then climbed another hill and reached our destination. I was back in my old home, and, journey or no journey, there I intended to stay for the next six or seven days.

[2]

Perhaps I should never have included Bradford in this itinerary. Obviously I cannot visit it in the same spirit in which I visit the other places. I am not merely returning to a city I know well, but to my childhood and youth. I left Bradford in September 1914, and have never lived in it, only stayed in it, since then. I have probably got just the wrong amount of knowledge of it now, being neither a citizen nor a complete stranger. I had better apologise now for everything that follows in this chapter. Nevertheless, I am determined to write it. This record would not be complete if there was not some such visit as this set down in it. I am not a citizen of this city, the Bradford of 1933. My Bradford ended in 1914. This must necessarily be a tale of two cities. They have much in common, and youthful memory may seize too eagerly upon what has been brought from that earlier Bradford; but I could not ignore the differences even if I wanted to do. I have changed, of course; but I think the place itself has changed even more than I have. And I am not thinking now of those inevitable alterations in the appearance of a large town; the new streets where once there were old pubs and shops; the miles of semi-detached villas where once I rolled among the gigantic buttercups and daisies. These changes are more significant. A sight of them here may give us a glimpse of two Englands, two worlds.

Bradford is one of those cities and towns that are products of nineteenth-century Industrialism. In 1801 it had a population of about 13,000. In 1901 its population had risen to nearly 280,000. (The only town in the country that grew faster was Middlesbrough.) It was very fortunately placed for its own staple trade of worsted and woollen manufacturing. It was near some large coal-fields, and what was even more important, it had an excellent supply of soft water free from lime, good for both washing wool and dyeing it. All the processes of worsted manufacture—combing, spinning, weaving, dyeing and finishing—are carried on in Bradford. It also deals in alpaca, mohair and silk.

DRUMMOND'S WOOL ROOM, c.1930 *Photographer Unknown*

Indeed, there is nothing that can be spun and woven that does not come to Bradford. I remember myself, as a boy, seeing there some samples of human hair that had been sent from China: they were pigtails that had been cut off by Imperial command. And there used to be one factory in Bradford that specialised in dolls' hair, those crisp curls you find in the nursery cupboard. When I was a rebellious lad, I used to think that a wool office—and I was sent to one for a season—was the very symbol of the prosaic; but now I see that I was wrong. Revisiting them again, I saw that these offices, with their bins of samples, blue-wrapped cylinders of hair, are really romantic. Take down some of those greasy or dusty samples and you bring the ends of the earth together. This wool was lately wandering about on our own South Downs. This comes from the Argentine, this from Australia. The dust and dried dung that falls out of this packet comes from the desert. Here, in this blue paper, is hair clipped from the belly of a camel. These wools and hairs will be sorted, scoured, combed, the long strands forming Tops, the short Noils, and these Tops and Noils, if they are not used locally, may be exported all over the place, from Finland to Spain. What they will end as, God only knows. Their adventures are terrific. Do the Bradford wool men, with their broad faces and loud voices, ever think about these things? I fancy they do, but they never mention them in public. Their talk is all of prices. You might think, to hear them, that they cared for nothing but 't'brass'. Don't you believe them.

It was after 1830 that Bradford began growing rapidly and piling up wealth. Apart from its natural advantages and the general state of trade, there was another reason for this, and that is that during the early and mid-Victorian periods, a number of German and German-Jewish merchants, with German banks behind them, came to settle in the town. Many of these merchants were men of liberal opinions, who knew they could be happier outside Germany. The results of this friendly invasion were very curious. Bradford became—as it still remained when I was a boy there—at once one of the most provincial and yet one of the most cosmopolitan of English provincial cities. Its provincialism was largely due to its geographical situation. It is really in a back-water. The railway main lines went to Leeds, ten miles away, and not to Bradford, with the result that Leeds, though it has never had the world-wide reputation of Bradford, is a larger city and of much greater local importance. It was Leeds, and not Bradford, that became the great marketing centre of West and Mid-Yorkshire. Leeds has a university and law courts; Bradford has not. I have always thought that there must be proportionately fewer university graduates in Bradford than in any other large town in England. Then again, the wool business was so much a local trade that a man might spend all his life in it, unless he happened to be sent out buying or selling, and never meet anybody but his neighbours. A city that has mixed trades will probably have some of its corners rubbed off; it must work with other places; but Bradford, with its one trade, was all corners, hard provincial angles. There was no mistaking a Bradford man. Moreover, Bradford was, and still is, on the edge of the moors, hardly more than a tram-ride from wild Pennine country. A man might spend his mornings in the Wool Exchange and then spend his evenings among moorland folk, who would not do badly as characters in the medieval Wakefield Nativity Play. Wuthering Heights are only just round the corner. The town did not gently fade away into regions decorated by landed proprietors and gentleman farmers. John Ball's old gibe, 'When Adam delved and Eve span, Who was then the gentleman?' had no application to Bradford, where everybody was busy spinning. A few were rich, and a great many were very poor, working from morning until night for miserable wages; but they were all one lot of folk, and Jack not only thought himself as good as his master but very often told him so. Bradford was not only provincial but also fiercely democratic. (The Independent Labour Party was born there.) If, having made some big lucky gambles in wool, you made a fortune there and determined to retire and set up as an English gentleman, you never stayed in Bradford, where everybody was liable to be very sardonic at your expense; but bought an estate a long way off, preferably in the South.

Yet at the same time—and this is what gives the place its odd quality—Bradford was always a city of travellers. Some of its citizens went regularly to the other side of the globe to buy wool. Others went abroad, from Belgium to China, selling yarn and pieces. They returned to Market Street, the same sturdy Bradfordians, from the ends of the earth. You used to meet men who did not look as if they had ever been further than York or Morecambe, but who actually knew every continental express. They would go away for months, keeping to the most complicated time-tables. When they returned they did not give themselves cosmopolitan airs; it was very dangerous in Bradford to give yourself any airs, except those by tradition associated with solid wool men. And then there was this curious leaven of intelligent aliens, chiefly German-Jews and mostly affluent. They were so much a part of the place when I was a boy that it never occurred to me to ask why they were there. I saw their outlandish names on office doors, knew that they lived in certain pleasant suburbs, and obscurely felt that they had always been with us and would always remain. That small colony of foreign or mixed Bradfordians produced some men of great distinction, including a famous composer, two renowned painters, and a well-known poet. (In Humbert Wolfe's *Now a Stranger* you get a glimpse of what life was like in that colony for at least one small boy.) I can remember when one of the best-known clubs in Bradford was the *Schiller-verein*. And in those days a Londoner was a stranger sight than a German. There was, then, this odd mixture in pre-war Bradford. A dash of the Rhine and the Oder found its way into our grim runnel—'t'mucky beck.' Bradford was determinedly Yorkshire and provincial, yet some of its suburbs reached as far as Frankfort and Leipzig. It was odd enough. But it worked.

The war changed all that. There is hardly a trace now in the city of that

German-Jewish invasion. Some of the merchanting houses changed their names and personnel; others went out of business. I liked the city better as it was before, and most of my fellow-Bradfordians agree with me. It seems smaller and duller now. I am not suggesting that these German-Jews are better men than we are. The point is that they were different, and brought more to the city than bank drafts and lists of customers. They acted as a leaven, just as a colony of typical West Riding folk would act as a leaven in Munich or Moscow. These exchanges are good for everybody. Just lately, when we offered hospitality to some distinguished German-Jews who had been exiled by the Nazis, the leader-writers in the cheap Press began yelping again about Keeping the Foreigner Out. Apart from the miserable meanness of the attitude itself—for the great England, the England admired throughout the world, is the England that keeps open house, the refuge of Mazzini, Marx, Lenin— history shows us that the countries that have opened their doors have gained, just as the countries that have driven out large numbers of their citizens, for racial, religious or political reasons, have always paid dearly for their intoler- ance. It is one of the innumerable disadvantages of this present age of idiotic nationalism, political and economic, this age of passports and visas and quo- tas, when every country is as difficult to enter or leave as were the Czar's Russia or the Sultan's Turkey before the war, that it is no longer possible for this admirable leavening process to continue. Bradford is really more provincial now than it was twenty years ago. But so, I suspect, is the whole world. It must be when there is less and less tolerance in it, less free speech, less libera- lism. Behind all the new movements of this age, nationalistic, fascistic, commu- nistic, has been more than a suspicion of the mental attitude of a gang of small town louts ready to throw a brick at the nearest stranger.

But our theme is Bradford. Not only have nearly all the big merchanting houses disappeared but a great many of the English firms too. Wool mer- chants, whose names seemed to us like the Bank of England, have vanished. Not one or two of them, but dozens of them. The great slump swept them away. Some of them, of course, had made fortunes before then. There were fortunes to be made in the West Riding during and just after the war. The money rolled in. I think this short period of artificial prosperity confused many people's ideas of trade. They thought, and still think, it represented some form of trading. When the slump came, many of them sat about, not bothering much and telling one another that there had been bad times before. I am no economist, but it is obvious even to me that this notion of there being a normal standard of trade is fallacious and dangerous. The situation is not merely changing temporarily all the time; it is also changing for ever. A set of conditions cannot exactly repeat themselves. The export trade of such places as Bradford was declining long before the war. We used to sell textile machinery to other countries and send out managers and mechanics with those machines. You cannot expect to teach other people to make goods and then expect them to go on still buying those goods from you. The war was a sharp break in this process of decline, a brief golden age of profits. Then reality broke in again in the early nineteen-twenties. The export trade, dependent on countries that had not the money to spend, rapidly dwindled. The very tide of fashion turned against the West Riding, which was still making solid fabrics for a world that wanted flimsy ones. Prices sank lower and lower. One firm after another staggered and then crashed. The raw wool business had always been a bit of gamble, but now it was a gamble at which you could not win. The wool trade suffered a great purge. The first to be swept away were the crowds of middle-men, who had been earning a living—and a very easy living—for years. Even when I was a boy, it had struck me that these gentry, with their one little room somewhere, their solitary clerk or typist, their hours of lounging in the cafés, playing dominoes or chess, had a remarkably easy time of it, that they had escaped very conveniently from the curse of Adam. I used to know dozens of them, and a very nice life they led, with the maximum of freedom and the minimum of responsibility. The air was fragrant with the latakia and old Virginia in their pipes. But not now. That fairy tale of trade has been rudely concluded. Those swarms of genial smoky parasites have gone. At the time of writing the wool trade is better than it has been for several years, but now it is a different wool trade, with none of that easy gambling and genial acceptance of good times and bad times. They snatch at every crumb of business. Every man has to do not only a day's work but a very canny day's work, using his wits all the time.

Everybody in the business I talked to confirmed this change. It was no longer the wool trade that I had known. 'And mind you, lad,' said one old merchant, 'they're beginning to say Bradford's makking money again. It's doing nowt o' t'sort. What bit o' money is being made's going to t'banks. It's banks 'at's makking money.' They are not enthusiastic about the banking system in these parts, for in a world demanding long credits, they say that the banks will give them no rope at all except the rope with which to hang themselves. The men who are managing to hold their own in this new and keenly competitive age are different from the old wool men. They are not such tremendous 'characters,' but, on the other hand, they are something more than lucky gamblers. They have to have a good many solid qualifications. I am thinking now of several men in their forties who have decent positions in the trade, chiefly on the export side. Let me make a tiny composite sketch of them. He is managing a firm, and therefore has under him various buyers, travellers, clerks, warehousemen. He has to have a good knowledge of raw wool, tops and noils, and there is a great deal to know about these commodities. Probably his knowledge was acquired in the first place from a course or two at the Technical College and then improved, and vastly improved, by practical experience. He probably knows German, French and some Spanish or Italian. He has to know something about the relative cheapness and efficiency of various methods of transport, shipping and railway lines, road and canal. He has to know something about finance, about drafts and bills from Gothenburg, Warsaw or Barcelona. And all the time he must watch the market, which is never still and never reliable. In my opinion he earns his money. And you can safely bet that his wife, unless he is unlucky, earns hers too. For she probably has only one maid or a daily woman, to help with the rough work, and yet not only keeps the house clean and comfortable and looks after the children, but carries on the Yorkshire housewife's tradition of cooking and baking everything (including the bread) herself. Unlike her mother, who probably did all this but tended to let the house and its work and worries crush and age her, she will probably keep herself smart and pretty and reasonably well-informed and be ready to join her husband at cards or golf or whatever pastime he favours. These two seem to me good citizens; and there are plenty of them, known to me by name, in the West Riding.

[3]

The re-union battalion dinner, which had brought me here when I ought to have been continuing my journey elsewhere, was held at a tavern on Saturday night. The battalion was the 10th Duke of Wellington's, of the 23rd Division, which did good work in France and then in the later stage of the war did equally good work on the Italian Front. It was not specifically a Bradford battalion. Most of the fellows I had known as a boy had not belonged to it, but had joined a Bradford 'Pals' battalion that had been formed rather later. There were a number of these 'Pals' battalions, and as a rule the young men in them were well above the average in intelligence, physique and enthusiasm. They were all sent to the attack on the Somme on July 1st, 1916, when they were butchered with remarkable efficiency. I spent my boyhood in a rapidly growing suburb of Bradford, and there was a gang of us there, lads who played football together, went 'chumping' (i.e. collecting—frequently stealing—wood for the bonfires) just before the Fifth of November, played 'tin-can squat' and 'rally-ho' round the half-built houses, climbed and larked about on the builders' timber stacks, exchanged penny dreadfuls, and sometimes made plans for an adventurous future. If those plans had been more sensible, they would still have been futile; for out of this group there are, I think, only two of us left alive. There are great gaps in my acquaintance now; and I find it difficult to swop reminiscences of boyhood. 'The men who were boys when I was a boy,' the poet chants; but the men who were boys when I was a boy are dead. Indeed, they never even grew to be men. They were slaughtered in youth; and the parents of them have gone lonely, the girls they would have married have grown grey in spinsterhood, and the work they would have done has remained undone. It is an old worn topic: the choicer spirits begin to yawn at the sight of it; those of us who are left of that generation are, it seems, rapidly becoming mumbling old bores. It is, however, a subject that has strange ramifications; probably I should not be writing this book now if thousands of better men had not been killed; and if they had been alive still, it is certain that I should have been writing, if at all, about another and better England. I have had playmates, I have had companions, but all, all are gone; and they were killed by greed and muddle and monstrous cross-purposes, by old men gobbling and roaring in clubs, by diplomats working underground like monocled moles, by journalists wanting a good story, by hysterical women waving flags, by grumbling debenture-holders, by strong silent be-ribboned asses, by fear or apathy or downright lack of imagination. I saw a certain War Memorial not long ago; and it was a fine obelisk, carefully flood-lit after dark. On one side it said *Their Name Liveth For Evermore*; and on the other side it said *Lest We Forget*. The same old muddle, you see: reaching down to the very grave, the mouldering bones.

I was with this battalion when it was first formed, when I was a private just turned twenty; but I left it, as a casualty, in the summer of 1916 and never saw it again, being afterwards transferred to another regiment. The very secretary who wrote asking me to attend this dinner was unknown to me, having joined the battalion after I had left it. So I did not expect to see many there who had belonged to the old original lot, because I knew only too well that a large number of them, some of them my friends, had been killed. But the thought of meeting again the few I would remember, the men who had shared with me those training camps in 1914 and the first half of 1915 and those trenches in the autumn and winter of 1915 and the spring of 1916, was very exciting. There were bound to be a few there from my old platoon, Number Eight. It was a platoon with a character of its own. Though there were some of us in it young and tender enough, the majority of the Number

Eighters were rather older and grimmer than the run of men in the battalion; tough factory hands, some of them of Irish descent, not without previous military service, generally in the old militia. When the battalion was swaggering along, you could not get Eight Platoon to sing: it marched in grim, disapproving silence. But there came a famous occasion when the rest of the battalion, exhausted and blindly limping along, had not a note left in it; gone now were the boasts about returning to Tipperary, the loud enquiries about the Lady Friend; the battalion was whacked and dumb. It was then that a strange sound was heard from the stumbling ranks of B Company, a sound never caught before; not very melodious perhaps nor light-hearted, but miraculous: *Number Eight Platoon was singing*. Well, that was my old platoon, and I was eagerly looking forward to seeing a few old remaining members of it. But I knew that I should not see the very ones who had been closest to me in friendship, for they had been killed; though there was a moment, I think, when I told myself simply that I was going to see the old platoon, and, forgetting the cruelty of life, innocently hoped they would all be there, the dead as well as the living. After all, there was every excuse that I should dream so wildly for a moment, because all these fellows had vanished from my sight for years and years and in memory I had seen the dead more often than the living. And I think that if, when I climbed the stairs of the tavern, I had seen my friends Irving Ellis and Herbert Waddington and Charlie Burns waiting at the top, grinning at me over their glasses of ale, I would not have been shocked nor even surprised, would not have remembered that they had returned from distant graves. Sometimes I feel like a very old man and find it hard to remember who still walk the earth and who have left it: I have many vivid dreams, and the dead move casually through them: *they pass and smile, the children of the sword.*

Never have I seen a tavern stairs or a tavern upstairs so crowded, so tremendously alive with roaring masculinity, as I did that night. Most of the faces were strange to me, but here and there, miraculously, was a face that was not only instantly familiar but that at once succeeded in recalling a whole vanished epoch, as if I had spent long years with its owner in some earlier incarnation. We sat down, jammed together, in a dining-room that can never have held more people in all its existence. It was not full, it was bursting. We could hardly lift the roast beef and apple tart to our mouths. Under the coloured-paper decorations, we sweated like bulls. The ale went down sizzling. But we were happy, no doubt about that. We roared at one another across the narrow tables. The waiters, squeezing past these lines of feasting warriors, looked terrified and about half life-size. The very bunting steamed. I was between two majors, one of whom was the chairman and (no cool man at any time, except no doubt at a crisis in the front line) now quite red-hot. With him I exchanged reminiscences that seemed almost antediluvian, so far away were those training camps and the figures that roared commands in them. The other major, unlike most of us there, was not a West Riding man at all, but a South Country schoolmaster, known to all his men as 'Daddy', and whose character and reputation were such that through him the whole affected tittering South Country was forgiven everything. In short, he was amazingly and deservedly popular. Rarely have I observed such waves of affectionate esteem rolling towards a man as I did that night. Those rough chaps, brought up in an altogether alien tradition, adored him; and his heart went out to them. I caught a glimpse then—and I am not likely to forget it—of what leadership can mean in men's lives. I had seen it, of course, in the war itself; but long years of a snarling peace, in which everybody tended to suspect everybody else, had made me forget almost its very existence. And I do not suppose that in all the years that had passed since the war any of those men had found themselves moved by the emotion that compelled them that night to rush forward, at the earliest opportunity, and bring themselves to the notice of 'good old Daddy'. In other words, they had known this endearing quality of affectionate leadership in war but not in peace. It is more than sentimentality that asks, urgently and bewilderedly, if they could not have been given an outlet for this deep feeling just as easily in a united effort to help England as in a similar effort to frustrate Germany. Are such emotions impossible except when we are slaughtering one another? It is the men—and good men too—who answer *Yes* to this who grow sentimental about war. They do not seem to see that it is not war that is right, for it is impossible to defend such stupid long-range butchery, but that it is peace that is wrong, the civilian life to which they returned, a condition of things in which they found their manhood stunted, their generous impulses baffled, their double instinct for leadership and loyalty completely checked. Men are much better than their ordinary life allows them to be.

The toast in memory of the dead, which we drank at the end of the dinner, would have been very moving only unfortunately when we were all standing up, raising our glasses and silent, there came from a very tinny piano in the far corner of the room what sounded to me like a polka very badly played. I tried to think, solemnly, tenderly, about my dead comrades, but this atrocious polka was terribly in the way. I sat down, bewildered. 'Damn fool played it all wrong,' growled the major, our chairman, in my ear. 'Should have been much slower. Regimental march, y'know.' That little episode was just like life; and I suppose that is why I am at heart a comic writer. You stand up to toast your dead comrades; the moment is solemn and grand; and then the pianist must turn the regimental march into something idiotically frivolous, and ruin the occasion. I am certain that if my friends ever want to drink to my memory, something equally daft will happen; and I shall murmur 'What did I tell you?' from the great darkness. Now more men came in; the temperature rose another fifteen degrees; the waiters shrank another six inches; and there were songs and speeches. The chairman made a good speech, and in the course of it told the lads that the last battle in which the battalion had been engaged, on the Italian Front, was the greatest pitched battle in the whole history of the world. As he talked about this battle and its momentous consequences, I stared at the rows of flushed faces in front of me, and thought how queer it was that these chaps from Bradford and Halifax and Keighley, woolcombers' and dyers' labourers, warehousemen and woolsorters, clerks and tram-conductors, should have gone out and helped to destroy for ever the power of the Hapsburgs, closing a gigantic chapter of European history. What were the wildest prophecies of old Mother Shipton compared with this!

I had arranged to meet, in a little ante-room, the survivors of my original platoon, and as soon as I decently could I escaped from the press of warriors in the big room, to revisit my own past. There were about eight of us present, and we ordered in some drinks and settled down to remember aloud. I had not seen any of these fellows for seventeen years. I knew them all, of course, and they seemed little older. The difference was that before they had all been soldiers, whereas now their respective status in civilian life set its mark upon them, and now one was a clerk, another a tram-conductor, another a mill-hand, and so forth. Nearly of all them remembered more than I did, although I have an exceptionally good memory. Details that had vanished for ever from my mind were easily present to theirs. Why? Was it because a defensive mechanism in my mind had obliterated as much as it could from my memory; or was it because much more had happened to me since the war than had happened to them and, unlike them, I had not gone back over and over again to those war years? (A third explanation, of course, is that, living in the same district and often running across one another, they had talked over those years far more than I had.) As figure after figure, comic and tragic, came looming up through the fog of years, as place after place we had been in caught the light again, our talk became more and more eager and louder, until we shouted and laughed in triumph, as one always does when Time seems to be suffering a temporary defeat. Frensham, Aldershot, Folkestone, Maidstone, Bully Grenay, Neuve Chapelle, Souchez—how they returned to us! Once again the water was rising round our gum boots. We remembered the fantastic places: that trench which ran in front of a graveyard, where the machine-gun bullets used to ricochet off the tombstones; that first sight of Vimy Ridge in the snow, like a mountain of despair. We recalled to one another the strange coincidences and dark premonitions: poor melancholy B. who muttered, 'I'll be lying out there to-night,' and was, a dead man that very night; grim Sergeant W. who said to the draft, 'This is where you can expect to have your head blown off,' and had his own head shattered by a rifle-grenade within three hours. And little Paddy O., who had always seemed such a wisp of a chap, with everything about him drooping, who looked the same as ever, ready to drop at any moment, though he never had dropped and the Central Powers must have spent hundreds of thousands of marks trying to kill him, little Paddy, I say, came close to me, finished his beer, and asked me, stammeringly as ever, if I remembered sending him from the front line for some water for the platoon, on a summer morning in 1916. 'Nay,' he stammered, 'I wasn't gone more than t-ten minutes, and when I c-come back, where you'd been, Jack lad, there was n-nobbut a bloody big hole and I n-never set eyes on you again till to-night.' And it was true. I had sent him away on a ten minutes' errand; immediately afterwards a giant trench mortar had exploded in the very entrance to the little dug-out where I was dividing up the platoon rations; I had been rushed away, and was gone before he returned; and it had taken us more than seventeen years to find one another again.

Several of us had arranged with the secretary to see that original members of the battalion to whom the price of the dinner was prohibitive were provided with free tickets. But this, he told me, had not worked very well; and my old platoon comrades confirmed this, too, when I asked about one or two men. They were so poor, these fellows, that they said they could not attend the dinner even if provided with free tickets because they felt that their clothes were not good enough. They ought to have known that they would have been welcome in the sorriest rags; but their pride would not allow them to come. (It was not a question of evening clothes; this dinner was largely for ordinary working men.) I did not like to think then how bad their clothes, their whole circumstances, were: it is not, indeed, a pleasant subject. They were with us, swinging along while the women and old men cheered, in that early battalion of Kitchener's New Army, were with us when kings, statesmen, general officers, all reviewed us, when the crowds threw flowers, blessed us, cried over us; and then they stood in the mud and water, scrambled through the broken strands of barbed wire, saw the sky darken and the earth open with red-hot steel, and came back as official heroes and also as young-old workmen wanting to pick up their jobs and their ordinary life again; and now, in 1933, they could not even join us in a tavern because they had not decent coats to their backs. We could drink to the tragedy of the dead; but we could only stare at one another, in pitiful embarrassment, over this tragi-comedy of the living, who had fought for a world that did not want them, who had come back to exchange their uniforms for rags. And who shall restore to them the years that the locust hath eaten?

[4]

There are nearly always compensations. Thus Bradford is a city entirely without charm, though not altogether ugly, and its industry is a black business; but it has the good fortune to be on the edge of some of the most enchanting country in England. A sharp walk of less than an hour from more than one tram terminus will bring you to the moors, wild virgin highland, and every mill and warehouse will be out of sight and the whole city forgotten. However poor you are in Bradford, you need never be walled in, bricked up, as a round million folk must be in London. Those great bare heights, with a purity of sky above and behind them, are always there, waiting for you. And not very far beyond them, the authentic dale country begins. There is no better country in England. There is everything a man can possibly want in these dales, from trout streams to high wild moorland walks, from deep woods to upland miles of heather and ling. I know no other countryside that offers you such entrancing variety. So if you can use your legs and have a day now and then to yourself, you need never be unhappy long in Bradford. The hills and moors and dales are there for you. Nor do they wait in vain. The Bradford folk have always gone streaming out to the moors. In the old days, when I was a boy there, this enthusiasm for the neighbouring country had bred a race of mighty pedestrians. Everybody went enormous walks. I have known men who thought nothing of tramping between thirty and forty miles every Sunday. In those days the farmhouses would give you a sevenpenny tea, and there was always more on the table than you could eat. Everybody was knowledgeable about the Dales and their walks, and would spend hours discussing the minutest details of them. You caught the fever when you were quite young, and it never left you. However small and dark your office or warehouse was, somewhere inside your head the high moors were glowing, the curlews were crying, and there blew a wind as salt as if it came straight from the middle of the Atlantic. That is why we did not care very much if our city had no charm, for it was simply a place to go and work in, until it was time to set out for Wharfedale or Wensleydale again. We were all, at heart, Wordsworthians to a man. We

have to make an effort to appreciate a poet like Shelley, with his rather gassy enthusiasm and his bright Italian colouring; but we have Wordsworth in our very legs.

Sunday morning, after the battalion dinner, opened wonderfully, so a little party of us took a car into the country. It was plain from the very first that the local enthusiasm had not vanished. All that had happened since the war was that it had taken a somewhat different form. Before we used to set out in twos and threes, in ordinary walking clothes, for our Sunday tramps. Now they were in gangs of either hikers or bikers, twenty or thirty of them together and all dressed for their respective parts. They almost looked German. We passed the hikers very early on our journey, and so I cannot say much about them, except to doubt whether this organised, semi-military, semi-athletic style of exploring the countryside is an improvement upon our old casual rambling method. These youngsters looked too much as if they were consciously taking exercise: they suggested the spirit of the lesser and priggish Wordsworth rather than the old magician who had inspired us. We saw a good deal of the cyclists, however, passing troops of them all along the road up to Grassington; and I remember wondering exactly what pleasure they were getting from the sur- rounding country, as they never seemed to lift their heads from the handlebars, but went grimly on like racing cyclists. They might just as well, I thought, be going round and round the city. But perhaps they call an occasional halt, and then take in all the beauty with a deep breath. There was plenty to take in too, that morning.

We went to Ilkley, then through Bolton Woods to Burnsall and Grassington, and never have I seen that country so magnificent. The long dry summer had given it an autumnal colouring that was past belief. The morning was on fire. The dry bracken and the heather burnished the hilltops; and all the thick woods beside the Wharfe were a blaze of autumn. The trees dripped gold upon us. We would look down russet vistas to the green river. We would look up, dazzled, to see the moorland heights a burning purple. If we had been ten years in a dark cell and newly released, we could not have stared at a world that seemed more extravagantly but exquisitely dyed. I have never seen Bolton Woods looking like that before, and hardly dare hope to see them like that again. It was their grand carnival, and it will riot and glow in my memory as long as I live. Grassington came, where several water-colouring friends of mine, as well as a number of wool merchants from Bradford, have made their

Opposite: KILNSEY CRAG, WHARFEDALE, 1935   *W. A. Poucher*

home; and after that we slipped into Upper Wharfedale, which is narrower and less wooded and far more austere than the lower reaches. There are great limestone crags for walls there, and between them the valley is smooth and green. Half-way up we passed the pleasant village of Kettlewell. I always like the story of the woman from one of the remote outlying farmsteads—they look like white crumbs on a vast rumpled green tablecloth—who, when asked by the parson why he never saw her in Kettlewell these days, replied: 'Oh, I used to like going into Kettlewell about once a week, but now I can't stand t'racket.' And I remember a woman who lived in one of these remote farmhouses, a solid West Riding countrywoman and not one of your fanciful arts-and-crafts misses, who swore that she saw fairies dancing on the hillside. (Have these lonely folk keener senses than ours, or do they merely take to imagining things? It is still an open question, and not to be settled by a report from a committee because a committee would never see anything.) We reached Buckden, towards the head of the Dale, and a notable goal for Bradfordians, who have emptied the barrels at the inn there many a time; and then we turned left, towards the long remote valley of Langstrothdale, up which you may go to Hawes in Wensleydale. We stopped, however, at Hubberholme, a tiny hamlet that had a fine little old church and a cosy inn. There we stayed for lunch.

Once up there you seem at first at the world's end; and indeed you are a long way from anywhere, certainly from a railway station. It is the internal-combustion engine that has brought such a place as this on to the map, just as it has changed—or is changing—the whole face of England. Before the Industrial Revolution, before the railways came, these dales were more thickly populated than they were twenty years ago. (Wensleydale, with its castles and abbeys and ruined farms, must have had quite a considerable population in the Middle Ages, whereas it seems almost empty now.) It was steam power that brought people swarming into a few centres or kept them close to the railway lines. Now, after less than a hundred years of this centralising and canalising influence of the railway, people are being spread out again. We thought the railway system would last for ever, and it is dying now and the whole movement of the population is being reversed. The very coaching inns are with us again, their grooms and ostlers transformed into mechanics and garage men. And what interested me at the inn in this remote Hubberholme was that the talk before lunch—with the landlord, a townsman here for his

Opposite: A CORNER OF KETTLEWELL, 1935   *Walter Scott*

health, leading it—was all about local festivities, dances here, concert parties there, all manner of urban jollification. You could hardly ask for a better example of the change that is taking place in the country than this, for here was a region remote enough, yet the younger folk were as bent on enjoying themselves as any in the towns. Some of them were bent on other things too, for I heard how two brothers, young farmers from up the dale, had hanged themselves; not at the same time but within a few months. There was nothing wrong, as far as anybody knew, with the affairs of either of them; they were ordinary pleasant sociable young farmers; but both their bodies had to be cut down in their lonely farmhouse and then brought to the village on a sort of improvised sledge. I wonder what strange story that farmhouse could tell. Before I leave this inn I will add that for lunch they gave us soup, Yorkshire pudding, roast chicken and sausages and two vegetables, fruit pudding, cheese and biscuits, and coffee, all for two and sixpence each. And that—when they have a mind to—is the way they do it in Yorkshire.

In the afternoon we returned down Upper Wharfedale, but then cut east and climbed up to Blubberhouses. The sun had disappeared; the day was cloudy and sagging, with imminent signs of rain. Now we got that other and familiar aspect of these moorlands, seeing them as a high, grey desolation, with the winds shooting over them, threatening to shatter the heavy clouds. The long stone walls and the few stone buildings did not suggest man's handiwork or his presence, but seemed to be natural outcroppings of the grey rock. Not a soul was about. A few birds went beating up against the wind and crying desolately, that was all. The country was Thibetan in its height and emptiness. It was impossible to believe that in half an hour we might have dropped into Harrogate and taken the waters. I tried to remember exactly where it was that, years before in this region, I had stumbled upon a genuine deserted village. There it was, on the moors, with two small factories and several rows of cottages, and completely uninhabited. (Something, I believe, went wrong with the water supply.) I remember eating my sandwiches inside one of the cottages from which most of the roof was gone. I stared at the gaping doorways and the grass-grown street; and not even a mouse stirred. No village I saw in the war area, I think, gave me the same complete picture of desolation as that empty shell of a moorland village did. And it was somewhere in these parts, though behind what misty ridge I could not remember. The sagging clouds broke, and it rained good and hard, as it always does up there. We

Opposite: HUBBERHOLME, c.1937   *E. W. Tattersall*

bounded down towards Otley, past the reservoirs, which were mysterious lakes in that fast scribble of rain, and ran on through Menston to Baildon, where we found friends and tea. Baildon is not far from Bradford but it is on the very edge of a little moor of its own, so nearly everybody who can contrive it lives out there. The population of Bradford must be nearly half as large again during working days as it is at night and on the census returns, for so many of its people live at Baildon, Ilkley, Menston, Harrogate, Grassington. Before the war, my friends and I used to camp in a wooden shanty on this Baildon Moor, and divide our time pretty cheerfully between opening tins of beans, washing up, reading Walt Whitman, and arguing or scuffling with one another. It was only an hour or so from Bradford, that camp, but I still think of it, as I did then, as if it were a lodge in Labrador. Quite right too. For it needs no effort, after twenty years, to feel the freshness and see the wide glitter of those summer dawns up there. Oh, spaces more wide and open to me than all Montana or the Rhodesian plains, bless you all, and may the lark sing to you for ever and the ling never cease to bloom! With you, have I not fleeted the time carelessly, as they did in the golden world?

[5]

We got back to Bradford, that Sunday evening, between six and seven. It was dark and miserably drizzling. I asked to be dropped in the centre of the town. 'But what are you going to do?' they cried, staring at me as if I had been suddenly shaken out of my wits. 'I don't know,' I told them. 'I want to see what there is to do in Bradford on a wet Sunday night.' 'But there isn't *anything*,' they almost screamed. I replied firmly, and not without a suggestion of the heroic, that I must see for myself. So I was dropped in Market Street. At first it did not look too bad. There were plenty of lights about, and though of course there were no shops open, some of the larger establishments had left their windows uncovered and illuminated. There were signs too that the evening was clearing up. Such drizzle as remained was not troublesome. I heard music and discovered that a Salvation Army band was playing just round the corner; it was playing quite well too; and a considerable crowd had collected. So far as I could judge only the innermost ring of this crowd was in search of salvation; the others were listening idly to the music, smoking their pipes, and waiting until the pubs opened. I stayed there a few minutes, and came to the conclusion that if I could persuade myself to believe in the Christian account of this life—and the essence of it, the self-sacrifice of a god for men, seems to me too good to be true, and the rest of it, the theological

GRASSINGTON SQUARE, 1933 *Walter Scott*

jugglery lit by hell-fire, not worth having—I should either join the Catholic Church or fall in with the Salvation Army. Both of them have the right religious attitude; that is, they are not afraid of being thought noisy and vulgar; they take the thing out into the street. After all, if you really believe that the gates of Heaven are swinging open above you and the pits of Hell yawning below, it is absurd to be merely gentlemanly about it, like the Church of England, or drab and respectable, like the Nonconformists. I felt that the early Christians, with their wildly poetical tales, their glittering eyes, their dooms-day-haunted looks, would be able to find a welcome among the incense-swinging Catholics or the drumming, roaring Salvationists, but would be rejected with horror by the good sober Church and Chapel folk, aghast at such Oriental extravagances. Having reached this conclusion, I walked out of the range of the converted euphonium players, and began to explore the rest of the town.

Although it was such a poor night, there were lots of people, mostly young men, hanging about the streets. What were they doing there? Some of them, no doubt, were waiting for girls, or hoping that in some miraculous fashion they would quite casually make the acquaintance of a pretty and amiable young woman. But most of them, I think, were not baffled amorists: they were there simply to pass the time. They had to do something with their Sunday evening. They might have attended at one of the many and various places of worship; but obviously they did not like places of worship. They might have stopped at home or visited a friend's house; but then it was probably neither comfortable nor convenient for them to stay at home or for their friends to stay at home. If you have a lot of people, of very different ages and tastes, all crowded into one small house, in which, willy-nilly, they all have to eat and sleep and wash and dress, spending a whole evening at home, for some of the residents anyhow, may be a most disagreeable and unprofitable business. Thus, if you like reading quietly in a corner, you are unlucky if the rest of the family, including your sister's young man and your brother's girl, have a passion for very noisy gramophone records or the wireless at full strength. Moreover, even if it is not too rowdy for your taste, you get sick of the miserable little hole. Far too many opinions about staying quietly at home happen to be expressed by comfortable professional men writing in warm, well-lighted, book-lined apartments thirty feet long by fifteen broad. And again, even if they have quite pleasant homes, the fact remains that most young people like to go out at the week-end: it is not some temporary aberration of the tribe: such is their nature. They want to go out, to get on with their individual lives, which have a secret urgency of their own at such periods, to join their friends, to stare at and talk and giggle and flirt with and generally begin operations upon the other sex. Many, too, have stirring in them a desire for colour, rhythmical movement and sound, drama; in short, for some form of artistic expression and appreciation. Such is their nature, fortunately for the history of the race. If the facts of our social life do not conform to this nature, then it is useless preaching sermons or writing grumbling letters to the paper about modern youth: the only thing to do is to alter the structure of our social life. Bluntly, the position is this: the good old-fashioned English Sunday—the Sabbath, as it is called by a great many people who do not seem to realise, first, that they are not Jews, and secondly, that anyhow they are a day out in their calculations—is still being imposed upon large numbers of people, especially younger people, who no longer want the good old-fash-

ioned English Sunday, any more than they want the good old-fashioned English side-whiskers, thick underclothing or heavy meals. It is imposed upon
them legally and by force, not by mere suggestion; and the reason that the
imposition is still successful is that in most provincial towns the authority is
largely in the hands of elderly men who are not in sympathy with the desires
of newer generations. And what these elderly men do not want, nobody else
shall have: their attitude is a thoroughly dog-in-the-mangerish one. For
obviously there is nothing to prevent anyone from having a quiet Sunday
night, church or chapel, then cold supper and an hour or two's reading, solemn
talk or meditation at home, if he or she really wants to have have one. You
can have a quiet Sunday evening of this kind in Paris or Buenos Aires. There
has never been any talk of compulsory attendance on Sunday nights at dance
and concert halls, theatres, cinemas, just as it has never been proposed when
discussing local option—and this would be the only sporting conclusion—that
in the event of the vote going against them, total abstainers should be compelled to take an agreed amount of wine and spirits. I myself happen to live
in a city and in a certain state of life that leave me free to spend my Sunday
evenings at theatres, cinemas, concerts, restaurants, and so forth; but as it
also happens that I have more time for these things during the week than
most people and I like to spend Sunday quietly at home or with my friends,
I rarely take advantage of this freedom, remaining as sedate on most Sundays
as a Baptist deacon. But that seems to me no reason why I should impose
restrictions on other people, with different tastes. I have the kind of Sunday
I like: let them have the kind of Sunday they like. There is in this country
far too much grudging envy—too much of the *I had a bad time, you can have
one now* spirit—masquerading as religious conviction and austere civic virtue.
As for the familiar argument of an open Sunday evening creating too much
Sunday work, it is not worth very much. Many of the people concerned are
only too anxious to do a bit of Sunday work. And I have noticed that the
objectors, in their passion for a workless Sunday, never seem to refuse such
things as newspapers and milk on Monday mornings. It is time, however, we
returned to Bradford on a Sunday night.

The rain stopped, but it remained a wettish raw night. I explored all the
centre of the city and discovered that there were one or two very small cafés
open and then, from seven o'clock onwards, all the pubs, and nothing else.
You could take your choice and either promenade up and down Darley Street,
North Parade, Manningham Lane, or go into the nearest pub. Ever since I
can remember, elderly citizens have been protesting against this practice of
promenading on Sunday nights. They have always been disgusted by the sight

of young people monkey-parading in this fashion. It is, however, these same elderly citizens who have seen to it that nearly all doors leading out of the street shall be locked against these young people. They cannot listen to plays or music, cannot see films, cannot even sit in big pleasant rooms and look at one another; so they walk up and down the street. No doubt some of them would always want to promenade—even on nights like this, though it seems incredible—but most of them would obviously prefer one of a dozen different ways of spending Sunday evening. They have, of course, to get on with their mating, whatever elderly persons may think of them; but they could easily do it in a much more civilised fashion than this of monkey-parading. Having seen the promenaders, I thought I would try the only places of entertainment allowed to open—the pubs. The first one I visited was very quiet—it was still early—and in the lounge I entered there were only five or six hobbledehoys drinking glasses of bitter and elaborately chaffing the barmaid in the traditional style. Nothing wrong with the place except that it was dull and stupid. The next pub, a large gaudy affair, was doing better business. Its chief customers were either young men who stared, whispered, suddenly guffawed, and a number of youngish females who, if they were not women of the town, had certainly taken the most astonishing pains to disguise themselves as such, even to putting on the swollen greedy faces of the type. Nothing much was happening in there: an occasional guffaw, another order for drinks, a move from this little table to that, with the women of the town grimacing over their stouts and ports and missing nothing. This is not an attack on the place; I have not the least desire to see it closed; but I am puzzled to know why it should be open when so many obviously better places—the Civic Theatre, for example—are shut; I cannot see why playgoing, listening to music, watching films, even dancing, should be considered so much worse—or at least more secular—than sitting and boozing with prostitutes. Incidentally, how ironical it is that the process of turning oneself into a street-walker should be still called 'going gay', for anything less gay, anything more monotonous, dull, dreary, senseless, sordid, than the whole way of life, the surroundings, habits, manners, outlook, of these women here in England, can hardly be imagined. They nearly always look exactly what they are—gross, greedy, and stupid, and worlds away from the frail butterflies, the lights o' love, sentimentalised over by very young novelists. I then had a short walk and ventured into pub number three, a large establishment that seemed to be doing a very brisk trade. This time the lounge, which was crowded with people and thick with smoke, boasted some little coloured electric lights. That was all; nothing else, not even reasonable comfort; but it was enough, and every table, every seat, was taken. Fifteen shillings' worth of coloured lamps: this was gaiety, this was life; and so the place was selling beer, stout, port, as fast as it could serve them, to patrons of both sexes. I do not think any of these people—and they were mostly young, pairs of boys, pairs of girls; with here and there an older couple—could be said to be really enjoying themselves; but at least they could look at one another, giggle a bit, talk when they found something to say, and admire the carnival splendour of the coloured electric lights. They did not want to go home, they did not want to walk up and down the streets, so here they were. I endured about a quarter of an hour of it, then marched out to walk the two miles or so to my home.

As I went, I considered the pitiful evening I had half passed in the centre of this city, with its three hundred thousand people. What a miserable barbaric affair! I asked myself what I would have done, supposing I were a young man who had come here to work and was living in not very comfortable or amusing lodgings. This was Sunday night, and a dark wettish Sunday night: a melancholy tract of time, with Monday morning waiting to pounce on me at the end of it. What would I have done? What was there to do? It is hard to tell, but I arrived at the conclusion that I would have found one of the quiet pubs and there floated the dismal evening away on a full tide of drink. And if I was tight at the end of it, I told myself, all the better. So much for this fine old provincial Sabbath. I told myself too that if I had a young son or daughter whose work took him or her away from home, to live in one of these towns, I should object if it were a Sabbatarian town of this kind, which could offer its young folk nothing on Sunday night but a choice between monkey-parading and dubious pubs. Please give me, I would say, a wicked wide-open city, busy dishonouring its Sabbath, blazing with lights on Sunday evening, with concerts, theatre, cinemas, dance halls, restaurants, in full naughty swing. There I could trust my innocent child. But not—oh, never— in this barbaric gloom and boredom. Thus ended, with myself addressing a full applauding meeting of selves, my Sunday evening.

[6]

Having arrived at my old home, I let the journey proper look after itself for a few days while I went prowling about, renewing the past and exploring the present. I did not remain in Bradford all the time, for one West Riding town is not distinctly separated from another and so you are tempted to roam, unless you are so sensitive—and silly—that the whole grim region frightens you into seeing as little of it as possible. I went to Leeds, that companion city which crazily ignorant Southerners are apt to confuse with Bradford, to the disgust of both sets of citizens. With its University, Law Courts, mixed industries, position as the shopping and amusement centre of the West Riding, Leeds is rather more civilised than Bradford, but to my mind— and remember, I am a Bradfordian—far more dismal and less interesting. It has not the authentic, queer, carved-out-of-the-Pennines look of Bradford and some of the other towns. It is a large dirty town that might almost be anywhere, and mostly built of sooty brick. Its cheap clothing trade has given it a big Jewish colony, formerly recruited, I believe, from the Polish and Russian ghettos. This Jewish element seemed to be far more in evidence before the war than it is now, possibly because the flow of Jews from Eastern Europe is drying up. But there is still plenty of Yiddish in Leeds, and I can still see on the surface of its life traces of that restless glitter which is the gift of the Jew. I had another look at Halifax, which is more interesting than Leeds as a genuine West Riding product. It must be the hilliest town of its size in England. There, factories and rows of houses seem to be sticking up and out at all mad angles. The trams, groaning desperately, go mountaineering; and at night they look like luminous beetles swarming up and down a black wall. It is a grim, craggy place, piercingly cold in winter. When I first enlisted I was sent to the barracks in Halifax. They were in Gibbet Lane. I was there in the early days of that fine September of 1914, but I never recollect Gibbet Lane offering us anything but a Siberian bleakness. The folk there are honest, sharp-tongued, but kindly; they make heavy woollen stuff and carpets; and they delight in singing Handel and the Gilbert-and-Sullivan operas. You can meet them, a trifle subdued perhaps but there to the last wart, in the solid downright fiction of my friend, Phyllis Bentley, who writes perched on that Halifax hillside. Beyond Halifax are rum desperate outposts like Sowerby Bridge and Luddenden Foot, and beyond them are the moors. These high moors form the western boundary for all this district: they are just the same as they always were; and there they wait, probably for the ruin of this trumpery textile trade, this flickering episode of man's activity and cunning. The West Riding keeps one eye on the mills and markets and the other on the moors. It is surprising how close their desolation is. One afternoon I ran out to see an old friend at Thornton, an industrial village hanging on the western edge of Bradford and only a threepenny tram-ride from the Town Hall. Ten minutes in a car from Thornton took us to Withens on the moor, where we had some tea while heavy sleet slashed at the windows. We might have been on the Outer Hebrides. Withens itself is a low, square stone building, half farmhouse, half inn, and it stands on the brink of nothing but bog and wild weather. You feel that at any moment

HALIFAX TOWNSCAPE, 1936   *Bill Brandt*

Heathcliff may be roaring in the doorway. It is only up here that you can
believe in such people as Heathcliff. But then up here you could almost believe
in anything. What you cannot believe is that the Bradford Exchange and the
Chamber of Commerce are only half an hour away. The world they represent
has dropped clean out of sight and mind. These winds, savage and exhilarating,
have never known a black load of smoke, and would, it seems, tear down
a factory chimney in two minutes. Withens—the very name whisks away all
the warehouses and streets and rows of houses and shops and traffic signs
and policemen and rate-collectors, and leaves you gasping on the brown wet
roof of England.

   Most of my time, however, I spent in Bradford itself, renewing old acquaintance with people and places. Among the latter was the covered Market, our
nearest approach to the Oriental bazaar. The stalls there are not temporary
affairs but permanent fixtures, shops without windows, and most of them have
been in the same hands ever since I can remember. On one side there are still
queer old-fashioned little eating places, where you tuck into boiled cod and
steak pie sitting in pews. On the other side are the music stalls, where if you
linger a second the assistants pounce upon you at once and conjure the florins
our of your pocket. It was at one of these stalls, years ago when I was a schoolboy, that I bought, in a lunatic fit, that most melancholy instrument, a one-
stringed fiddle. It cost a pound or two, and I paid for it, laboriously, in shillings
and sixpences. 'You oughtn't to do that,' observed the assistant, a supercilious
young man. 'Looks as if you've been saving up.' And as that was precisely
what I had been doing, I was lost in shame. (A month or two afterwards,
I swopped that one-stringed fiddle for a deer-stalker hat, owned by a friend
of mine, who had about as much use for it as he would have for the fiddle,
or as I really had for either.) Between the music at one extreme and the boiled
cod in pews at the other, there are rows and rows of drapery, boot and shoe,
confectionery, grocery stalls. There are several bookstalls, and the owner of
one of them grabbed hold of me and said in that aggressive tone we use with
one another in Bradford: 'Nah, ah've got summat to show you. You've got
a minute to spare, haven't you? All right then. Nah just come with me.' He
led me from his stall to the Market entrance, where we climbed some stairs.
At the top there were rooms and rooms lined with new books. 'Stock, that
is,' he told me, waving a hand. 'All stock. And then they'll tell you there isn't
a bookshop of any size here. Look at that lot. All sorted out too—proper
alphabetical order. What d'you think o' that?' I told him it was a noble sight
and a prodigal display, and did not dare to hint that there seemed to me to
be very few good books in this vast collection. But if it was a question of

quantity, not quality, he had certainly justified himself. I think that if I had a shop in Bradford, I should insist upon its being in the Market, where they all know one another and are always having cups of tea. You see Funeral Wreaths hobnobbing in a genteel fashion with Cheap Biscuits, Dress Goods and Fents listening to the troubles of Toffee and Humbugs. Ladies' Shoes smiling over the teapot at Scarves and Jumpers. I might do worse, when I am old and out of fashion and bankrupt of ideas, a faded scribbler, than return to my own town and take a bookstall in the Market, there to smoke my pipe, have my cup of tea like the rest, and lend a benevolent ear to the confidences of the girls in the Sheet Music and the Cut-Price Grocery lines. I should be snug all day under that great roof, could stare at the bright little pageant of humble commerce, could eat frugally in the neighbouring pews, and when I died there might easily come my way a free Funeral Wreath, only a trifle damaged.

I sought out some old business colleagues, for I was once, before the war, in the wool trade, though only in a vague fashion. I returned to the dark interior of wool offices and warehouses, with their great bins of blue-wrapped samples, their counters littered with strands of tops and bits of noil, their dim recesses, in the warehouses, where the massive bales await the sorters, their curiously heavy, greasy smell, their men and lads all in blue 'brats', which is our name up there for overalls. A.W., once a clerk with me, though my senior, I found in his private office, for he is now in charge of the business and has to pilot it through shallows and whirlpools unknown in the old tranquil days. With him, as warehouseman still, was my old friend N., who looks just the same as he did twenty-odd years ago. He is a grand type of north-country working man, and I was glad to see him still cheerfully pulling the bales about, though he is in his sixties, and to learn that his two sons are both doing well, one in a shop of his own, the other in the city's largest store. N. was a trooper, forty-odd years ago, and was wounded by a spearthrust in the Khyber Pass. He and I talked about our old boss, who died a few years ago, and was an odd character, quite different from the usual run of wool merchants, who then were earthy, hearty fellows, fond of good living. Our old boss lived only for his business: he was a bachelor, a teetotaller, a non-smoker, who fussed away morning and night with every precious detail of his business, who would come down even on Bank Holidays to brood over his ledgers or write long letters to our foreign agents. It never occurred to him that the rest of us did not necessarily regard the exporting of wool tops as the very centre and peak of our lives, and when he kept us at it night after night, sometimes hours after most decent offices had shut down, he probably imagined that he was doing us a kindness, by not compelling us to go out into the dreary world that lay outside the office, by offering us an hour or two more of this colour and glamour of business. To me, in those days, he did not seem a real person at all, so far removed were his interests from anything that I could enjoy; and I saw him as a sort of powerful robot. It was like working for a Martian. He left about a quarter of a million sterling—mostly to charity, for he was a dutiful kind of man—and I am certain that he never got a tenth as much out of life as his warehouseman, my friend N., on his pre-war wages of twenty-seven or thirty shillings a week and his two-pound-ten now. N. and I talked about him, among the bales in the dim greasy warehouse. 'Nay, Jack lad,' N. observed, 'Ah don't know what t'owd chap lived for. He got nowt aht o' life, did he? Ah've had more fun i' one night than Ah bet he had i' thirty year. He'd no mates. He nivver went onywhere an' enjoyed hisself. He'd all that brass an' didn't know how to spend it. Ah don't believe he'd ivver owt to do wi' a woman. Nay, you can't imagine him, can you? But mind you, Jack lad, he worn't a bad sort. He wor *peculiar*, as you might say, but not a bad sort. He wor better to get on wi' nor So-and-So.' I agreed, having had trouble with So-and-So myself. 'Ah remember one morning,' N. continued, 'when So-an-So rang me up at t'warehouse abaht some bags. An' he called me a 'silly blockhead' cos Ah told him we hadn't got 'em. Ay, he called me a "silly blockhead". So Ah went straight down to t'office and Ah says to him, "Did you call me a silly blockhead"?' But it is impossible to suggest in print the menacing deliberation of this in an aggressive Yorkshire voice: it is tremendous. 'So he says, "Ah dare say Ah did," and Ah says to him, "Well, don't do it again then, 'cos neither you nor onnybody else is going to call me a silly blockhead. an' we haven't got them bags either," An' he wor careful what he called me after that,' N. concluded. Then he added: 'You know, Jack lad, you wor t'only one o' them lads in t'office who wor nivver frightened o' So-and-So, and Ah've allus said that about you. You didn't give a damn for him or onnybody else, did you? Ah've had monny a good laugh thinking o' things you used to do. Ay, you wor a cough-drop.' Good old N. If ever I go back to that warehouse and find him gone, that day will be very black for me.

For once, I was lucky in my traffic with old friends. I called at a house I had not been to for many a long year, a house I had visited a great deal at one time, for an old schoolfellow had lived there and his parents still lived there. When I called, one evening, the house seemed very quiet and there was a dim light in the bedroom. My heart sank: I had a vision of death, long dreadful illness, misery and evil. Dubiously, tentatively, I tried the bell. Mr.

W. himself opened the door and peered at me through his steel-rimmed spectacles. We had not seen one another for at least ten years. Recognition, joy; no death, no dreadful illness! He and Mrs. W. were sitting in the back room, and there I sat with him, and we talked of old times in that house and of their son, my former schoolfellow and friend, who had collected several University degrees and diplomas and now held a very important post (you may have heard of him) in another and larger city. Mr. W. had recently retired and brought back his bag of tools from the mill for the last time. And now I can confess that it was from him that I took a good many hints for my Jess Oakroyd; borrowing his trade and something of his appearance, his mixture of simplicity and real shrewdness, of independence and deep affection. What were sharply different were their respective domestic lives, for this real man had—and still has—a wife in a thousand, and both a son and a daughter he is proud of. And, for once, it had all ended happily. The tremendous sacrifices these two good folk had made for their son, so that he could collect his degrees and diplomas and solid jobs—and I well remember the extent and severity of those sacrifices—had not been made in vain; he and his wife had recently been staying there; and in a week or two these old people were off to stay with them. It had all turned out as events in the more respected contemporary novels are not allowed to turn out, for the best. And Mr. W., beaming, fetched in a jug of beer, in the time-old fashion, and over it we exchanged reminiscences, and he pointed the stem of his little pipe at me, as of old, when he delivered some shrewd thrusts at the Government and the City Council and the pompous bigwigs. Of course, it is shocking that a man of this kind, a sound conscientious hard-working craftsman, should have had to make such sacrifices, should have received so narrow a slice of the good life. Anybody with a glimmer of a notion of what social justice should mean ought to be ready to fight for him and his kind. But on the other hand I for one am equally ready to fight against any scheme that would turn him and his kind into different beings. Bernard Shaw once declared that all he wanted to do was to abolish the working class and put in its place some sensible people. But for my part, I would as soon see England filled with men like Mr. W. or old N.—and, mark you, it is not filled with them, otherwise it would be a different England— as I would see it populated by average members of the Fabian Society. After all, such men as these, like Mr. Shaw himself, stand on their own feet, do their jobs with a will, stoutly resist stupid opposition but give way to affection, and, like him, are grand lumps of character. What—in the name of every thing but supermen—more can you want?

You find people writing now about women working in Russia as if this was some new thing in the world's history. Women have always worked in these textile trades, which could not exist—on their present economic basis—without them. One unmarried elderly woman of my acquaintance, up there, had just retired, after working fifty years as a weaver in one mill. Fifty years. During that time, she and her relatives and most of her friends had not only worked in that enormous mill but had lived all their lives in its shadow. Time for them had been marked by the sound of its hooter—locally known as a 'whew'. Fifty years, only broken by an occasional four or five days at Morecambe or Blackpool. Fifty years, living in the same back-to-back houses, just behind the mill. Millions of yards of fine fabrics had gone streaming out, from their hands, to almost every part of the world, to be cut into the fashions of the 'eighties, the 'nineties, the Edwardians, the Georgians. Fifty years of quick skilled work, with hours, in winter, lasting from dark to dark. If a world that once went bare is now partly clothed and decorated with fabrics, then these folk may be said to have lent a hand in the great processes of civilisation; they have not been passengers in the ship; a brief childhood at one end and a few sinking weary years at the other end, and between them these five solid decades of work: that is their record. Such services do not go unrewarded, of course. A weaver fit to be kept on working for fifty years has proved herself a valuable old servant of the firm. Therefore she receives a pension of five shillings a week from the mill, five shillings to do what she likes with; and when to that is added the ten shillings that the rashly generous state is flinging her way, it will be seen that she has a whole fifteen shillings a week for herself, which, if she had only herself to consider—and unfortunately, in this instance, she had to help an invalid sister—would undoubtedly leave her splendidly idle and luxurious at the end of her fifty years. It is a pity that she has somebody else to support, because otherwise, no doubt, in this pensioned ease, she could see something of the world for which she has been weaving so long, could be waited on for once in her life, could look at the big shops and buy pretty little presents for her grand-nieces and nephews, could, in short, have a wonderful time with her fifteen shillings. But perhaps it is as well that she cannot go splashing her fifteen shillings about, because if she could, although she is old and heavy and tired, she might arouse the indignation of those honest fiery Tory patriots who write articles for and letters to the newspapers, protesting against the treatment afforded this pampered class, talking like the noblest Romans of us all in this later age of bread and circuses. Perhaps she is better as she is, wishing she had strength enough to work more than those fifty years, wondering how to get through the coming week, and never asking herself, as she stirs in the dark mornings when she hears the hooter blowing and the clatter of feet outside, whether mills were created for men and women or men and women for mills. She does not complain much, perhaps because she realises, like all the protesting gentlemen who lounge before large club fireplaces, that if, during and after her fifty years of toil, she had been treated with any more consideration it would have meant the ruin of a great country. And, not being a literary sentimentalist, she does not say that a country in these years has no title to greatness, had better face and risk ruin, if it still allows its people to suffer such damnable injustice.

[7]

I had time to note a great many changes in my Bradford, and as some of them may be taking place in a good many other provincial towns, they are worth recording here. I think a few, however, are probably peculiar to Bradford. For example, that sad dwindling of the foreign community in the city, and with it the decline of many things they fostered, notably music. The very building in which I heard the orchestras of Richter and Nikisch when I was a boy, the old St. George's Hall, has been turned into a permanent picture theatre. Bradford has no proper concert hall now—more shame to it. The old Theatre Royal too, where Irving played for the last time, has also been turned into a cinema. The city used to have three newspapers of its own, one morning and two evening papers; but now it has only two, and one of them is certainly not as good as it was before the war, when, as I well remember, it was publishing some of the earliest travel essays of H. M. Tomlinson. The Arts Club still exists but in a very modest fashion, and is not the institution it was. There is not, to my mind, the wealth in the city there used to be. This is not merely because the wool trade has not been producing the wealth it used to produce, but also because the richer merchants and manufacturers no longer live in the city. They work there, but live well outside, Ilkley, Harrogate, Grassington way. The motor has, of course, encouraged this migration, which is common, I suspect, throughout the north, where the wealthier industrialists are busy turning themselves into country gentlemen and are leaving the cities to the professional, clerking and working classes. (This change may bring about some curious results very soon.) When I was a boy, we had certain wealthy families of manufacturers who came as near to forming an aristocracy as such a democratic community as ours would allow. Now they are gone, and their places have not been taken by other families. That chapter is closed. The main shopping streets have turned with the tide, and a glance at their windows shows that the shopkeepers are now trying to attract a much larger if poorer public. And of course you no longer notice much difference between members of various classes. Clogs have disappeared, for though they were really very sensible footwear for work, being healthy, comfortable and cheap, they carried a bad social stigma on them, even when I was young. The working woman's shawl is disappearing too. But such changes are general.

Bradford has a Civic Theatre, of which I happen to be President, so I came into contact with the dramatic folk of the city. This Civic Theatre, which used to be a branch of a similar movement in Leeds but now has an independent standing, is an organisation of amateur actors, with professional producers, who give throughout the winter months a series of good plays, for which they do not charge admission. People who subscribe a few shillings to the Theatre are given priority in booking seats, but the seats themselves throughout are free, though of course there is a collection to which audiences are expected to contribute as generously as possible. Even now, many people do not realise that there is a chain of such theatres, small intelligent repertory theatres organised on various lines, stretching across the country. Most of them have to struggle along, hardly paying their way; they have not as yet produced any brilliant new schools of drama or acting; they have probably not succeeded yet in creating a public of any real size for intelligent drama; but nevertheless I do not think my own personal interest in the theatre is deluding me when I declare that this dramatic movement, which came into existence after Hollywood had nearly wrecked the declining professional theatre of the provinces, is of immense social importance. To begin with, it is a genuine popular movement, not something fostered by a few rich cranks. The people who work for these theatres are not by any means people who want to kill time. They are generally hard-working men and women—small business men, teachers, clerks, artisans—whose evenings are precious to them. And they are tremendously enthusiastic, even if at times they are also—like all theatrical folk everywhere—given to quarrelling and displays of temperament. Many of them have not only had to work extremely hard for their theatres, but they have also had to face a certain amount of ridicule; and all this with only their own encouragement, and not—as it so often happens nowadays—with that of the Government or the newspapers. In short, this is a genuine spontaneous movement. If you reckon its supporters merely by quantity, it may seem unimportant; but if you begin to take quality into account, it is a different story. These theatres are attracting to themselves the more eager, impressionable, intelligent younger people in these industrial towns, where depression has hung like a black cloud for the last few years. Some of them, in various places, have told me what this dramatic work has meant to them, and in many instances the persons in question have not been producing, designing scenery, playing big parts, but may only have been selling programmes, taking tickets, or doing the accounts. A dozen of such folk, who use their own wits and form their own judgment, are more significant than a thousand members of that crowd which is at the mercy of all the forces of publicity and advertisement. For this reason we must not allow a mere consideration of numbers to influence us. These theatres are very small and have to fight for their very existence; but the more I have seen of industrial England, the more firmly I am convinced that it would be easier to under-estimate than over-estimate their significance. I see them as little camp-fires twinkling in a great darkness. I am not writing now as an occasional dramatist, whose plays are being performed in such theatres, but as a novelist desperately turned social historian, addressing himself to readers who may possibly not care twopence if every playhouse in the country should close to-morrow. The point is, that in communities that have suffered the most from industrial depression, among younger people who frequently cannot see what is to become of their jobs and their lives, these theatres have opened little windows into a world of ideas, colour, fine movement, exquisite drama, have kept going a stir of thought and imagination for actors, helpers, audiences, have acted as outposts for the army of the citizens of to-morrow, demanding to live, though they should possibly have less food on their table and shabbier clothes on their backs, a life at once more ardent and more thoughtful than their fathers and mothers ever knew.

There is something very ironical about Bradford's present position as a theatrical town. (And much of what follows, I believe, applies to a good many of the industrial towns in the north.) While the professional theatre regards it as a very poor place indeed, hardly on the map any longer, actually it is theatrically-minded to a most fantastic and droll degree. It is a city crowded with amateur actors. I have never known anything like it. Operas, musical comedies, farces, dramas, the place hums with them. Every second typist is an ingénue lead somewhere, every other cashier a heavy father or comedian. Acres of canvas are being transformed into rural scenes and library sets every week. All the young electricians can rig you up floats or battens or spots at a moment's notice. The local papers print whole pages of amateur stage photographs. Nearly every organisation appears to run a dramatic society as an off-shoot. The young man frowning into vacancy, at the other end of the tram, is probably busy working out the movements of the first act of *The Silver Box*. The large man who just nodded to him is probably about to turn himself into the comic bailiff in *Tilly of Bloomsbury*. There are soubrettes and tragediennes in all the shops. The very factories produce their own revues and pantomimes. All the town's a stage. If all this seems so much fanciful exaggeration, I can offer cold figures. During the last municipal year, the number of amateur dramatic licences issued in Bradford passed the total of 700. And here at least there is a distinct local drama, written by local men and women in the West Riding dialect. Though the royalties paid by these modest dramatic societies must obviously be very small, there are so many of them that I know at least two local dramatists who are almost entirely supported by such royalties. I am quite ready to believe that Bradford, which, after all, has not a peculiarly histrionic population of its own, is by no means alone in this recent and astonishing passion for theatricals. It is, of course, symptomatic of a change in the whole temper and outlook of the industrial north, of a general desire for more movement and colour and imaginative activity in life, and of a new and healthy protest against that merely passive amusement which is regarded as one of the weaknesses of our mechanical civilisation. To me, a pre-war Bradfordian, some examples of this changed outlook took my breath away, as, for instance, when I heard that one middle-aged couple of my acquaintance, both products of a fairly grim Nonconformity, were having their little girl, the youngest child and the apple of their eye, seriously trained as an acrobatic dancer. It did not take much of that to send me wandering about dazed, a stranger in my own town.

'And what seem to you the greatest changes here?' I asked a very intelligent middle-aged woman, an old Bradford friend. She thought for a moment, then startled me by demanding, 'Where are the men?' I asked her to explain, and she continued: 'There never seem to be any men about nowadays, whatever you are doing or wherever you go. Plenty of women, but no men. It doesn't matter what it is—a dramatic society, or lectures, or at the theatre, or even a political meeting—they're all women. Where *do* the men go nowadays? In the old days, there used to be at least as many men interested in everything as women—it was half and half—but now it isn't. Yes, I know there was the war—but even that doesn't explain it. After all, there's another generation grown up since then. And you see the girls in at everything, but not the boys and the men. What *do* they do with themselves? They don't go to the pubs every night, as they used to do. It's not that. It isn't even the pictures, because they're mostly women there too. Do they just sit at home and play with the wireless, or what? I tell you, it's a mystery to me, and nobody I know can explain it.' Neither could I, though the problem reminded me of what I heard so often in London, from persons who knew more than I do about the youngest generation of adults, especially in the upper middle-class, namely, that in this generation the young men are far more subdued, far less enterprising and am-

bitious than the girls, who seem to have mysteriously acquired all the dash
and virility. Whether this is true everywhere, I do not know. Indeed, I do
not know if it is true anywhere; and I suspect it to be one of those grand
conclusions drawn from a few hasty glimpses of young people at parties and
dances. Certainly, there seemed to me plenty of young men about in Bradford.

I met one man I was glad to meet, for it proved, as I thought it would,
a most odd and illuminating encounter. I was introduced to him on the ground
floor of a very dingy warehouse, where he was doing an odds-and-ends sort
of business in various textile commodities. He was a man who had been a
legend up there ever since the war. I had never heard of him before the war,
but afterwards I hardly ever heard about anybody else. He was easily the
richest man the West Riding had recently produced, and he was also a character. (And still is.) Nobody knew how much he was worth, at the time when
he was bestriding the whole wool trade like a Colossus, but I gather that it
was between five and ten millions. His operations were vast and mysterious,
and did not stop at wool business, combing and spinning mills, and the like,
but at last even including West End theatres, in which he lost a lot of money
finally by speculation and by putting on expensive musical comedies. There
was a wonderful crop of stories about him, in the usual West Riding vein,
but the only one I remember that pleased me went something like this: at
the time when he still controlled this staggering array of properties, extending
from remote industrial villages in Yorkshire to Shaftesbury Avenue, but when
the slump was just beginning, somebody asked him how things were, and he
replied: 'Nay, out of all t'lot, there's nowt paying but eighteen milk bee-asts
Ah've got up i' North Yorkshire.' This story may not be true, but I can certainly imagine the man I met making this reply. He was a tall, well-covered
man, with a face at once forceful and droll, like that of a comic pirate. I have
not the least idea whether he was a good financier or a bad one, a mediocre
man who was lucky for a season or a clever man who was ultimately unlucky,
but I do know that he was—and is—a character. I have never understood
exactly what happened to all his combines and properties. Apparently the
whole pagoda-like edifice collapsed, leaving him—and I will swear, with a droll
look—among the ruins. He did not go bankrupt and he had the sense and
courage—unlike so many of these financial Napoleons—not to blow his brains
out. He began all over again, in a small way; and there he was, on the ground
floor of a dingy warehouse. It is quite probable that if I had met him when
he was a multi-millionaire, I should have disliked him; but as an ex-multi-
millionaire—not, I imagine, the easiest of situations—he seemed to me very
good company. It is a pity he could not write a perfectly frank autobiography.

In America, where the law of libel does not run as swiftly and remorslessly as it does here, they frequently take you behind the scenes in this super-variety show of high finance; but here in England we are allowed few such visits and a discreet silence is maintained until somebody happens to reach the Old Bailey. Until they are openly proved to be crooks, our own financial jugglers are regarded as distinguished if somewhat mysterious figures, so many benevolent wizards. Nobody but prosecuting counsel, at the right time and in the right place, is permitted to 'de-bunk' them and their world. My Bradford acquaintance had some amusing things to say about this world, things that confirmed much of what I, an ignorant man of letters, had very privately guessed about it. The height of folly, in that world, is to be clumsy, as Hatry was. It is, I gather, a sphere of action in which all depends on your being able to 'get away with' certain things. In lower spheres, where more stupid fellows are merely trying to do, to the best of their ability, the jobs for which they are paid—they may be making a chair, installing a hot-water system, even writing a book—it is not simply a matter of 'getting away with' things; but then it is not here we find the supermen, the wonder chaps, who have to work with one eye on Maidstone Gaol and the other on the House of Lords. It would be better to set up a Monte Carlo of our own than to let our men with Monte Carlo minds, men with 'a system', loose upon the city, there to play with the nation's wealth. We ought to have got past the gambling era now. My Bradford man solemnly warned me against rash speculation: 'You let some brass stick to your fingers, lad,' he said, more than once. There is no advice I can give him, twenty years my senior. But I take him to be a forceful and astute personality, something more than a dashing gambler; and I do not think that he ought to be starting all over again on the ground floor of a dingy warehouse. Nor do I think that he ever ought to have been in control of more factories than he could ever visit or to have been juggling with half-a-dozen West End theatres when he knew nothing about the drama but only about wool, tops and yarn. I do not blame him in particular, I blame us all for allowing such a daft chaos to go blundering on, wasting men who might otherwise have proved themselves first-class servants of the community. Metaphorical language is sometimes extremely significant. There is only one sphere of action in the more civilised countries to-day in which men find it necessary, when describing the ordinary operations there, to use metaphors and similes drawn from medieval brigandage or the early life of the Wild West; and that is the world of high finance. Thus I cannot help feeling, in my innocence, that there must be something strangely anachronistic, crude, violent, barbaric, about that world; and that therefore it is time it was brought into the twentieth

MARKET STREET, BRADFORD, 1930 *Walter Scott*

century, cleaned up and civilised. I hinted as much to the fallen Titan in the warehouse, and wish I could have complimented him upon bringing out of his crazy vanished Eldorado so much humour and courage, two notable West Riding qualities. But we never pay compliments in Bradford. We are, as we readily admit, not good at expressing our feelings, which only means, of course, that we are bad at expressing our pleasant feelings, for I have noticed that we give tongue to the other kind with great frequency and force. I feel that now is the moment when I should put down some memorable concluding sentence of praise about the whole of the West Riding and its people; and of course I cannot do it. But then I am one of them, and they are the very people who will understand why I cannot do it. So—well, I'm off. Behave thi'sen, lad!

CHAPTER NINE

To the Potteries

[1]

The thread of my journey proper was waiting to be picked up again, and I found it in the Potteries. I carried with me to the Potteries a full load of ignorance. I knew that cups and saucers and plates were made there, and I had some acquaintance with them, in the form of the Five Towns, in Arnold Bennett's novels. And that was all. Though Bennett, I think, told us a good deal about his birthplace, oddly enough I do not think I heard his name mentioned once during all the time I was in the Potteries. In a Year Book of the district, several years old, that someone gave me, though there were thousands of names mentioned in it, I never caught sight of his. Very odd, this. There is a great deal in this Year Book about the products of North Staffordshire. Surely Bennett and his excellent novels deserve a place among those products. And what single man in our time did more to make the Potteries known to the rest of the world than Bennett did? Why no sort of memorial to him anywhere? And why are third-rate politicians in this country still considered to be far more important than first-rate artists of any kind? It is because there is always a chance that the politician may be able to wangle something, whereas no real good can come of artists? I wonder if there is a country in Europe in which musicians, painters, authors, philosophers, scientists, count for less than they do in this country.

Bennett's famous Five Towns consist of six towns, Burslem, Fenton, Hanley, Longton, Stoke and Tunstall, which have now been merged into one city, called Stoke-on-Trent. This city has a population of nearly three hundred thousand, but it has no real existence as a city of that size. There is no city. There are still these six little towns. After federation into one city had been first suggested, the inhabitants of these towns argued and quarrelled most bitterly for years. Finally, the obvious advantages of federation carried the day, and there appeared, on paper, the mythical city of Stoke-on-Trent. But when you go there, you still see the six towns, looking like six separate towns. Unless you are wiser than I was, you will never be quite sure which of the six you are in at any given time; but at least you will be ready to swear that you are nowhere near a city that contains three hundred thousand people. There is now a civic centre in Stoke itself, but even that will not persuade you. For what distinguishes this district, to my eye and mind, is its universal littleness. Everything there is diminutive. Even the landscape fits in, for though there are hills, they are all little ones. I seemed to be paying a visit to Lilliput. The region is a clutter of small towns, as I have already remarked, but inside these towns everything is small too. Not a single thing sends you staring upward. The pottery manufactories—known locally as 'potbanks'—have nothing big about them, no six-storey factories or towering chimneys. You see no huge warehouses, no high public buildings. The houses, which stretch out in a ribbon development for miles and miles, are nearly all workmen's cottages, and if they are not actually small of their kind, they contrive to suggest they are. Down one road I noticed some cottage houses and tiny bungalows that had boldly labelled themselves *Commercial Hotel*, and I will swear that in any of them the arrival of two travellers at once would have wrecked the establishment. I cannot believe that in any other part of England such preposterous dolls' houses could have passed as hotels. And unless I am sadly wrong, unless I was so dominated by this idea of littleness that I could not use my eyes, the very people are small; sturdy enough, of course, and ready to give a good account of themselves; but nearly all stunted in height. Even the smoke—and there is plenty of it in the Potteries—does not hang well above the towns like a dark cloud, as it does in other industrial districts, but seems to drift heavily just above the roofs. Never before have I seen such a Lilliputian region. It is a marvel to me that the cups and saucers turn out the right adult size.

It resembles no other industrial area I know. I was at once repelled and fascinated by its odd appearance. Perhaps it was all the more curious to me because, being a Yorkshireman, when I see so much grimy evidence of toil, I also expect to see the huge dark boxes of factories and the immensely tall chimneys with which I am so familiar. Here, however, although there was more smoke than I had ever seen before, so that if you looked down upon any one of these towns the drift over it was so thick that you searched for the outbreak of fire, there were no tall chimneys, no factory buildings frowning above the streets; but only a fantastic collection of narrow-necked jars or bottles peeping above the house-tops on every side, looking as if giant biblical characters, after a search for oil or wine, had popped them there, among the dwarf streets. These, of course, are the pottery kilns and ovens, which are usually tall enough to be easily seen above the rows of cottage houses. I never got used to their odd appearance, never quite recovered from my first wild impression of them as some monstrous Oriental intrusion upon an English industrial area. But without these great bottles of heat, there would be no

Potteries. They represent the very heart and soul of the district, as you very soon learn; and unless you are prepared to take a deep and lasting interest in what happens inside those ovens, it would be better for you to take the first train anywhere. This is no region to idle in, and the pity of it is that, what with the decline in the American trade for the better-class china and the triumphant competition of other countries in the cheaper lines of earthenware, so many good workmen here, men who have learned a fine old craft, are compelled to remain idle. This is not a place designed to comfort and compensate such idlers. I do not know what Nature originally made of it, because nearly all signs of her handiwork have been obliterated. But man, who has been very thorough here, has not made of it anything that remotely resembles an inland resort. For a man of the Potteries, it must be either work or misery. For the man who is in regular work at decent wages there are some definite compensations, as I shall presently try to show; but as a district to do anything but work in, it has nothing to recommend it.

To begin with, it is extremely ugly. You can see open spaces everywhere—'fields', the local people call them proudly—but these are no Arcadian pastures, to be idle and poetical in. You can, if you are young, kick a ball about on them, but they cannot be fit for much else. I have seen few regions from which Nature has been banished more ruthlessly, and banished only in favour of a sort of troglodyte mankind. Civilised man, except in his capacity as a working potter, has not arrived here yet, just as the real city of Stoke-on-Trent, which will no doubt be a monument of civic dignity, has not yet arrived. The small towns straggle and sprawl in their shabby undress, following the ugly fashion of industrial small towns. They are neither old and charming nor bright and new, but give the impression of having been hastily put up seventy or eighty years ago, like frontier outposts or mining camps, and then left to be sooted over. Their excellent services of buses, which have replaced the actual trams but not always the tram-lines and posts and wires, simply take you from one absence of civic dignity and urban gaiety to another. These six towns are not exactly alike; even I could see that there were differences, but these differences are minute when compared with the awful gap between the whole lot of them and any civilised urban region. I do not mean to suggest that there are not schools and museums and shops and cinemas and those public halls in which the musical citizens can indulge their passion for oratorio. These amenities exist, and may be as plentiful per head of the population as they are in any other place. But the general impression is of an exceptionally mean, dingy provinciality, of Victorian industrialism in its dirtiest and most cynical aspect. The look of these places bears no proper relation to the work that

BOTTLE KILNS AT ETRURIA, c.1935   *Harold White*

goes on in them. It seems to me monstrous that good craftsmen, whose families have been working for generations perhaps with Wedgwoods or Adams or Spode, should be condemned to live in such miserable holes as these. It would not seem so odd if they were all making excavating machines or dredgers or torpedoes; but they are not, they are shaping and colouring things like cups and saucers and plates and vases. That anything even vaguely decorative should come from these places seems a miracle. That a craft, perhaps the most ancient known to us, should still be carried on here is incredible. It is as if nobody had any eyes to see outside the workrooms. The men of the directing and managing class can, of course, slip into their waiting cars and return to a home that is in pleasant country, from which the Potteries are only seen as a distant haze. The others are doomed to live in one or other of these six towns, and no doubt when they are working hard, life is not so bad. But it must be a sorry business for them when they are thrown out of work or compelled to retire. What compensations are there here? The green fields and the bright streams have gone, and the real city, which would at least offer something to the eye and the mind, some suggestion of dignity or gaiety, an amusing stir of life, has not yet arrived. We shall be told at once, of course, that 'they are used to it', that after all 'this is their home'. But what a grim process, getting used to this! What a home!

Certain amusing traits of Arnold Bennett's odd but engaging character, his knowing air, his passion for excessively smart cosmopolitan ways of life, his delight in being 'in the swim', were always explained by the fact that he was very much the provincial come to town. The explanation never entirely satisfied me because so many English authors, perhaps the majority of them, are also provincials who have arrived in town, and yet few of them shared Bennett's boyish enthusiasm for all that was metropolitan, fashionable, anything-but-provincial. The very first morning I spent in the Potteries gave me the clue. Coming from this part of the world, Bennett was not merely a provincial but a super-provincial. He came—perhaps in reality, he fled—from a region that contains the very essence of remote provinciality. Though the Potteries lie between, and no very great distance from, Liverpool and Manchester in the north and Birmingham in the south, though they can communicate easily with nearly any part of the country, occupying as they do an almost central position, there is something so self-contained about them and their peculiar industry that they convey a most unusual impression of provincial remoteness, an impression heightened by their odd littleness and shabbiness. You feel that nobody comes to the Potteries and nobody—except Arnold Bennett—has left them. The same firms, none of them very large though several, of course, are famous, go on from generation to generation, throughout a century employing workmen from the same families. There is something to be said for this cosy, personal sort of industry, as I shall indicate later, but this too helps to make the district self-contained and to confirm it in whatever kind of life it has adopted or made for itself. And now it may be retorted upon me that obviously the people who live in the Potteries like this kind of life, however unlovely it may seem to a hasty visitor, otherwise they would be restless and not show themselves so unwilling to leave it. But what roots them there, I suspect, is their work, their ancient craft, which so far I have been careful to disengage from the general way of life there, the thick drift of smoke, the huddle of undignified and ugly little towns, the rows of dingy dolls' houses, the narrow streets that lead from one dreariness to another. If Bennett had been either a master potter, on the one hand, or a 'thrower' or 'jollyer', on the other, probably he never would have left his Five Towns, and we should have had a few more good pieces of crockery but not *The Old Wives' Tale* or *Riceyman Steps*.

In short, the Potteries are not worthy of the potter. If you are working hard there, then you are not too badly off, because, as we shall see, the work is frequently good work, in which a man can take a personal pride. But if you are not working there, if the depression in America or the triumphant competition of the cut-price countries has thrown you out, then God help you, for nothing that you will see or hear or smell in these six towns will raise your spirits.

[2]

Cups, saucers, dishes, plates, jugs, mugs, teapots, basins. For nearly forty years I had been making use of them. Had I often wondered how they were made? I had not. In all those years I had never spent five minutes wondering how these things were made. They might have grown on trees or been fished out of the sea, for all I knew or cared. Now I look back on this old ignorant pre-Potteries self with the contempt the fellow deserves. I have been behind the crockery scenes. I am almost one of the Pottery lads. When I dine out, I often turn the plates over and see who has made them. (Many of my friends, I am sorry to say, are using foreign ware, and some of those who have bought English stuff have been fobbed off, I am afraid, with *seconds*. This last is a technical joke, only meant for my colleagues in the trade.) I know how jugs acquire their handles and teapots their spouts. I have been in at the birth of giant meat plates. I could sketch you, with these two hands, the early life-

THE ART OF THROWING, c.1934 *Photographer Unknown*

history of a vase or a litter of egg-cups. How do cups and saucers and plates come to have gilt lines and floral decorations and even whole pictures on them? You—I am now addressing the vast oafish lay public—do not know. But I know, having actually been there when the trick was done. And those very imposing vases and mugs that have Greek damsels and cupids on them standing out in clear relief—you may not admire them very much; I don't myself— but how are they made? Where do the damsels and cupids come from? Scarlet with shame, again you have to confess your ignorance. But I know, I know. I could not make one myself, but I believe I could give rough—perhaps very rough, far too rough—directions as to how they should be made. All this weight of knowledge comes of visiting the Potteries. I thought I should like to obtain a glimpse of the trade. There are, however, no glimpses in the Potteries. Either you stay outside the works or you come in and take a good long look. They are nothing if not thorough.

This trade has a language of its own, a smattering of which I acquired. The stuff that has to be shaped and fired is known as 'body'. Its varying thickness is referred to as its 'strength'. In its early liquid state it is called 'slip', and the separate ingredients of 'slip' are called 'slop'. The process of shaping the clay on a revolving disk—the time-old business of the potter's wheel—is known as 'throwing'. If you work at the stuff inside a mould, you are, I believe, either 'jollying' or 'jiggering'. The Potteries are filled with cunning men of their hands who are divided into 'throwers' or 'jollyers'. (My vote is for 'throwing', as we shall see.) North Staffordshire provides the master potters, the 'throwers' and 'jollyers' and the rest of them, and it has the coal for the ovens, but it no longer provides its own 'slop'. In other words, the original ingredients come from outside the district, china clay from Cornwall, flints from the South Coast, and so on. The flints are calcinated, and are then ground into a smooth paste. I saw a very ancient machine doing this—it had been revolving and grinding there for generations—and was told it had not been improved upon yet. This paste is mixed with various earths and clays, and then most of the moisture is pressed out of the mixture. There is in all these works a fascinating machine called, I think, 'a pug', and out of this the firm clay glides in a continuous square column, to be cut into the necessary lengths. With the addition of varying amounts of water, it can now be shaped by the 'thrower' or pressed into moulds. But the basis is still the ancient potter's wheel. There are scientists and engineers at work now in these places, but the fundamentals of the craft remain unchanged. These North Staffordshire workmen and the potters of Ancient Egypt share the same skill, and if they could meet and find a common language, no doubt they would have a lot to say to one another. Here, in short, you have a modern industry rooted in a traditional craft. Moreover, there is tradition at work even among these modern employees. I watched a man performing the difficult operation of 'throwing' large meat dishes. These are made by taking a piece of clay that has been roughly pounded down to the required area and thickness and then quickly placing it on a plaster-of-paris mould. This mould is revolved at varying speeds, and as it goes round, the 'thrower' rapidly and deftly adjusts the clay to it and evens out the thickness of the embryo dish. As the movement is circular and the dish is not, this process is extremely difficult and demands a very fine trained sense of touch, which I discovered, after one humiliating half-minute, that I did not possess. But this man had been throwing dishes and plates all his life, and his father and his grandfather before him had been throwing dishes and plates. By this time, it had become a family craft. For all I know, they were beginning to be born with the 'throwing' facility, and threw small imaginary dishes in the very cradle. What is certain, however, is that this sound element of craft, in which they can, and do, take a personal pride, removes all these men from the ordinary ranks of modern workmen. They are not merely doing a job for so much a week. They are craftsmen. They are doing something that they can do better than anybody else, and they know it. When they come to their work, they do not dwindle, as most people do nowadays, people who have to leave their personalities behind as they 'clock in'; on the contrary, these men—and no doubt many of the women too—become more themselves, enlarge their personalities, just because it is here that they can use their skill and find an outlet for their zest. Nearly all of them are on piecework, and I have more than a suspicion that, the pottery trade being what it is to-day, they have to make full use of that skill and that zest in order to take home at the week-end a decent living wage. Nevertheless, I am convinced that most of these men would scorn to do a poor job, even if it were in no danger of being discovered. Their pride would not allow them to be slovenly. For this reason, they are left to themselves to get on with the job, are trusted and respected. The happy result can be read in their faces. You have to go a long way these days to find that look.

I went through one long clayey slippery room after another, and saw ladies and gentlemen of all ages and sizes shaping cups, saucers, teapots, jugs; cunningly sliding on handles and spouts (one flick of a little knife through the clay and they get just the right angle for the handles to meet the curved side of the teapots and jugs); putting on transfer papers that would leave patterns on the ware; spraying revolving vases with colour (a fine messy job this, half an hour of which, with glorious blue or scarlet in the spray, would take me out of many a fit of depression); or painting gilt lines or green leaves or pink roses on the superior ware, most of which, I think, would be still more superior if it did not reflect the taste of the 'fifties and the Great Exhibition. Some of these better firms are now beginning to make use of the services of real artists, but they have still a good deal to learn about the æsthetic demands of this present decade. I did not like to say so at the time—and I do not enjoy saying it now, for this is a poor return for hospitality—but these firms are at their worst when they are told to spare no expense, for then they fairly riot in artiness, in dreadful elaborations of cupids and roses. The craftsmanship behind these pieces of super-ware is astonishing, but, unfortunately, so are the pieces themselves. They are difficult and it seems a pity they are not impossible. But I can understand the excitement there used to be in these works when Russian grand-dukes or American millionaires gave *carte blanche* orders for dinner services. I wish, for all their sakes, these fairy-tale orders still arrived every month or two. But where are the grand-dukes? Where, indeed, are the American millionaires? These firms used to make a very good thing out of what seemed to me a very queer American custom, that of having what are

TURNING AND DECORATING, c.1934   *Photographer Unknown*

known as 'service plates', which are never loaded with food but are placed
before guests between courses, to be looked at and admired. These luxury
plates were usually very ornate and would be specially made, here in the Potteries, for each customer. Some Americans like to have a picture of their college
on their plates, and in one of these rooms there are probably transfer pictures
of all the American colleges—a solemn thought. But all this trade has declined
rapidly. It may never come back. Americans, in their new austerity, may never
again flaunt their 'service plates' or eat off a Staffordshire transfer of the good
old campus. If all this should suggest that the products of these firms are all
unpleasing, I must make haste to correct the impression. Some of their ware
is very charming indeed, notably the eighteenth-century china glazed hand-
painted ware and the deep blue printed ware of the early nineteenth century.

The firing is done in old-fashioned bottle-shaped ovens. They are bigger,
especially when inspected from the inside, than they first appear to be. The

things to be fired are packed in 'saggers' or 'seggers', round, flat-bottomed containers that are built up inside the oven, in which no space is wasted. The fires, of course, are in the wall of the oven. One firing may take twenty tons of coal. There are two or three men in charge of an oven that is being fired, and these men stay on the job until it is finished. I talked to two who were sitting by a hot oven, occasionally getting up to peep into one of the fires. They looked as if they had been there for weeks, as if they lived by the side of this monstrous hot brick bottle, and had a very red-rimmed appearance. Apparently it is quite a highly-skilled business, this of firing an oven, and the men have to be intimately acquainted with the whims of these bottles. The two I saw were smoking short pipes and were, I fancy, philosophers. If they were, they had all the necessary warmth of climate.

[3]

Wedgwood's works are in a place that the famous original Wedgwood christened *Etruria*. All that returns to my memory concerning Etruria is that it was by the side of a very dirty canal. I might have remembered more if I had not spent such an amusing day inside those works. I had a guide, with brown overalls, a pleasant but sententious manner, and a habit of referring to all and sundry as 'ladies and gentlemen'. There were long, long walks through sheds and rooms. For the first hour or so I said nothing. We watched some very good 'throwing' in one big well-lighted room, where everybody seemed to be busy and cheerful. Then we watched some gentlemen putting various round articles, bowls and jugs and the like, on lathes and turning them, or putting in decoration with funny little odds and ends of tools. All these articles were made of a heavier clay, which lent itself in the most accommodating fashion to these fascinating methods of treatment. To stand there and see the particles of clay fly from the sharp edge of the tool was very tantalising. I am not—and never have pretended to be—a man of my hands. No great craftsman was lost when I took to scribbling for a living. But there was something very tempting about these surfaces of hard darkish clay. In some instances these surfaces were rather rough and had to be turned on the machine to make them deliciously smooth. In other instances, the fine smoothness was there and now had to be dug into cunningly to make the necessary decoration. Never have I seen another substance that set up such an itch in the hand. All one's manhood—or boyhood—ached to be at it. The lovely stuff simply asked for trouble. This was not a feeling peculiar to me, the mere visitor. Quite obviously all the men there were in thrall to it too. They had been working with this

OVEN-FIRING AT ETRURIA, c.1934   *Photographer Unknown*

stuff for years and years, had served seven years' apprenticeship to it, but they too were still happy to be setting about it. *Whirr!*—and there was a tiny dark cascade of clay, the tool went biting in and in, until the man on the job suddenly stopped, took a pair of calipers, made a swift measurement, and found that his eye had been right and no more was necessary. Do not tell me that those fellows were not enjoying their work. If one of them had been compelled to stay in the room without laying a finger on a bit of clay, he would have gone mad.

'Can't I have a shot at this?' I asked the guide, piteously. He said I could, but he would take me to a special little department where a very experienced and high-skilled man did the turning and decoration of the more important pieces. This department turned out to be a queer little eighteenth-century cabin, which looked at first like an old curiosity shop. It was crowded with a glorious hotch-potch of plaster moulds, blue prints, vases in various stages of completion, rum little tools, clay shavings, and a hundred-and-one other things. It looked like the mad jumble one sees in pictures of old alchemists' chambers. There ought to have been a stuffed alligator hanging from the roof, and a few skulls about. In the far corner was an old treadle machine, probably the darling of the original eighteenth-century Wedgwood. The treadling was worked by an elderly comfortable-looking woman. At the other end of it, attending to the decorating of the revolving vases, was an elderly comfortable-looking man. There was quite a Darby-and-Joan atmosphere about these two, though actually they were only two old colleagues. The guide explained that I wanted to try my hand at a little decoration. The craftsman was affable, though I thought I caught a sardonic gleam from his spectacles. He put a small black basalt vase on the machine and then showed me how to apply to it, as it revolved, the various foolish little tools that were there. He gave me a short demonstration. It looked very easy. But wisely I refrained from saying so. I took up my position. 'Right, Mary,' he said, and Mary treadled and the vase went round and round. 'Press harder,' he said. I did, nervously, jerkily. 'Not so hard,' he said. I thought—and still think—that I did the flower-and-leaf decoration at the top very well; and was not bad at the bit of cutting out at the bottom. But the middle part, in which one had to shave a small slice away at equal distances all round the vase, was not good. It did not look good then; it does not look good now. Yes, I have that very vase, which was afterwards fired for me and now is a deep black and almost like metal, here in the house, and when it first arrived the children pretended to admire it. Every time I look at it I wish I could try that middle bit again. Some day I shall make a special journey to Wedgwood's to see if I cannot do better in the middle with another vase. Possibly, however, they would not let me in again, for they may easily have had quite enough of me that day. It was now the lunch hour—how time hurries away with us craftsmen!—and I joined three very pleasant and intelligent young men, who appeared to be in complete charge of the big complicated works. This in itself was a happy change, for as a rule one sees nothing but middle-aged or elderly faces round these directors' dining tables. After a lot of good talk about the Potteries and trade and America and wages and whatnot, I told them that they would never get me out of their works until I had done a little 'throwing'. If I could not 'throw' something that very afternoon, I should go down to the grave dissatisfied. So it was arranged that I should 'throw'.

These people may talk of 'jollying' and 'jiggering' and mixing the 'slop' and 'pugging the slip' and designing moulds and making moulds and printing transfers and hand-painting and gilding, until their voices are no more than a hoarse rattle, but they will never persuade me that the very heart and soul of the craft is not the glorious 'throwing', which has in its essence come down to us through the mists of antiquity. I had watched these fellows as I used to watch Cinquevalli the juggler. But they are better than he ever was, for their juggling is creative. Indeed, this process looks more like original creation itself than any I have ever seen. It is miraculous. The 'thrower' sits on a small high seat well above his wheel, which here is a horizontal rotating disk, driven automatically but controlled by a foot pedal. He takes a lump of clay, wets it with water, then first 'centres' it by letting it spin rapidly between his hands and gently increasing the pressure until it rises in a whirling column that very quickly becomes symmetrical. He can then play with it as he pleases. A downward and outward pressure and it instantly turns into a bowl. An upward pressure transforms it into a vase. If there is a more fascinating operation than this in all man's varied handiwork, I have never had the luck to see it. I want no conjuring trick more enchanting than this of the spinning clay instantly flowering into bowls and jugs and vases of every known shape. Here is the supreme triumph of man's creative thumb. The combination of eagerness and docility in the spinning moistened clay was entrancing. If the far slower and more arid work of the turning machines and the little digging tools fascinated me and made me itch to be at work, what then can be said of this marvellous operation, this essence of rapid creation? I guessed of course that it could not possibly be as easy as it looked, that men do not have seven years' apprenticeship for nothing, but I did not care how big a fool I made of myself before these grinning lads and lasses; I had to try my hand at it. And of course I cherished a vague hope, which was perhaps less vague after lunch than before, that I would prove an exception to this rule of craftsmanship, that I would be miraculously endowed with potter's thumbs at once ('Why, you were born with the touch, sir,' they would cry, startled and admiring), and that I might achieve, within a single hour, that Priestley bowl, that Priestley vase, which would open a new chapter in the history of this famous old firm. (For more than thirty years now I have never tried to do anything new without cherishing this wild hope, that God would let me play tennis or billiards or the violin wonderfully at first sight, allow me to display myself suddenly as a heaven-born orator or singer. No such miracle has ever happened. Nobody yet has been startled by my exhibition of unsuspected skill. Yet I know I shall go on hoping in this same foolish fashion right to the very end, when, the silliest old man in England, I shall be hoping to die in some neat clever new way.) Now I put on a suit of overalls. So much wet clay had dried on them that they were as stiff and thick as armour. I climbed on to the little high seat, and then tried revolving the 'wheel'. I found the foot pedal hard to regulate and very uncomfortable. They gave me a good lump of clay and I set it whirling and tried to 'centre' it. At first I did not press hard enough, and then I pressed too hard, with the result that the clay shot up into a frightening lop-sided tower and wobbled desperately between my hands. It took me some time to make any kind of reasonable shot at 'centring'. After that I began to try and make things. But my vases had a nasty trick of growing very tall, then very wide at the mouth, and then of releasing most of themselves from the bondage of the wheel altogether. Often, in my excitement, I would forget that my right foot was supposed to be controlling the speed, and, grappling manfully with the clay, I would let my foot press down, with the inevitable result that the speed increased enormously, the clay went round too fast and could not be manipulated, indeed, could not be kept in any kind of order at all and would reach up and try to strangle me or would fling a long strand of itself at a couple of grinning lads five yards away. I decided to experiment with bowls instead of vases, for as soon as the clay was more than about six inches tall it could not be controlled by me. At first the bowls seemed much easier, but time after time something went wrong. The rims would become too thin; or there would be air-bubbles in the clay; or when I tried to shape the outside, towards the bottom, I would press too hard and the whole wretched bowl would begin rising in the air.

I was a great success as an entertainer if not as a potter, for all the other folk roared with laughter. I spent almost the whole afternoon wrestling with innumerable lumps of clay. My hands were lost in the greyish wet stuff, and it was all over my face and in my hair. The foot that was more or less on terms with that pedal developed very early a cramp that soon took possession of my entire right leg. But I was determined to make something that afternoon, even if I had long ago abandoned all idea of noble vases and had shrunk to considering, even wistfully, any sort of little ashtray that would stand up at all. I managed it in the end too: a sturdy little bowl that you could use for sugar or sweets or as an ashtray; not one of these inhumanly symmetrical and smoothly finished things, but a bit knobbly and rough, one of your genuine hand-made articles. They promised, almost with tears in their eyes, to be kind to this little chap, to fire him and glaze him and then pack him carefully in straw and wood and send him to me. He has not turned up here yet; though that black basalt fellow I decorated (in my opinion, an inferior production) has been here some time. If Wedgwood have lost or destroyed it or, in their jealous rage, have locked it away in the safe, I warn them that I shall return to the Potteries and 'throw' again, 'throw' like mad. I have half a mind to install a wheel here—and one more easily controlled than theirs—and have clay sent down by the ton, so that I can tackle this vase-and-bowl problem again at my leisure. One thing is certain, that the guide was right when he said there was life in clay. Set it spinning and there is far too much life in it. You feel it fluttering and straining between your hands like a captured wild thing. Oh—with a little pressure of the palm there, a flick of the thumbs here, to be able to make it flower into every imaginable shape! William de Morgan, after being a potter most of his life, took to writing novels at the end of it. If I had more confidence in my thumbs, I would reverse the process.

Early in this chapter I declared that the Potteries were no place to be out of work and idle in, but were excellent for the man hard at it in the local trade. You can see why now. This is an industry that is still a craft. In the cheaper branches of it, more and more may be done by machinery; but the element of craft, of work demanding personal skill and quick judgment, still remains. I never saw people in any industrial area who looked more contented during their working hours than these Staffordshire folk. And as it is still diffi-cult to run 'a potbank' on a gigantic, joint-stock, inhuman scale, the trade has largely remained cosy and homely and is given to using Christian names. It is chiefly made up of small family businesses, in which the employer is well acquainted with all his workpeople. It is for these reasons that serious labour troubles have been rare in the Potteries, though the folk there are sturdily independent. The Potteries seem to me unique. They look like no other indus-trial region. They are unique in their remote, self-contained provincialism. And they are unique in their work, an industry that is still a craft, and one of the oldest in the world. We ought to keep that craft here, even if it means looking

ETRURIA, c.1931   *Harold White*

at the trade mark when we buy a cup and saucer and being ready to spend
a little more on them. We must have our own 'throwers' and 'jollyers'. Why
should we subsidise other people's fun? 'Throwing' and 'jollying' should begin
at home. I shall never look at a piece of crockery with the same eyes that
I used in my ignorant pre-Potteries days. I shall feel the reverberation of every
fresh blow that strikes the industry, because I shall know that it means that
a few more deft thumbs are robbed of their clay, that some will 'throw' and
'jigger' no more, and that some good folk who only ask to put their time-old
skill at our service will go to join the unhappy idlers who hang about the dingy
little streets in the dingy little towns that are still a city only on paper. May
the orders pour in; may prodigious and unheard-of quantities of 'slop' be
transformed into 'slip'; may cups and saucers and plates and teapots rush
like magic out of the clay; may the ovens never grow cold; may Stoke-on-
Trent, a real city, spacious and gay, fit for good craftsmen to live in, rise high
and white; and may the blanket of smoke, the sooty dolls' houses, the blackened fields, soon be nothing but a memory, a tale of the old pioneers.

CHAPTER TEN

To Liverpool and Manchester

[1]

I have never been near Liverpool in spring, summer and early autumn. My visits have all been wintry. I find it impossible to imagine what the city looks like in clear bright sunshine. I think of it existing in a shortened year, only running from November to February, with all its citizens for ever wearing thick overcoats. Just before you reach Lime Street Station your train runs into a deep cutting and daylight promptly vanishes, never returning, I feel, until your other homeward train has left Lime Street and Liverpool well behind. It has, in my memory, more fog about than other cities, not excepting London. The centre is imposing, dignified and darkish, like a city in a rather gloomy Victorian novel. Does spring ever arrive in St. John's Gardens? Do the birds ever twitter and flutter before the solemn façade of St. George's Hall? Is there a Mersey, so much green flowing water, not simply a misty nothingness hooting dismally? I must go there in June, some time, to find out.

There was no deep dark railway cutting for me on this occasion, for I arrived by road, and in place of the cutting were streets that went on and on and on through dreary regions infested by corporation trams. The surface of these streets was a slippery abomination; though we were going very slowly, three times we were nearly on top of pedestrians who started up not three yards from our radiator and slithered about as if bent on suicide. When I was able to think, I began to gather together what I knew already about Liverpool and remembered what I could of previous visits. Well, there was the Playhouse, and its director, my friend William Armstrong, who considers himself—probably with some truth—the busiest man in the city, for he is always watching one play, producing another, and making plans for the production of two more. His, I suppose, is the best repertory company in the kingdom; no other, except perhaps Birmingham in its heyday, has sent so many brilliant young actors and actresses to the West End; but I decided there was no room in this chronicle for William and the Playhouse. On two previous visits I had been given a dinner at the University Club. A very jolly little club it is too, where they know how to turn Liverpool winter into something like summer, at least for one evening: pleasant journalists, with Mr. Macleay, of the *Liver-*

pool Daily Post, at the head of them; smiling professors and their ladies; young barristers and shipping men: all very good company and as hospitable as you please. Let me admit that their Liverpool exists, and does it admirably. But it was not the Liverpool I wanted now. The surgeons in Rodney Street (where Gladstone was born), with its fine late eighteenth-century fronts? The Cathedral, which remained in my memory as a vast dark-red bulk, immensely impressive but tantalising because it just missed being a noble expression of our own age? The great buildings down by the river, such as the Dock Board Offices, the Cunard and Royal Liver palaces? Unusual for England—as if Liverpool had had so many peeps at New York's water-front that it felt it must do *something*—but not material for me. What else was there? Birkenhead, where the middle-class folk have comfortably established themselves in villas on the hill? I had had a lunch and tea or two over there, in solid Victorian comfort, but this time I wanted to see something quite different. The cotton brokers and the shipping men? I had met both kinds, and no doubt they would have a lot to say to me—and what they would say would be well worth hearing—if I met some of them again. They were genuine Liverpool, I admitted to myself, but even they did not fit into this mysterious composition that so far was purely negative.

We had now arrived in the heart of the big city, and as usual it was almost a heart of darkness. But it looked like a big city, there was no denying that. Here, emphatically, was the English seaport second only to London. The very weight of stone emphasised that fact. And even if the sun never seems to rise properly over it, I like a big city to proclaim itself a big city at once. If it must have a thousand Corporation trams lumbering and screeching and groaning about the place, let it build up and up, as Liverpool has done, to dwarf the mournful beasts. We had cut and curved our way to the very entrance, the imposing entrance, of the Adelphi Hotel. I believe that the Adelphi was originally built for the first-class Atlantic passenger traffic, and unfortunately for Liverpool and its luxury hotel that traffic was immediately afterwards diverted to Southampton; with the result that the Adelphi has been hot from mingled shame and vexation ever since, rather too hot for my comfort, even in the dead winter of Liverpool. But there I was, signing my name in the register, and as yet I had no programme of exploration. There was a Liverpool I wanted for this book, and I had still to decide which it was. But I knew it was something quite unlike the interior of the Adelphi, which is an hotel that no producer of musical comedy would object to using for his big set in the Second Act. What was it then? Up in my bedroom I reminded myself that it was probably Liverpool the seaport that contained what I wanted. I had been to Southampton and Bristol; I was on my way to the Tyne and Hull; but there was something here that none of these ports could show me. The search was narrowing. I began telephoning to one or two newspaper acquaintances in the city. I was on the trail.

It led me to the vicar of the queerest parish in England—his own description, and I am not going to quarrel with it. He was an elderly man and had been there a great many years, during which time, knowing so much about his people, he must have accumulated enough of the raw material of fiction for a batch of Balzacs. There was nothing of the mild, faintly scholarly dodderer about him. He was still a sturdy figure, and as downright as a bo'sun. We set out to explore this queer parish of his, which was in the very middle of Liverpool's more picturesque and exotic slums, populated by the human flotsam and jetsam of a great old seaport. We had not gone twenty yards when he pointed his stick at some figures mooching in the square. 'I call that the fo'c'sle walk,' he remarked. 'Old sailors. Just watch them. You see? A few short paces one way, then the same number back again. They do it all day. It's the result of spending years in ships. Yes, that's the fo'c'sle walk.' We passed near the men and he waved a greeting with his stick. The neighbouring streets and squares all belonged to one period, the Regency or a little earlier. Here, a hundred years ago, the comfortable Liverpool merchants lived, going in and out of these charming doorways and beneath these fine old fanlights, thinking about their cargoes of cotton and tobacco from New Orleans and of rum and sugar from Jamaica. You had only to half-close your eyes as you looked at these charming and dignified façades to feel that the past was reliving itself for you. Liverpool must have been a town worth loitering in then. All this area of it must have been as pretty as an old print. (And why is it that in 1833 you could still order a house from the nearest builder and it would be something fit to be seen, whereas, after a hundred years of astonishing progress, in 1933 the nearest builder would probably erect a monstrosity and you have to find a really good architect, who in turn has to find a really good contractor, before you can be sure of getting a decent house? And I write not as a worshipper of the past, an antique snob, a connoisseur, but as an ordinary ignoramus who happens to use his eyes.) But one good look and that charming vision vanished. The fine lines and the carefully designed doorways remained; but they had suffered a sad sea change. The owners lived here no longer; the crew had taken possession. These were all slum tenements, like those Georgian streets in Dublin, where the country gentry once had their town houses. Every bit of woodwork was fast losing its last flakes of paint. The windows were broken, boarded, raggedly curtained. The open doorways gave out a reek of unwashed humanity. The buildings were rotting away, and some of the people were rotting with them. Faces that had shone for a season in brothels in Victoria's time now peered and mumbled at us. Port Said and Bombay, Zanzibar and Hong Kong had called here. The babies told the tale plainly enough. They were of all shades, and Asia and Africa came peeping out of their eyes. 'That little chap there,' said the vicar, pointing with his stick at an ochreous baby lad who might have just been plucked out of a rice-field, 'he's one of four. All with different fathers. And his mother's a nice woman, a very good sort.'

We hurried off to the local school that all these half-caste children attended. By the time we got there the little ones were leaving, and my companion singled out several of them, who answered his smiling questions very softly and shyly. All the races of mankind were there, wonderfully mixed. Imagine an infant class of half-castes, quadroons, octaroons, with all the latitudes and longitudes confused in them. I saw all their things, baby-size, neatly put away in cupboards; and they had done this themselves. They could have been pictured in the act, not as a Liverpool infants' class but as the human race, which is probably still a baby, trying to tidy up. On the floor above a class of older children had not yet been dismissed, and the vicar marched me in to look at and listen to them. There cannot be a queerer class anywhere in the world. The woolly curls of the negro, the smooth brown skin of the Malay, the diagonal eye of the Chinese, they were all there, crazily combined with features that had arrived in Lancashire by way of half a dozen different European countries, from Scandinavia to Italy. Nor did their appearance tell the whole tale; indeed, it could be oddly deceptive. A boy could look pure Liverpool and prove to be three parts Chinese. The negro influence was the most obvious. One little girl looked ready to bud into another Florence Mills. A handsome sturdy lad, with a fine head, proudly carried, and big flashing eyes, was the grandson of an African chieftain. As the class finished their work for the day, the vicar, who knew all about every one of them, softly poured a stream of information into my ear. We spoke to several of the children when the class broke up. The boys rushed down to the tiny schoolyard at the back, and there, in the dusky half-light, had a glorious scuffle with a small ball. We could see them down there, like a miniature League of Nations assembly gone mad. Meanwhile the vicar went on telling me things. The children with Chinese strains in them interested him the most. Many of the boys, he said, would probably go to China within a few years. An uncle of one of them was now an important official in the Chinese Republican Government; and he too had once been a boy in Liverpool and was now bitterly opposed to Britain and

PITT STREET, LIVERPOOL, 1937 *L. J. D'Andria*

British influence because of the life he had once been compelled to lead in the slums of Pitt Street, Liverpool. It was more than likely, he continued, that most of the little half-caste girls—those smiling exotic dolls—would, within a year or two of leaving school, become prostitutes, following the female family tradition of the quarter. I suggested that some of them, especially those with negro blood in them, might prove to have theatrical talent, like the 'high yallers' of Harlem; but he replied that in his experience they had never shown any signs of possessing such talent. (But have they ever been given a chance? I doubt it.) A rosy little boy, who had been kept behind on some monitor's job, came up, and we had a word or two with him. When he had gone the vicar said: 'Now that boy looks English enough, doesn't he? But as a matter of fact, he's half Chinese. Yes, and he's *all* Chinese inside. He has dreams, that boy, and they're all Oriental dreams. Queer, isn't it?' He went on to outline briefly a theory of his, born of long experience of these people of mixed blood. 'The real nature of these half-castes,' he said, 'is always the opposite of their appearance. If they look European, then you can depend upon it that inside they're almost entirely Chinese or negro or whatever it is. If they're born half and half, and look Chinese or negro, then you'll find that their nature is European. It's very odd, and I don't know why it should be so. But it is so. I've proved it over and over again.' As things are, there is something very cruel about this relation between appearance and character, for clearly the unfortunate half-caste will be always most attracted to the very people whom his looks will alienate, and will always belong at heart to the particular society not prepared to welcome him.

There was something deeply impressive, almost moving, about the sight of these strange children, here in this slum corner of Lancashire. Although they had mostly been begotten, born and reared in the most pitifully sordid circumstances, nearly all of them were unusually attractive in appearance, like most people of oddly mixed blood. (A really first-rate film-producer could make a film of exceptional interest, probably of real beauty, out of these children.) Looking at them, you did not think of the riff-raff of the stokeholds and the slatterns of the slums who had served as their parents: they seemed like the charming exotic fruits, which indeed they were, of some profound anthropological experiment. (And that woman who had had four children all by different fathers, probably all of different race, surely deserves a subsidy from some anthropological research fund.) Perhaps we have been given a glimpse of the world of 2433, by which time the various root races, now all members of a great world state, may have largely inter-married and inter-bred. Knowing gentlemen from the tropics or the East always tell us emphatically that the half-caste is no good, a poor specimen combining the vices but not the virtues of both his parent races. That is what they tell us, and most of us who listen, perhaps sceptically, cannot marshal enough examples to prove the contrary. We can only remind ourselves that while violent racial prejudices still exist, all the dice are loaded against the children of mixed blood, the very circumstances of whose parentage have probably been unfortunate. But Nature herself, whatever she may do to them in later life, displays no sharp animosity against these half-caste infants but takes care to work most cunningly and beautifully with their physical characteristics. And I wish it were possible to learn what happens to all these quaint children, where they go, what they do, what manner of men and women they turn into. Will some of them, after extraordinary adventures and vicissitudes, be found, years hence, negotiating with us in China and defying us in Africa, inspired by memories of England that do not extend beyond tenements and dark streets in a dock-side slum?

Liverpool's Chinatown is rapidly dwindling. There are only a few hundred Chinese left there. In the quarter we explored, now gathering mystery in the dusk of a November afternoon, there were still some signs of their occupation. You noticed a Chinese Republican Club and a Chinese Masonic Hall. There were a few Chinese shops, selling ivories and tea. We wanted some tea ourselves, so climbed the stairs of a Chinese eating-house. The room was deserted

LIVERPOOL'S CHINATOWN, 1937   *H. A. Smith*

except for two Chinese, one of them, I think, the proprietor, playing a card game in a corner. A shy girl, who appeared and disappeared like an Oriental ghost, brought us some good China tea, and over it we talked in whispers. I learned that there were two good reasons why this Chinatown was rapidly disappearing. The first was bad trade, for the Chinese go where there is money to be made, and there has not been much money to be made in Liverpool during these past few years. The second reason is that the Chinese find that they cannot live here as they would like to live, there is too much interference with their customs. After all, I suppose if our countrymen who carry the white man's burden in the East suddenly found themselves prevented from indulging in sport, meeting in clubs, and drinking gin and whisky, they would not linger long in exile. The Chinese, I believe, are very fond of gambling, have a weakness for secret societies, and like to smoke opium; and no doubt this makes them liable to be brought before a magistrate, who himself, perhaps, has been known to have a flutter on the turf, is a Freemason, and is always irritable after dinner unless he smokes his usual *Larranaga*. Not all the Chinese who used to live here have gone back to the East. A good many of them, I was told, have moved to Rotterdam. There used to be racial street fights here at one time, but there has not been one now for several years. Perhaps they are having them in Rotterdam. We did not stay long over our tea, but moved on through the narrow darkening streets. Many of the houses in these streets used to be brothels, and some are still. Women are being smuggled into Liverpool even yet, in spite of a determined local effort to stop the supply. It made me wonder where on earth such women came from, if they could allow themselves to be smuggled into these holes and could consider a life behind these yellowed lace curtains as a career.

We made for the docks. I had seen these docks before, but oddly enough, although I have sailed to or from Hull, Goole, Harwich, Tilbury, the Pool of London, Dover, Folkestone, Newhaven, Southampton, Plymouth and Avonmouth, I have never either arrived at or departed from this port of Liverpool. Nor am I sorry, for they have always seemed to me most gloomy docks. The romance of the sea, about which we have always heard and read so much, has to set its opening chapter in some very dismal quarters of this country. Trams going whining down long sad roads; a few stinking little shops; pubs with their red blinds down and an accumulation of greasy papers under their windows; black pools and mud and slippery cobblestones; high blank walls; a suspicious policeman or two; that is usually the opening scene. You see it in London. You see it in Liverpool, miles of it. Docks and slums, docks and slums. We are an island people; even now we owe nearly everything to the

SALTHOUSE DOCK BY NIGHT, c. 1933   *S. Charles Dietterle*

sea; our foodstuffs are brought in ships and our manufactures are taken away
in ships; but when you visit most of our larger ports you see nothing but slums.
'Welcome!' we cry to the sailor, and immediately make him free of Wapping,
London, and Wapping, Liverpool. If there is anything to choose between these
two Wappings, the London one has it. I caught a glimpse of the other that
afternoon. We reached the docks, put out our pipes and entered their precincts,
where a vast amount of gloom and emptiness and decay was being carefully
guarded. It was deep dusk. There were some last feeble gleams of sunset in
the shadowy sky before us. Everything was shadowy now. The warehouses
we passed seemed empty of everything but shadows. A few men—far too few—
came struggling along, their day's work over. We arrived at the edge of the
Mersey, and below us was a long mudbank. The water was a grey mystery,
a mere vague thickening of space. Something hooted, to break a silence that

immediately closed up afterwards to muffle the whole spectral scene. We walked slowly along the waterfront, from nothing, it seemed, into nothing; and darkness rose rather than fell; and with it came a twinkle of lights from Birkenhead that reached us not across the river but over a gulf that could not be measured. I have rarely seen anything more spectral and melancholy. It was hard to believe that by taking ship here you might eventually reach a place of sharp outlines, a place where colour burned and vibrated in the sunlight, that here was the gateway to the bronze ramparts of Arabia, to the temples and elephants of Ceylon, to flying fish and humming birds and hibiscus. With our hands thrust deep in our overcoat pockets, we trudged along and talked about Liverpool's trade, a fitting topic for the time and place.

On the way back from the docks I was shown the David Lewis Club and Hostel. The Club is largely maintained by the profit on the Hostel. It looked a good place. There is an amusing little theatre on the premises, with a room below filled with bits of scenery, half-painted canvas cloths, odd 'props'. There are reading, chess and card-rooms. I was told by one of the officials that the Club had a contract bridge team; this is the first time I have heard of working men playing contract bridge, to say nothing of playing in tournaments. There is a chess team too. If I lived in the district I do not suppose I should be able to win a place in either team, but it would not be for want of trying, for I should certainly spend a lot of my time in the Club. It is a rather old-fashioned building and needs some brighter decoration, but with its cosiness, recreations and companionship it must seem like heaven after those long dark slummy Liverpool streets. The Hostel is next door, and an enormous establishment. A man can live there on one-and-ninepence a day, but he will not have to be very sensitive about his surroundings. It has a very grim institution look. The distempered walls and old-fashioned tiles cry at once: 'No nonsense here, my man.' That hundreds of men have been glad of its existence I have no doubt whatever; but I cannot imagine one of them, returning after an absence, breaking down in the hall and sobbing at the sight of the dear old hostel. Nowadays it is only about half-full, because of the trade depression, which means that there are fewer casual labourers and the like drifting into the city. But though only half-full it smelt completely full. It was not exactly a dirty smell—for the place was clean enough and, I should imagine, well disinfected—but it was like that of the thick air that meets you when entering the Underground. The dining-room was very large and had a counter in one corner, where you bought your food. I saw a man buying a plate of stewed steak. This was sixpence and the dearest item on the menu; but you got a good plateful. The lodgers all have boxes in lockers, and keep tea things in them. I noticed several of them making their own tea. They can do their own washing too, though I did not chance to see any of them doing it. Upstairs are floors and floors of cubicles, dreary little holes. Not much seems to have been done at any time to make the building cheerful and attractive. The men I saw in there were a fairly mixed lot, with elderly casual labourers in the majority. There were one or two intensely respectable-looking middle-aged men, spruce as bank managers; and they were all busy writing letters, probably the sort of begging letters I am always receiving, in which the writer is nearly always an elderly ailing woman with any number of sick children. Many of the men who lodge here are married, and sometimes their wives come looking for them and make trouble. There is very little trouble with the men themselves, few roaring drunks and mad fighting men. All quiet, tamed, broken in, nearly broken down. Walking round, not very hopefully, I asked myself how long I could stick it, living here on my one-and-ninepence a day. I came to the conclusion that if I felt it was a purely temporary lodging, a half-way house in a journey between two homes, I could stand weeks, months of it. I should be living not in this Hostel but simply in hope and faith. I should sit near that stove in the dining-room, plotting like mad and probably turning out some pretty artful begging letters. I should dream dreams in my little cubicle. But if I was convinced that for the rest of my life it would be either this Hostel or something worse, I think I should leave it and for one night, one very long night, take a room somewhere with a gas fire. Such places as this seem peculiarly pitiful because they are so largely occupied by elderly men. Young men have always hopes of a better job; they can go out and lark about or fall in love; they can make light of the discomforts and indignities. After all, I lived under much worse conditions than these throughout most of the war. But elderly men have none of these compensations; they are on the wrong side of the hill, with darkness below them; they need comfortable little homes of their own, some dignity, and peace. Some day perhaps they may all have their chance of these things, even the feeblest little shuffler and idler. Yes, why deny even that poor creature his fireside and his armchair at night? We can create a society big and generous enough to give away these pathetic little comforts and to be sorry for the pathetic fellow who receives them, because he is so weak and purposeless and is condemned to be among those who take but cannot give.

There is a very large Irish quarter in Liverpool. Two cheerful young journalists took me across the city to see it. Paddy's Market was about to finish business for the day. A few Lascars, like men cut out of brown paper, lurked in the entrance. All the seamen know this covered market, where they frequently come to replenish their wardrobes. Even those natives who have never

REPAIRING NETS IN CANNING DOCK, 1936   *J. E. Marsh*

seen England before and speak no English can ask for 'Paddee Markee', as if the place were our pride and joy, the diadem of the Empire. It is surrounded by slum streets, dirty little pubs, and the Irish. A great many speeches have been made and books written on the subject of what England has done to Ireland. I should be interested to hear a speech and read a book or two on the subject of what Ireland has done to England. If we do have an Irish Republic as our neighbour, and it is found possible to return her exiled citizens, what a grand clearance there will be in all the Western ports, from the Clyde to Cardiff, what a fine exit of ignorance and dirt and drunkenness and disease. The Irishman in Ireland may, as we are so often assured he is, be the best fellow in the world, only waiting to say good-bye to the hateful Empire so that, free and independent at last, he can astonish the world. But the Irishman in England too often cuts a very miserable figure. He has lost his peasant virtues, whatever they are, and has acquired no others. These Irish flocked over here to be navvies and dock hands and casual labourers, and God knows that the conditions of life for such folk are bad enough. But the English of this class generally make some attempt to live as decently as they can under these conditions: their existence has been turned into an obstacle race, with the most monstrous and gigantic obstacles, but you may see them straining and panting, still in the race. From such glimpses as I have had, however, the Irish appear in general never even to have tried; they have settled in the nearest poor quarter and turned it into a slum, or, finding a slum, have promptly settled down to out-slum it. And this, in spite of the fact that being an Irish Roman Catholic is more likely to find a man a job than to keep him out of one.

The two journalists and two trams brought me back to the centre of the city, whose essential darkness made a good background for quite a metropolitan display of Neon lighting and flashing signs. Cinemas, theatres (though Liverpool could do with several more), dance-halls, grill-rooms, boxing matches, cocktail bars, all in full glittering swing. The Adelphi Hotel had dressed for the evening, was playing waltzes, and for the time being did not care a fig about the lost Atlantic traffic. In the restaurant there were little birthday parties, tender re-unions, and commercial gentlemen entertaining foreign customers (I heard them) and exchanging slow little speeches in which the syllables were all spaced out as they are in children's reading primers. In here, as they might have said, it was all very plea-sant and com-fort-able and ev-en gay and lux-ur-ious. I had had a long day and was tired and rather depressed. I wished then I had had someone dining with me, if only as an excuse to do the pair of us proud, to order a lot of food and drink, and chatter and laugh a good deal. I am not old enough yet (perhaps I never will be) to sit down solemnly and do myself proud, going through the full ritual of food and liquor. I still eat quickly, swallow one glass of something, and go on thinking all the time. And, that night, this was all wrong. I did not want to go on thinking. I wanted to eat and drink and have a party, chiefly because I could not get it out of my head that here I was, perched on a little lighted apex and that going down on every side were very long dark slopes. It was the beastliest pyramid you can imagine. I did not want to be at the top, but still less did I want to be further down, on any of those horrible slopes. I wanted to be off the thing altogether, and enjoying myself. Miserably I decided that somebody else must give a plain fair account of this great city: the task, in the time, was beyond me. So I bought myself a good cigar.

[2]

There was a time when Manchester was known as the 'home of living causes', but exactly what living causes are finding a home there now I do not know. It was also said that 'what Manchester thinks to-day England will think to-morrow.' But that was before our time, though we still see some of the results—let us be fair, the worse results—of what Manchester thought in what has been left us, to mourn over, by the vast, greedy, slovenly, dirty process of industrialisation for quick profits—and damn the consequences. Still, when I was a boy, Manchester had the best newspaper and the best orchestra in the country, which is saying something: its citizens, who could read the *Manchester Guardian* in the morning and listen to the Hallé under Richter in the evening, were not badly off and could be said to be in touch with civilization. (They had too, at that time, the best repertory theatre in the kingdom, and their own considerable school of dramatists and dramatic critics. It is perhaps significant that the critics were better than the dramatists. Manchester, I suspect, has always been more critical than creative; but that, let us admit, is much better than being neither.) Both the newspaper and the orchestra, like the cotton trade, are still there, but, also like the cotton trade, are not quite what they were: though both are much more like what they were than the cotton trade.

On paper, in official returns, Manchester has a population of about three-quarters of a million. In actual fact, it is much larger than that. All manner of towns pretend to be independent, and produce separate population figures of their own, when for nearly all practical purposes they have been part of Manchester for years. The real city sprawls all over South Lancashire. It is an Amazonian jungle of blackened bricks. You could take trams in it for hours and hours, never losing it and arriving into broad daylight. The real population of Manchester must be getting on for two millions. You seem as long getting at the heart of the city as you are when driving into London itself. Unlike Liverpool, all this is Lancashire proper. Liverpool is simply Liverpool. Its people—or at least the uneducated among them—have an accent of their own; a thick, adenoidy, cold-in-the-head accent, very unpleasant to hear. Once you touch Manchester or any of its satellite towns you are really in Lancashire. The people talk with a Lancashire accent, and if you are a Southerner you may imagine that you have landed among a million music-hall comedians. Why Lancashire should have become almost the official accent of music-hall humour is something of a mystery, for there are plenty of droll folk and music-halls elsewhere. But that rather flat but broad-vowelled speech—much less attractive, to my ear and mind, than the companion speech of Yorkshire—is admirable for comic effect, being able to suggest either shrewdness or simplicity, or, what is more likely than not, a humorous mixture of both. It lends itself, too, to ironical under-statements. It may add no charm or prettiness to a woman's talk, but it can give it flavour, body, character, as it does in the songs and patter of Gracie Fields, who is not only the most popular and most dominating personality of the English variety stage but is also a sort of essence of Lancastrian femininity. Listen to her for a quarter of an hour and you will learn more about Lancashire women and Lancashire than you would from a dozen books on these subjects. All the qualities are there: shrewdness, homely simplicity, irony, fierce independence, an impish delight in mocking whatever is thought to be affected and pretentious. That is Lancashire. The danger is, of course, that you may miss a lot by always being in terror of seeming affected or pretentious. The common denominator is a good sound one, but too many people may be reduced to it. There is a Lancashire standard—and no paltry one either—but it is apt to be applied too ruthlessly. Swaggering bad poets for example, would have a wretched time of it in these parts, but so too would really good ones. The working folk of Lancashire have much in common, of course, with their Yorkshire neighbours; but in my time we in Yorkshire considered the Lancastrians as people worth considering as people, real folk (not like the vapouring creatures from the South Country), but inclined to be frivolous and spend-thrifts, so that we shook our heads at the thought of their annual goings on in Blackpool. (The annual burst at the seaside, where you spent in one delirious week the savings of months, was a Lancashire and not a Yorkshire working-class custom.) We were quieter, less sociable and less given to pleasure, more self-sufficient and more conceited, I think, than the people at the other and softer side of the Pennines. That people from other parts of the country could—and still do—see little or no difference between the two sets of folk—could even confuse them— matters nothing, except as yet another proof of human stupidity and blindness: or so it seemed to us, and indeed still seems to us. The sad irony of it all now is that we should have disapproved of the Lancastrian because he had so much money to chuck about and *did* chuck it about, the sight of Blackpool's tower and great wheel goading him into a frenzy of spending. (There was more female labour, certainly more highly paid female labour, in the cotton than in the wool trade, and in the old days the whole family in Lancashire would be working at the mill, and though their individual wages might not be very generous, the total family income was often considerable and so afforded chances of grand annual sprees.) Now the Yorkshire folk would be only too glad if their Lancashire neighbours still had the money to chuck about, had money enough for any kind of holiday. We still shake our heads over them, but now our heads have very different thoughts buzzing inside them. We think of the ruined trade, the empty mills.

We arrived in Manchester that afternoon just in time to see a fog descend upon the city and to escape its worst consequences. Manchester weather is a popular joke. And I do not care what the local meteorological statistics are, that joke has a solid basis. It is true that I have never visited Manchester in summer, but at every other season I have visited it the weather has been foul, combining in varying proportions rain and sleet and fog. The city always looks as if it had been built to withstand foul weather. There is a suggestion of the fortress about it. You always seem to be moving, a not too happy dwarf, between rows of huge square black warehouses. Even the public buildings—and there are plenty of them, big solid impressive fellows—look as if they are slowly transforming themselves into square black warehouses. Perhaps it is these warehouses—or the suggestion of them, the warehouse *motif*—that make the weather in Manchester seem worse than it is, turning the showers that fall into the dark gulfs of street between them into apparent downpours, thickening and yellowing and blackening mere patches of descending mist into blankets of fog. I know that during several visits I have often passed close to the City Art Gallery, which contains some good pictures, but have always postponed my inspection for lack of a reasonable amount of daylight. On that afternoon of my most recent arrival there daylight had vanished, and we crawled to the Midland Hotel through a turgid sooty gloom that was neither day nor night.

I was not here in Manchester entirely on your business, as readers of this book. I had other business of my own to attend to, and was at the old, difficult, never-turning-out-quite-satisfactorily trick of trying to kill two birds with one stone. The larger bird, at that hour, was a new little comedy of mine that was being 'tried out' in Manchester before opening in London. A great many pieces are performed for the first time in Manchester nowadays, and the reason given—in interviews to the local Press and grateful speeches from the stage—is that Manchester audiences are good judges of the drama and that what pleases Manchester is sure to please the easy idle set of playgoers in London. This is the reason given—and complacently accepted. For my part I like Manchester audiences, but I doubt if they are any better judges than audiences in most large cities, and they show exactly the same characteristics, among which is a tendency to be very slow and cautious about attending the theatre when a fairly intelligent play is being presented, so that the seats only begin to go when the play is nearly ready to go too; and the companion tendency to book up in advance the entire theatre to see some piece of musical comedy nonsense that they probably do not enjoy, if only because it has been carefully assembled, to the last leg and dirty joke, to please an altogether different kind of audience. Probably the real reasons why Manchester is so frequently chosen now for these 'try outs' are that it has some fine big theatres that serve an enormous population, is easy to reach from London but is not too uncomfortably near (because of that doubtful Third Act, which may have to be re-written).

Here I was then, no longer the enquiring traveller but a worried dramatist, with a new little comedy still untried, a company somewhere on a train and perhaps lost in the fog, a stage manager and a carpenter probably trying to find the set and 'props', a producer brooding over his lighting and that curtain to Act Two, and an enormous theatre now rapidly filling with that specially thick brand of fog that finds its way into Oxford Street, Manchester. There were more seats in the dress circle of that theatre than in the whole auditorium of the little playhouse where we were to appear in London, and for which the production was designed. It was a grand theatre, terrifically impressive— like the dim vast buildings in dreams—when you prowled about in its foggy interior on a Sunday afternoon and peered down at the stage across the mountainous slopes of the empty dress circle or the gallery. I have a weakness for these big old-fashioned theatres, which can seat twice as many people as the new theatres (and let them all hear too), and yet contrive to appear far cosier and more intimate and homely. Too many of the new theatres look like lecture halls, and their straight-fronted balconies, which do not go round at each side to meet the proscenium, cut the audience off from the stage and produce a chilly effect. I admit that intimacy was the last quality that, at first sight, I would have associated with this Manchester theatre; but I realised afterwards that for its enormous size it created a surprisingly intimate feeling, once it was filled with people. At first, looking down from the gallery on the vast proscenium arch, I told myself that the fantastic spread of curtain there could reasonably be raised only to reveal a full set of a city square, in which fifty baritones in the uniforms of Ruritanian Hussars were welcoming the Crown Prince on his return from Paris. It was absurd to think that very soon it would go up to show, like something that had been casually dropped into the opening, my modest little set of a suburban dining-room. And there were problems of lighting to be solved. We shouted to one another, through the gathering fog, from various parts of the house, while Bert and Sid and the rest played about with the coloured lights. 'Give us a bit more pink, Bert,' was cried.

'Sid, take out your ambers.' And steadily there was mounting inside us that tide of excitement, sometimes foaming into hysteria, which inevitably rises when a play is being produced. You may have very little at stake in the venture, may even regard the whole thing as almost a spare-time hobby, but that does not matter. The theatre gets you. The play binds you, body and soul. There seems to be nothing else worth talking about. If the papers announced that half a continent had been blown into the ocean, you would not spend five minutes talking or thinking about it. You say the same things to one another over and over again. For two or three days you are like a child that has been allowed to stay up far too late; indeed, all the time you feel that it is three in the morning. Thoughts go round and round in your mind like mad circus horses. You eat and drink at odd hours, and though terribly in need of food and liquor, you consume them in a dream. Only the people connected with the show and the theatre are real: all the others, the citizens in the crowded streets, the fellow-guests in the hotel, are mere shadows. Their lives are nothing to you; they seem like civilians, while you are troops opening a campaign. The whole life of the city, except in so far as it touches your theatre, is nothing. You and your colleagues might be members of a secret society, working feverishly to strike a sudden blow at authority. You have nothing to say to the mere population, the good bourgeois. When you are tired out and exasperated and screaming with nerves you pretend to envy these solid sensible folk—who, when the play is running, will become the famous 'they', the audience—but there is no real envy in your heart any more than there is when you see some cattle quietly grazing. The whole business is maddening, but for the time being it is all that matters and you would not be out of it, merely one of 'them', for a fortune. What they are worrying about does not concern you, even though local finances and the state of trade may make a great difference to the size of your audiences. The real questions are: 'Will Bert manage that five seconds fade out all right?' and 'Is Miss So-and-so going to get that move right at the end of Act Two?' Thus you soon understand why theatrical folk usually know so little about anything outside the theatre, why actors can visit a city time after time without ever acquiring ten solid facts about it, why at heart the players are still the rogues and vagabonds that society once held them to be. Into this world of bohemians who will slave day and night at a crisis, this world where idle make-believe is desperate work and all other work seems no weightier than a distant game, I was, then, deeply plunged.

PALACE THEATRE, MANCHESTER, 1938 *Photographer Unknown*

That meant—and this explains why the previous paragraph should have a place in this chronicle—that I was not really in Manchester at all. I was living in a private nightmare city, bounded in space by the Palace Theatre and the Midland Hotel. I did contrive, however, to obtain a few glimpses of the real city. The day after my play had opened, when I was flapping about in that mid-air between the world of the theatre and the world of real walls and real hair and day-light, I was the guest of a lunch club, whose members were jovial business men, hearty unpretentious chaps, who met once a week in the upstairs room of a small pub. I had some difficulty finding this pub, which was in a rather old part of the city I had never been in before, not at all like the Manchester I have already described. There were no huge square black warehouses, but little old houses, narrow streets, and odd shops and stalls. The upstairs room was very small and the lunch-club members were there in force, so that we were all packed in close together and had to be merry or die. My hosts were commercial travellers, under-managers, and buyers, many of them from the Co-operative Wholesale Society, which has its head-quarters in Manchester. We drank beer, and a great deal of it. The food was Lancastrian. The first course consisted of a notable local delicacy, namely, Bury Black Puddings, all made by one little shop that was famous for them and had been producing them for generations. I have never cared for black puddings before (in Yorkshire we used to say that they were made of blood and sawdust), but these were very good, once you had recovered from the sinister look of them. The next course was meat pie, another stout Lancastrian dish. After that there were cheese and biscuits, if you had any appetite left. And all the time an amber stream of beer flowed into us. The club's speech-makers were all the same type: large robust men who stood up boldly, with wooden faces, and then humorously insulted the other speakers and the officials of the club and told funny stories, sometimes using a word or two that cannot be put down here. The wooden face that they could all achieve was obviously part of their performance as droll speakers, and I suspect that the grins and giggles of the London after-dinner speakers, who want you to realise at once that they do this sort of thing awfully well, would have been frowned upon here. Some of the stories, told in broad Lancashire, were excellent; they had the right grimly ironical quality. Here is one that I happen to remember, of those that can be repeated for a mixed audience. A weaver up Blackburn way had just lost her husband. 'Where yer going to bury 'im?' a neighbour asked her. 'Ah'm not going to bury 'im,' she replied. 'Well, what *are* yer going to do wi' 'im?' she was asked. 'Ah'm going to 'ave 'im cremated,' she replied. The neighbour was impressed. 'But whatever will yer do wi'

LANCASHIRE FUNERAL, 1937   *Humphrey Spender*

th'ashes?' she enquired. 'Ah'll tell yer what Ah'm going to do wi' th' ashes,'
said the widow. 'Ah'm going to 'ave 'em put into an egg-timer. Th'owd devil
wouldn't ever work when 'e were alive, so 'e can start doing a bit now 'e's
deead.' That still seems to me a very good story, even though I am no longer
under the influence of beer and Bury Black Puddings. It is a fair sample of
Lancashire's grimly ironic humour. The lunch itself was perhaps typical. There
was at work in it a spirit at once realistic and grim and yet uproariously festive.
That story, you notice, introduces death and cremation and ashes into its nar-
rative. (Even the food—with its emphasis upon Bury and Black—has a graveyard look.) No dodging the hard facts of life here. Whatever has been happening to cotton, life for the common folk in Lancashire has never been easy.
The men are tough, and the women are tougher still. (I suspect that it is really
the women who keep Lancashire going.) But what is surprising about them,
where they chiefly differ from working folk elsewhere in the North, is that
with their grimly realistic outlook and brutal speech they combine a gaiety
of their own, a zest for pleasure, sheer gusto. After a funeral—and they like
a funeral—they all pack into a room crammed with food and drink and tell
funny stories. But you must not look for this unique temper in Manchester
itself, which is now too big and mixed and dignified. Lancashire is there all
right, but no longer on parade. You must go outside, to that smudge of towns
to the north and west.

WASHDAY, BOLTON, 1937   *Humphrey Spender*

CHAPTER ELEVEN

To Blackpool and Blackburn

[1]

Between Manchester and Bolton the ugliness is so complete that it is almost exhilarating. It challenges you to live there. That is probably the secret of the Lancashire working folk: they have accepted that challenge; they are on active service, and so, like the front-line troops, they make a lot of little jokes and sing comic songs. There used to be a grim Lancashire adage: 'Where there's muck, there's money.' But now when there is not much money, there is still a lot of muck. It must last longer. Between Bolton and Preston you leave the trams and fried fish shops and dingy pubs; the land rises, and you catch glimpses of rough moorland. The sun was never visible that afternoon, which was misty and wettish, so that everything was rather vague, especially on the high ground. The moors might have been Arctic tundras. The feature of this route, once you were outside the larger towns, seemed to me to be what we call in the North the 'hen runs'. There were miles of them. The whole of Lancashire appeared to be keeping poultry. If the cotton trade should decline into a minor industry, it looks as if the trains that once carried calico will soon be loaded with eggs and chickens. It is, of course, the extension of what was once a mere hobby. Domestic fowls have always had a fascination for the North-country mill hands. It is not simply because they might be profitable; there is more than that in it. The hen herself, I suspect, made a deep sub-conscious appeal to these men newly let loose from the roaring machinery. At the sound of her innocent squawking, the buried countryman in them began to stir and waken. By way of poultry he returned to the land, though the land he had may have been only a few square yards of cindery waste ground. Now, of course, sheer necessity plays its part too. We were going through the country of the dole.

Beyond Preston, in a flat and characterless countryside, all the roads suddenly become very straight and wide and display large cheerfully vulgar advertisements. That is because they, like you, are going to Blackpool. Even if you did not intend to go to Blackpool, once you had got beyond Preston you would have to go there. These roads would suck you into Blackpool. That is what they are there for. There is no escape. Blackpool has a comparatively long season, but it does not include November. It starts at Easter and then goes through to October, reaching its height in July and August. For a week or so about Christmas the hotels and larger boarding houses are full and noisy again. But November is dead out of season. The great roaring spangled beast is hibernating. I came into the town near the South Shore, where the enormous amusement park, with its terrifying giant coasters and other fantastic idiocies, was submitting silently to the wind and the rain. As I intended to put up for the night at the other end of the town, I sent the car and my luggage along the length of promenade ahead of me and got out and walked. I realised then that no genuine fresh air had come my way for days. I had been living on stuff that had been used over and over again, thick warmed-up trash. Here there was air. It blew in great salty gusts. Within five minutes I felt half drunk. I was sober enough, however, to notice that Blackpool was deserted or asleep. Its bravery was very tawdry, after being neglected only a week or two in that Atlantic weather. They had all gone, the fiddlers, fortune-tellers, pierrots, cheapjacks, waiters and sellers of peppermint and pineapple rock. Nobody was demonstrating, with voice, piano and saxophone, the *Season's Hot Suc-*

cesses. Nobody was cooking or enjoying or touting for those *Nice Hot Dinners.* There was, in short, nothing hot left. All was chill and wet but gloriously fresh. The three piers had done with frivolity for this year and were now engaged in their proper stern task of holding up against the dark raging sea. There was only a glimmer of light from the famous tower, and the great wheel was gone for ever. Nobody was suggesting a nice hour's sail. I was not asked to buy anything along the whole length of the promenade. Blackpool the resort was dead, and even the residential town, which is of a considerable size, was moribund. Only the weather was awake, and that was tremendously alive. The sea roared in the deep dusk and sent sheets of spray over the glistening wet railings and seats. And this was, for the time being, all the Blackpool I wanted.

The hotel was empty and stuffy. In the old-fashioned lounge, well-padded and too warm, an indifferent little orchestra was playing to two middle-aged ladies with fancy-work, one middle-aged gentleman with yawns, and five waiters who tried to pretend they were busy, chiefly by moving ashtrays from one table to another. After a cup of tea and a gloomy stare at an illustrated paper two months old, I went out again, this time for a sharp walk along the promenade that runs north, out Fleetwood way. Blackpool has built miles and miles of these promenades, sometimes in tiers—tiers from the depths of some divine despair—and very soon it will have fortified about half the Lancashire coast against the Irish Sea. I trudged on like some purposeful little insect moving on a dark wet shelf. The only people I passed were mysterious raincoated figures, optimistically busy with electric torches and tins of bait and rods; though what they hoped to draw out of that thudding darkness I cannot imagine: it seemed no place for gentle angling. There was nothing to look at and my track was as inevitable as that at Brooklands; I was not exploring, but was there simply for air and exercise; so as I went I thought about Blackpool. There is a good deal to be said about it and for it. To begin with, it is entitled to some respect because it has amply and triumphantly succeeded in doing what it set out to do. Nature presented it with very bracing air and a quantity of flat firm sand; and nothing else. There is no less charmingly situated resort anywhere. Its citizens must have realised at once that charm and exclusiveness were not for them and their town. They must have decided immediately to make a move in the opposite direction. They would turn it into a pleasure resort for the crowd, and especially the Lancashire crowd from the cotton mills. Blackpool should give them what they wanted, and make no bones about it. Blackpool did. Compared with this huge mad place, with its miles and miles of promenades, its three piers, its gigantic dance-halls, its

NO FRIVOLITY ON THE PIER, 1937 *Humphrey Spender*

variety shows, its switch-backs and helter-skelters, its array of wine bars and oyster saloons and cheap restaurants and tea houses and shops piled high and glittering with trash; its army of pierrots, bandsmen, clowns, fortune-tellers, auctioneers, dancing partners, animal trainers, itinerant singers, hawkers; its seventy special trains a day, its hundreds and hundreds of thousands of trippers; places like Brighton and Margate and Yarmouth are merely playing at being popular seaside resorts. Blackpool has them all licked. It has recently built a bathing pool that does not hold mere hundreds of people but thousands, the population of a small town. It has decided that it ought to extend its season into October, while the beds are still aired and the frying-pans hot, and so now every autumn it has the whole front, miles of it, illuminated with coloured lights, not a few thousand coloured lights but hundreds of thousands of them. That is Blackpool. It is a complete and essential product of industrial democracy. If you do not like industrial democracy, you will not like Blackpool. I know people who would have to go into a nursing home after three hours of it. (In the season, of course.) I am not one of those people. I have never actually been in Blackpool at the crazy height of its season, during the various

Lancashire 'wakes' weeks; but I knew it before the war and I have seen something of it since. It is not, in my opinion, as good as it used to be. There are various reasons for this. One of them is that like all originators it has suffered from the mere passing of time, during which time others have been able to follow its example. Thus, for years before the war, public dancing on a big and rather luxurious scale was part of Blackpool's programme, and the great ballrooms in the Tower and the Winter Gardens, where spinners and weavers by the thousand could dance on perfect floors to the music of good orchestras, were famous throughout the North. Now, public dancing of this kind is to be found everywhere. Even the Potteries have got an enormous new dance-hall, in which on occasion notable dance bands from London scream and croon. The rest of the world, we can say, is catching up with Blackpool, our first great entertainment caterer to the sixpenny crowd. There is, however, another and better reason why I think it is not as good as it was. From the few glimpses I have had of the place since the war, I gather the impression that it lacks something of its old genuine gaiety. Its amusements are becoming too mechanised and Americanised. Talkies have replaced the old roaring variety turns. Gangs of carefully drilled young men and women (with nasal accents), employed by the music publishers to 'plug' their 'Hot Broadway Hits', have largely replaced the pierrots and nigger minstrels. The entertainers are more calculating, their shows more standardised, and the audiences more passive. It has developed a pitiful sophistication—machine-made and not really English—that is much worse than the old hearty vulgarity. But then in the meantime there have been changes in the class for which it caters. One section of it has gone ahead and does not want the new Blackpool and would probably have rejected the old: it does not care for mass entertainment and prefers to spend its leisure in quieter places, cycling and walking and playing games in the sun. There are plenty of young working-class people of that quality now in the North. The rest of them, the less intelligent and enterprising, are, I feel, fit patrons of the new Blackpool, which knows what to do with the passive and the listless, but would not have been quite up to the energetic old Blackpool, crowded with vital beings who burst out of their factories for the annual spree as if the boilers had exploded and blown them out. In those days, I remember, they used to descend upon the town as if it were about to be besieged, for they were loaded with eatables, whole boiled hams and sides of bacon and round tin trunks filled with cake. More often than not, they paid for their lodgings on arrival, for then they knew that every penny left could be spent; and they returned home with a stick or two of pink or yellow Blackpool rock, a plush-framed photograph of the Tower and the Wheel, the

other half of their excursion ticket, and nothing else. And for the next week
or month at home, they had to live on 'tick' or 'tally'. But they had enjoyed,
rapturously enjoyed, their Blackpool, and had never once insulted its breezy
majesty by singing about their 'blues'. In those days you did not sing the woes
of distant negroes, probably reduced to such misery by too much gin or co-
caine. You sang about dear old Charlie Brown and his pals, and the girls,
those with the curly curls. These songs were nonsense too, but they were our
own silly innocent nonsense and not another country's jaded weary nonsense;
they had a fresh lilting quality, and expressed high spirits not low spirits. The
Blackpool that sang about Charlie Brown and the girls with their curly curls
was the Mecca of a vulgar but alert and virile democracy. I am not so sure
about the new Blackpool of the weary negroid ditties. It would not be difficult,
I feel, to impose an autocracy upon young people who sound as tired as that.
Fortunately, there are other young people who do not come this way at all,
but go climbing on to the moors, into the sun, and they may have their own
ideas about politics just as they apparently have about holidays.

I returned to the hotel after four or five miles of this dark wet promenade,
blown about and a bit weary, but feeling that some air had found its way
into my lungs at long last. I had a drink in the only bar there, an American
bar with a white-coated young man in attendance. I was his only customer,
and we had some talk, chiefly about his trade of cocktail-shaking. He had
just been away for a week, it appeared, and had spent a good part of that
week seriously investigating the cocktail-shaking and American Bar situation
in other parts of the country. He talked very solemnly about other bars, their
decoration, prices, and so forth. His considered opinion was that prices were
far too high, and anybody would have thought he was discussing the cotton
trade itself. It is an odd thing that all the people connected, in their work,
with the fashionable frivolities of the day, against which sermons are preached
and passionate letters written by elderly moralists to the newspapers, are sober
and solemn and heavily serious. This young barman might have been a favourite disciple of Dr. Smiles. I have met others of his kind. Lads who toot on
saxophones in dance bands talk as if the weight of the world were on their
shoulders. I once talked to a young man who was a professional dancing
partner in a fashionable West-End restaurant, and if he had been the Under-
Secretary for Foreign Affairs he could not have taken himself more seriously.
Some youngster who has written the music for a dirty song in a revue will
talk of his 'work' as if he were composing Beethoven's Tenth Symphony for
him; while the agonising conscientiousness of the youth who has been given
the job of designing costumes for five chorus girls in a cabaret is painful to

witness. It looks as if this age were only frivolous in its values, which are about the only things sensible people take seriously. I can see excuses for the age, however, and probably they will be found scattered among these pages. That night, thanks to Blackpool air and my walk, I had about eleven hours of deep untroubled sleep. Considering the time of year and the deserted state of the town, I thought my bill excessive, but paid it without a frown. After all, there had been no extra charge for that air, those eleven glorious hours; and now I was ready to discover what was happening elsewhere in Lancashire. At the moment all that was happening here—and probably it was happening all over the county—was a downpour of rain so fixed and implacable that it looked as if it were going on for ever.

[2]

We went splashing through that rain, back along those big wide roads, through Preston, past innumerable soaking 'hen runs', until we reached Blackburn, where I met a friend of a friend, to whose kindly hospitality I had been recommended. He took me at once to his house, which was well out of the sad-looking town. It was high on a hill-side, with a bit of moorland not half a mile away. But though the air was as clear and the view as broad and fine as you could wish, it was dead in the centre of the more northerly cotton country, with mills not far away in every direction. The land on which we were perched, my host told me, had belonged to his family for over four hundred years. He himself was not in the local trade—if he had been I might not have had so bright a fire and so many good Lancashire meals—but a professional man in his office hours, and a man of parts outside those hours. One of the first things I noticed, when the dripping miserable day had been banished and we were all cosy, was the number of good pictures about the place. I then discovered that my host was not only an excellent judge of pictures but was himself an enthusiastic water-colourist of some merit, who had exhibited a good deal. Nor was that all. Upstairs, in a corner, I was surprised to find a number of beautifully made bows, fit for Agincourt. Discovery number two was that my host had in his time been champion archer of England, and still was famous in toxophilite circles. We can say of him what they said of old Double: 'He drew a good bow—he shot a fine shoot.' And when he found that I was amused and interested, he brought out bows and arrows and told me more about the ancient craft than I ever knew could be told in these days. All this delighted me. I like a man of parts. England is England still, even if the cotton trade is returning to the hell from which it probably

BLACKPOOL LIT-UP, 1937 *Humphrey Spender*

came, when a middle-aged professional man and father of a family can leave
his office and suddenly turn himself into either a water-colour painter or a
master bowman, brightening at the sight of either a camel-hair brush or a
goose feather. These are the men for my money, solid fathers and good citizens
in whom the active boy and the dreaming youth are still alive. While Lancashire can still produce them—and it can—Lancashire is all right, cotton trade
or no cotton trade. It will win through yet, even if it has to do it with paint-
brushes and longbows.

But although there was much talk of art and archery during these next few
days, talk that was welcome enough, if only as a relief from gloomier matter,
there was still more talk about the life and work of the district. Even if I had
come there on another errand or merely to idle away a few days, I think there
would still have been this talk. You cannot, in fact, keep away from it up
there, any more than one could stop talking about the war between 1914 and

1919. There is no escape. The whole district had been tied to prosperity, to its very existence, with threads of cotton; and you could hear them snapping all the time. I did not know anything about the cotton trade before I went up there; I do not know a great deal now; but I know too much for my peace of mind. Whichever way you looked there was the same tragic situation. In this house there was a little housemaid called Alice. Her mistress, noticing that the girl's boots were in poor shape and deciding to buy her a pair, asked her what size she took. Bewildered, Alice could find no reply. It turned out that she had never had a pair of new boots and so knew nothing about sizes. That is the kind of wonderland that this Alice is in. Her father, mother and brother are all out of work. Their club pay ceases at the end of this year, but their real life ceased some time ago. So even if I had stayed indoors all the time, with cottonwool in my ears, there would still have been no escape: I should have caught sight of Alice and have been reminded that there was a war on. But I neither stayed indoors nor kept my ears shut, but went about and talked to all manner of people. They had all the same tale to tell.

That very day a mill, a fine big building that had cost a hundred thousand pounds or so not twenty years ago, was put up for auction, with no reserve: there was not a single bid. There hardly ever is. You can have a mill rent-free up there, if you are prepared to work it. Nobody has any money to buy, rent or run mills any more. The entire district has been sliding towards complete bankruptcy for years. The tales of men driven out of business were innumerable. I heard of one former cotton king who was seen picking up cigarette ends in the street. Another is a bus conductor, another has a stall in the open market, another is a barman. A few of them have got jobs as clerks, and others are still hoping. Many, of course, have quitted a world that must have seemed to them to have gone suddenly and tragically mad. Those who have struggled on, pleading with the banks for more time, desperately trying to get a few orders at cut-prices, sacking old employees with whom they have been on Christian name terms for perhaps twenty years, have led the lives of hunted men. Every day found them in a new and more terrible dilemma. I heard of one oldish man whose mill had just gone. He started the mill himself forty years ago, and recently had been losing £200 a week trying to keep it going, having lost altogether over £100,000. My informant said that there were tears in this man's eyes when he spoke of his workpeople. (Though he added, in characteristic Lancashire fashion: 'Ay, it troubles some—but not so many.') But of course there have been millions lost in cotton during these last few years. There had been bad times before, notably during the American Civil War, when the raw material was not available, and at various times during the last quarter of the nineteenth century, when the depreciation of silver low-ered the purchasing power of the Eastern countries. Actually, the comparative decline began years ago, as it did in most of our major industries; but still, cotton was cotton, and Lancashire knew what to do with it. You could put your money into cotton: and they all did. There was the one gilded Oriental basket, with all their eggs snugly inside it.

Compared with my old trade, wool, England's oldest industry, cotton is a mere upstart. It was nothing before the Industrial Revolution. But when it grew, it grew quickly. In 1781 we imported 5,000,000 lb. of raw cotton. Twenty years later we were importing 56,000,000 lb. The first steam engine was installed in a Manchester cotton mill in 1789. At the same time the South-ern States began sending their cotton to us. Thus we had the new steam power and immense new sources of supply all at the same time. In 1806 the power loom arrived, and the industry was further mechanised, though not, of course, without violent opposition. It was making extensive use of machinery long before the wool trade. Incidentally, a Blackburn man told me something about John Osbaldeston, who invented the weft fork that was a vital part of the power loom, and is, I believe, still in use. 'They'd got to know he'd invented something,' said this Blackburn man, 'these cotton and engineering heads, and so one night they got him drunk and wormed the secret out of him. And Osbaldeston died in the workhouse. Thirty years ago,' he continued reminis-cently, 'I used to talk with an old man of ninety who knew 'Owd John' well and saw him taken in a cart to the workhouse.' There are a lot of stories like that in the histories of the textile trades, which are a monument to man's ingenuity and industry on one side, and on the other a pitiable record of his stupidity and greed and selfishness. It was not long before cotton headed our exports. About the middle of the last century its value was somewhere near a third of the total value of our exports. Cotton was the Victorians' pride and joy. Those were the days when Manchester, having more muck and money than any other city, spoke for England. The shiploads of raw cotton clouded the Mersey with canvas. There was an endless stream of cotton yarns and calico going out from Lancashire. We held the gorgeous East in fee. More and more mills were built, and with them rows and rows of little houses, all alike, for the weavers. More money, more muck; more muck, more money: the only flaw in the system being that the money tended to go in an opposite direction from that of the muck. There was, of course, even a cotton school of political philosophy, usually known as the Manchester School. It believed in Individualism and Free Trade, and Money For Some and Muck For All. You catch a glimpse of the system at work in Dickens's *Hard Times*, though

it is as well to remember that the man was a novelist, and a sentimental caricaturist at that. I have before me, as I write this, a very well-produced photograph, labelled *Industrial Lancashire: a typical cotton spinning district*. It is
a modern photograph, but it must have been taken a few years ago, because
all the tall chimneys in it—and I can count twenty-five—are smoking furiously,
belching out thick dark clouds that look as if they will descend on the ugly
conglomeration of roofs below. That is what it must have looked like throughout all the great days of the industry. It was then that all these hideous towns
were built, towns meant to work in and not really to live in. However, the
work was there, not too well-paid perhaps, but steady work. An energetic
deft woman could always get her four looms to look after. As Mr. T. Thompson tells us, in his very vivid and truthful novel of pre-war Lancashire working-
class life, *Blind Alley*, a woman who had left the mill on her marriage could
always reply to any taunt or threat from her husband: 'Ah con allus get four
looms.' The trade boomed, and was sturdy enough to carry an immense load
of bad organisation, unnecessary specialisation, a pipe-smoking army of middle-men. But Time has a loom too, and on it there began to appear a most
sinister pattern.

I met a most pleasant youngster who had a job in a firm that makes automa-
tic looms. They sell these in Lancashire, and immediately put a few more
weavers out of work. They have been selling them for years all over the world,
and every time one is loaded on to a ship at Liverpool a good piece is snipped
off Lancashire's trade. And then there began to appear, at places like Blackburn's Technical College, which is, of course kept going with public money,
certain quiet, industrious, smiling young men from the East, most anxious
to learn all that Lancashire could teach them about the processes of calico
manufacture. They sat through their courses, missing nothing, smiled at their
instructors for the last time and disappeared into the blue. A little later, as
a result of this—for we live in a wonderfully interdependent world—there also
disappeared into the blue a good deal of Lancashire's trade with the East.
Most of those students came from Japan. It is worth remembering that in
the seventeenth century the Japanese, after observing with some astonishment
and alarm the quarrels of the various groups of missionaries, Catholic and
Protestant, that had been sent to civilise them, decided to expel these turbulent
visitors and, having done that, passed laws forbidding any dealings with foreigners or even the building of ocean-going vessels. They wanted to be left
alone, and for two centuries were left alone. In the middle of the last century,
however, representatives of Western civilisation, arriving in ships of war, per-
suaded them to come out of their cherry-blossom dreams. Once out, they have

stayed out. One of the innumerable results of this is that cotton magnates in Lancashire are found picking up cigarette ends, and some of their weavers have not seen a loom or a week's wages for years. We live, you see, in an interdependent world. We insisted upon proving that fact to the dreamy and exclusive Orientals last century, and now in this century they are only adding further proofs. There is no escape now on this planet. I remember travelling, three years ago, when the great slump had just begun its operations on the grand scale, to the other side of the world, among the islands of the South Seas. There, behind the coral reefs and shining lagoons, in these tropical and salty Arcadias, you would think that a man could completely forget the dwindling trade returns of Europe and the financial crashes of America. But not a bit of it. The slump was there too. The natives were not getting the old prices for their pearls and copra, could not buy as many cigarettes and trinkets, and were gloomy about it. There is no escape. We may be under fifty different national flags, but we are compelled to serve now under only one economic flag. We do not know who designed it and ran it up, but there it is, and the more often we try to desert from it the more brutally we shall be starved into submission. It is as if a supernal being were determined to make this planet one whole or depopulate it. Lancashire is learning a lot about this queer interdependence of things. There were those smiling students from the East. And then there were those events in India. A rum little chap called Gandhi, who provided the most promising raw material for music-hall jokes, was going about there, spouting and spinning a fatuous little wheel. What had his antics to do with the stout cotton men, grinning in their clubs, the weavers roaring in the music-hall gallery? Nowt at all, it seemed. And then all manner of unpleasant things began to happen in India. The peasants were poorer than they had been, owing to bad harvests. Then there was strong local competition in the cotton trade. Then heavy import duties on Lancashire cotton. And then a boycott of English goods. The whole Indian trade, which had taken millions and millions of yards of the cheap grey stuff woven in Blackburn and district, was crumbling away; and the next thing they knew, firms went out of business, mills were idle, then empty, and folk by the street and by the town were thrown out of work.

The tragic word round there, I soon discovered, is *dhootie*. It is the forgotten 'Open Sesame'. A *dhootie* is the loin-cloth of India, which even Gandhi did not disdain to wear, and it is also the name of the cheap cotton fabric from which these loin-cloths are made. Blackburn expected every man to do his *dhootie*. This fabric was manufactured in the town and the surrounding district on a scale equal to the needs of the gigantic Indian population. So colossal was the output that Blackburn was the greatest weaving town in the world. It clothed the whole vast mad peninsula. Millions and millions of yards of *dhootie* cloth went streaming out of this valley. That trade is almost finished. Few of them there now believe that it will ever return. Those firms that were able to survive the crash have made desperate attempts to find openings in the markets for the fine fabrics. Lancashire, with its industrial resources, which have always kept pace with every new development in the industry, its long experience, its excellent workmanship, should be always able to sell its more expensive cotton fabrics, which must still be the best in the world. But this trade is limited; the prosperity of Lancashire was chiefly based on the gigantic output of cheap stuff for the East. The result is that in these smaller remaining markets there is now the most desperate cut-throat competition. I talked to some elderly cotton men in one of the clubs up there, tough fellows who had been brought up in a grim school, who almost shuddered when they mentioned the competition there was now in the few selling lines. Decent men were forced by circumstance into the most terrible positions. 'Damn it,' cried one of them, exploding, 'an employer in this business *can't* be honest to-day.' And these men who were talking were the comparatively fortunate ones. They must have been, for they were sitting in a club and had just had a good lunch. I hope they are all still there, snug in their leather chairs. But I doubt if they are. There's a war on in Lancashire, and by this time that club will have provided a few more casualties.

[3]

When I was travelling in the Midlands on this journey, I met a woman I know who had just come back from this Blackburn district, which was her original home. She had not been back for some years. 'It's awful,' she said. 'They've got no work at all. And I hardly recognised the place. It's all becoming *clean*. The smuts are wearing off because so few of the mills are working. The brick and stone are beginning to show through. I hardly knew the place.' This was not irony. She was genuinely distressed. They had left the money so far behind that even the muck was going now. I am not sure that a stranger would guess that there was something desperately wrong with these towns. He would notice, of course, that many of the mill chimneys were innocent of smoke. If he were an astute observer, he might notice the absence of heavy commercial traffic in the streets. But that, I think, is about all. These Lancashire towns— and this excludes industrial villages, one or two of which, I believe, are completely ruined—have not the derelict look of some places elsewhere, to be

LANCASHIRE MILL-GIRL, 1937   *Humphrey Spender*

described later in this book. The streets are not filled with men dismally loafing about. You do not see abandoned shops, which look as if they are closed for ever, down every street. Everything that was there before the slump, except the businesses themselves, is struggling on. In nearly every instance, the whole town is there, just as it was, but not in the condition it was. Its life is suffering from a deep internal injury. All the people who matter there know that in Lancashire now you are on active service. I spent a morning with one of these people, who worked in connection with some local fund and had to leave his business that morning to go round distributing food tickets. He was an elderly man and a middle-class employer (not in the cotton trade): but all the men and women we visited called him 'Richard'. Nothing better illustrates the genuine and deep-seated democracy of Lancashire than this practice of using Christian names. It is, I think, a sounder democracy than those that insist upon 'citizen' or 'comrade'. One day perhaps, when we have sense and energy and vision enough, we might build on this good foundation a society that would astonish and shame the rest of the world. Meanwhile, however, I had to see what was happening in the society we have got. The houses we visited were all in one neighbourhood, on the side of a hill, with all the short rows of cottage houses running sharply down to the great black wall of a big mill at the bottom. The street that was just behind the mill was, as usual, the worst, like a dark gully of brick, where the children played as they may have done in the caves of ten thousand years ago. Though looking miserable enough outside, the houses were usually very clean inside, for the Lancashire woman is proud and a worker. We were not calling on specially hard cases, but merely doing an average round of unemployed who happened to be helped by this fund. And here are the notes I made about them. I will leave them as notes; I shall be under less suspicion of monkeying with the facts; and also for this one paragraph I may be admired in some quarters as a stylist in the best modern staccato manner.

First house, an elderly couple. Long, toothless man, just got up and now sitting down to bowl of sensible soup. This made by wife, jolly woman who said: 'Ay, there's been lots worse off nor us,' and meant it. These two lucky. Man been out of work between four and five years. All savings went. Lived on 10s. a week. But my friend Richard got him temporary job as night-watch-man. 6 p.m. to 6 a.m. for 6 days a week, 72 hours, pay 36s. a week, and much troubled on the job by rats, large and ferocious rats. But job regarded as a godsend, and couple overjoyed with good fortune. Rent of house, beautifully kept, 6/9 a week. Next, oldish widow drawing 10s. a week pension, rent of house 7/11 a week. Daughter, formerly a weaver, and daughter's husband, sturdy young Irishman with sullen bovine look, living with her. Daughter, a pretty young woman, now big with child and came back from Ireland to have it at home. Irish husband cannot get work. Neither of them on the dole. Three of them helped by relatives and friends, not money but bits of food, or could not exist at all. By this time, there will be another in the family. All like bewildered children. House Number Three occupied by fat man with broad grin and no teeth, his wife and daughter. All weavers and been out of work three years. Man gets occasional temporary job. Draw 32s. a week dole and pay 8s. for rent. Fat man a character, with passion for cricket. Once bought, in happier times, a phrenologist's head, to amazement of neighbours. Last time Richard called, found him deep in Ruskin's *Stones of Venice*. He complained, comically, of still having enormous appetite, and might well have, being a big man. Probably does not know that Ministry of Health consider he is living in luxury. Doubt if Minister of Health, though brave man, would care to try and prove it to him here. Must have been grand jolly family when working. Now making best of it, but shadows of people they must have been once. Next house, little thin worried man and dumpy smiling wife. Out of work four years. Tries hard to get jobs. Is going to try again this Christmas for temporary job in Post Office. Never managed it but is still hoping. Two enchantingly pretty little girls, Joyce aged nine, Muriel aged four, fair-haired elves wearing tiny clogs; much too small and slight for their ages. Very shy but are induced to accept coins from large staring stranger. Income here 29/3 a week, with rent about 8/6. All living in luxury according to Ministry of Health, but do not seem to realise this, not having scientific and official minds. Wonder what will happen to Joyce and Muriel. Last house. Childless middle-aged couple, both people of character, the kind who like work and are good at it, both cotton operatives and out of work for last three years. Bought their house while still working, paid about £100 off. All savings gone. Have to pay interest and rates. Their dole about 25s. Had been doing some whitewashing that morning. We caught them sitting down to dinner, big meal of day, fried potatoes, bread and margarine, and tea. (A rotten diet. Pity they have not more sense about this.) Man pointed out he had worked for over thirty years in plain weaving, and if it had been fancy weaving, would have been working yet. Just bad luck. One looked as good as the other when he started. Now one finished, the other still going on. Both of them, good independent folk, insisted that they didn't want to ask for anything. Lots worse off than them. They all say that. Return with Richard to main road, where Arctic wind is blowing, and feel like comfortable newspaper proprietor who has just inspected front-line trench (in safe sector) and is now leaving the brave boys to it, thank God! But have horrible conviction—and still have it—that all these decent people, good citizens, are being wasted, their manhood and womanhood, their energy and skill, their self-respect, all flung on scrap-heap, and that the dole is a dreary and short-sighted device for keeping them existing until—well, what, when? A typical solution of a problem offered by the official mind. But in all this where is the creative mind, bringing life?

After lunch, that same day, I met the treasurer of Community House, Blackburn, who took me with him to see what the younger unemployed men were doing there. This is a voluntary effort, and it needs no praise from me. But if I criticise what I saw, I do not intend by that any reflection upon the grand work of this voluntary scheme. I am criticising the nation. Community House is doing all it can within the limits imposed upon it, and it is the country at large that is responsible for the fact that those limits are so narrow. The work here was going forward in a building that had once been an elementary school but had recently been condemned. If you know what many elementary schools are like, you can easily imagine what sort of building a condemned specimen is. It was a dismal hole in a dark back street. In the first room, some youngish men were at work. One or two were cobbling boots, chiefly soling and heeling, for which they pay—in order to cover the bare cost of leather—a shilling for men's, ninepence for women's, and sixpence for children's boots. The other men were making things out of wood. They were mostly things for their homes, such as cupboards, book-cases, coal-boxes, and little desks for children; these last, I imagine, something of a local fashion. They were also making toys for Christmas, clumsy but effective wooden engines and model airplanes and the like. There is some compulsory work on these toys, which are given to unemployed men's children. All the men seemed to be immensely proud of their handiwork, and they were generally so anxious to get a thing finished, the instructor told me, so that they could show it to admiring mothers or wives at home, that they were liable to scamp the later stages of the work. This instructor, paid by the voluntary society, was busy all day giving out wood and tools and showing his men what to do. The wood is supplied without charge to the men, and one of the instructor's duties is to find quantities of it at the lowest possible price or at no price at all. He showed great ingenuity in this, and made me peep into an ancient little classroom in which he was storing his rum bits of timber. He said that the men were not very good craftsmen, and tended to be imitative and careless, but that many of them were very keen and did their best. The next room was used as a club room. Notices of sing-songs and socials were pinned on the wall. Two lads, who had been brought up in a world of unemployment and were not worrying about it, were playing table tennis with very rough home-made bats. When they had done, I challenged one of them to a game, and just managed to beat him. I was told that he was not one of their better players, which I can well believe, for many of these unemployed lads, playing the game for hours nearly every day, are very good at table tennis. Probably by the time the North of England is an industrial ruin we shall be able to beat the world at table tennis. In the next and largest room of all a public assistance class in woodwork was being held. The young men come here instead of breaking stones in the workhouse. At first, the instructor there told me, they resented any attempt at discipline and tuition. They felt they had been dragooned into messing about with bits of wood in this ex-schoolroom. They would not do what they were told. They were careless with tools and material. They did not want to make anything, and if they did decide to make something, they would do it their own way, and were not going to be treated like kids by any bloody instructor. That was their attitude during the first weeks. But after that, almost in spite of themselves, they gradually acquired an interest in their jobs at the benches; they began asking one another the best way to do this and that; and finally were glad of advice from the qualified instructor. There was something rather touching in this, the emergence of the natural craftsman that is buried somewhere in every man. The lads there looked to me a good sturdy lot. They were better off at those benches than doing some futile time-killing job of work or mooning at home; and they would be better off still, I thought, if they could spend a few years in the ranks of a sort of labour army, an organisation on semi-military lines that would supply mobile labour wherever it was wanted and would at the same time give these lads a certain amount of discipline, hard work, travel, adventure, comradeship. I do not like armies and navies, but as a rule I like soldiers and sailors, who are much better specimens of young manhood than street loafers and corner boys. It is a great pity that we did not devise some national scheme on these lines, forming a peaceful army of young men disciplined and trained to do big jobs of work. I do not pretend to know what the economic consequences of such a scheme would have been, but I know the social results would have been almost miraculous. We should have bred men, thousands and thousands of strong, capable, self-respecting men, instead of a crowd of bewildered, resentful or indifferent idlers who have lost the decent boyhood we gave them only to drift towards a shady and shiftless manhood.

I do not know what will happen to the cotton industry. Possibly this is only the worst of its periodic collapses. I suspect, however, that not all the re-organisation and rationalisation and trade agreements and quotas and tariffs and

embargoes in the world will bring back to Lancashire what Lancashire has lost. The trade grew like Jack's beanstalk, and it has lately been dwindling in the same magical fashion. It would have been better for Lancashire if we had been a less optimistic people, if we had said good-bye for ever to the belief that somehow God was always on our side, if we had opened our minds to the fact that our export trade was rapidly declining and that soon we might lose our best customer for cotton, the East. With her trade leaving her, her businesses going bankrupt, her mills silent and vacant, her workpeople by the thousand losing their employment, Lancashire needed a plan.

Lancashire must have a plan. What is the use of England—and England in this connection, of course, means the City, Fleet Street, and the West End clubs—congratulating herself upon having pulled through yet once again, when there is no plan for Lancashire. Since when did Lancashire cease to be a part of England? Under what flag are little Joyce and Muriel and their parents in that Blackburn back-street? They might be worse off. And so might we all. We might be all down on our bellies in the mud, grubbing for roots, or fighting our neighbours in the fields for the last few turnips. But we have marched so far, not unassisted in the past by Lancashire's money and muck, and we have a long long way to go yet, perhaps carrying Lancashire on our backs for a spell; and the hour for complacency, if it ever arrives at all, will strike long after most of us are dead. No man can walk about these towns, the Cinderellas in the baronial household of Victorian England, towns meant to work in and not to live in and now even robbed of their work, without feeling that there is a terrible lack of direction and leadership in our affairs. It does not matter now whether Manchester does the thinking to-day and the rest of England thinks it to-morrow, or whether we turn the tables on them and think to-day for Manchester to-morrow. But somebody somewhere will have to do some hard thinking soon.

And on this most unsatisfactory conclusion, asking myself, over and over again, what must be done with these good workless folk, I took leave of my kindly host and his family, of water-colours and toxophily and *dhooties* and black puddings and pretty stunted children in clogs, and made for the bleak and streaming Pennines, on my way to the Tyne; with the weather, like my journey, going from bad to worse.

Opposite: COLLAPSE OF THE COTTON TRADE, 1932 *T. C. Egan*

CHAPTER TWELVE

To the Tyne

[1]

I suffer at times from damp snivelling colds in the head, which descend upon me quite suddenly, turning me into a helpless and disgusting red-nosed and red-eyed animal feebly crying for still more handkerchiefs. Now my doctor had found some stuff for me that immediately dried up these colds. It did not cure them but it drove them, so to speak, from the surface. After a dose or two of it, I am no longer helpless and sodden, but am able to carry out— perhaps rather drearily—an average programme of work or play. In the car travelling north, I realised that a particularly nasty cold was threatening and that unless I grappled with it at once I should be unable to see anything for days and my journey would be wasted. So I began dosing myself with this mixture. (It contains belladonna; you take it before food; and for a few seconds, as a result of its drying-up properties, it makes you feel rather sick.) As the cold seemed to be of gigantic size and strength, I had to keep on dosing myself all the week. I was able to do all that I had arranged to do. Nobody knew that I had a cold. But my inside was the arena for a grand seven-day contest, Giant Cold v. Belladonna Mixture. This meant that throughout these days I was not quite my usual self. (I have been told since, by a competent medical authority, that I probably had a temperature all the time.) The result was that I moved in a world that was not quite the ordinary real world: it wobbled and bulged at times, like the world we know in dreams. A more marked subjective element, I suspect, was present in my field of observation. Hence this paragraph, which is not an attempt to force upon you a more than usually disgusting bit of autobiography, but a possible explanation of why things looked very queer indeed and were a little larger and wilder than life during these next few days. I ask the reader to remember the swarming bacteria, the drenchings with belladonna, the rising temperature.

We reached the Great North Road. Along its deserted length the raindrops were bouncing merrily. There was no more colour in the day itself than there is in a bundle of steel rods, but up to Darlington the red ruins of autumn were still about us. At the great divide of the North Road, Scotch Corner, which ought to be the most romantic spot in the country but somehow is not, we turned right for Darlington; and while the rain still spouted into the main street there, I sat upstairs in a café and ate roast mutton and treacle pudding behind the *Yorkshire Post* folded against the water jug. The waitress who attended me was tall, frail and looked tubercular. (Probably my own temperature was beginning to rise then. Still, it is surprising how many waitresses in these cafés are tall, frail and look tubercular.) We ran through County Durham, which offered us nothing but distant glimpses of coal-pits and mining villages. There was a nightmare place that seemed to have been constructed out of small army huts and unwanted dog kennels, all sprawling in the muck outside some gigantic works. What they made inside those works I did not discover, but even a Kaffir would not have envied the employees if it was they who lived in those forlorn shanties. A dingy huddle of cottage houses, bethels in corrugated iron, picture palaces with hardly a flake of paint left on them butchers' windows decorated with offal, all announced that we were arriving at some great industrial centre, that soon we should be in civilisation again. First, a mile or two of Gateshead (to which we shall return later), then a great bridge across steaming space, and we were in Newcastle. I had been in these parts only once before, and that was during the war, not long after I had left 'a convalescent camp' at Ripon. Then I lived for some weeks in a pier pavilion at Tynemouth, doing odd and mostly unpleasant jobs. During this brief stay at Tynemouth I roamed about a good deal when off duty and so made the acquaintaince of most of the Tyneside towns, North Shields, South Shields, Jarrow, Gateshead, and the metropolis, Newcastle, which promised us, after a dash by electric train, a good tea and a show at the Hippodrome or the Empire. I have a very distinct recollection of taking a great dislike to the whole district, which seemed to me so ugly that it made the West Riding towns look like inland resorts. The people were not bad once you got to know them, though even to a Yorkshire lad they appeared uncouth. And I disliked— as I still do—their accent. As a rule I like local accents, and have kept one myself. They make for variety in speech and they give men's talk a flavour of the particular countryside to which at heart they belong. Standard English is like standard anything else—poor tasteless stuff. Probably if I had spent most of my impressionable years near the Tyne and had known the ecstasies of first love in Newcastle's Jesmond Dene, I might have discovered treasures of cadence in the local accent; but as it is, I can find nothing pleasant to say about it. To my ears, it still sounds a most barbarous, monotonous and irritating twang. Every short phrase rises in exactly the same way, almost to a scream: *taw taw ta ta tee tee ti ti*. The constant 'Ay-ee, mon,' or 'Ay-ee, yer b——' of the men's talk and the never-ending 'hinnying' of the women seem to me equally objectionable. It is probably difficult for a visitor to make all necessary allowances for the effect of the local accent upon his opinion of a place, if that accent produces a slight but perpetual irritation. One ought to allow a liberal discount for its bad influence.

The centre of Newcastle, into which we had now landed, has a certain sombre dignity. The streets are fairly wide; the shops are good; and there are more impressive buildings than one would expect. It is chiefly built of a stone that has turned almost a dead black. Newcastle is even blacker than Manchester, and might almost have been carved out of coal. The sad trade depression into which most of the district has fallen is not immediately noticeable here in its capital. The city looked busy and quite prosperous. After casting about a bit, I found an hotel that looked as if it might be reasonably quiet at night and in the early morning. (It was, but only because I took a gloomy little back-bedroom.) I unpacked my bag, sniffed a bit, took another dose of the mixture, then said to myself: Well, here I am in Newcastle. I had then to consider the next move. The afternoon was nearly done. It was still raining, though not hard; and the whole city seemed a black steaming mass. I had not a friend in the place. At that moment I was not even sure that I had a friend in the world. I sent out for one of the local papers, and then wasted an hour staring gloomily at it rather than reading it, and smoking a pipe that appeared to be rapidly losing its flavour. I ought, I know, to have been busy and elated, for this was the most northerly point of my journey and soon, very soon, I would be turning round again and making for home. But I sat there in my little bedroom, like a man marooned in Lapland. I said bitter things about those two publishers who, far away in London, after having lunched well, were now brisk and cheerful and in their respective private offices, probably arranging for some other poor fool of an author to leave home for months. And I was enormously sorry for myself. Then, remembering that I had a job to do, I climbed out of this morass of silliness and set about exploring the Tyneside. I did explore the Tyneside, and have not been genuinely sorry for myself since; though at times I have caught myself at the old drooping tricks and have been ashamed. There is, you see, something bracing about the Tyne. After you have seen it, you realise that it is not for the likes of us to be sorry for ourselves.

[2]

I made a start by remembering that I had had some humorously aggressive correspondence with a bookseller in this city. I would look him up. It proved

TRAIN LEAVING NEWCASTLE, 1936   *Bill Brandt*

to be an excellent move. I found him in and not too busy; he gave me a cup of tea; and we settled down before the fire in his office for a good talk. He is in the rare-book-and-first-edition branch of the trade, which has suffered a great deal from the depression in America. Nearly all booksellers of this type have been most unlucky in the number of bad debts they have had in America, where bibliophiles seem to be rather casual in money matters. I care very little about rare books and first editions. I write books and I read plenty of them, but I am no 'bookman' or 'book-lover', no collector. I have never even understood the first-edition man at all: he seems to me the most foolish of collectors. And when I find the prices of these early editions being raised a pound or two because of a dropped letter on the title-page or a misprint in the first chapter, I feel I am spying upon lunatics. In spite of these opinions, which I openly acknowledged, I got on very well with my Newcastle bookseller, though he was no mere tradesman but, like most of his kind, himself an enthusiast, whose mouth watered at the thought of a dropped letter. He was a man of my own age; and no dreamy bookman but one who lived vividly in the present. This was fortunate for me. When he asked me what I was doing in Newcastle, I replied that I did not know but that I should like to look round the district. This pleased him, and he said he would like to show me what there was to be seen. Meanwhile, that evening he had one or two calls to make—he did some work with the People's Theatre—but otherwise was at my service. Let him do whatever he had to do, I suggested, and I would go with him, if I was not in the way; and so in this easy fashion I might contrive to see something of Newcastle life on a black wet November night.

It worked very well. First, we had some food (not bad) in a very hot grill-room that he recommended. After that we ran and dodged and ran through the pouring rain to a tram, which took us to the bottom of a narrow hilly road. At the top were some bedraggled women trying to sell peanuts; a square building; some men and lads hanging about, as if it were June; and a pay-box. This was the St. James's Hall, where boxing shows are held nightly. I asked for two ring-side seats. The man said, 'Sevenpence each.' For the next half-minute we were at cross-purposes; I wanted better seats than sevenpenny ones; and he thought I was trying to get to the ringside for less than sevenpence. It appeared that on ordinary nights, there were only two classes of seats: the threepenny balconies and the sevenpenny ringside. I think sevenpence was a fair price for what we saw. The square hall, with its rows of seats climbing steeply all round the ring, looked almost empty when we first went inside, but I soon discovered that it was deceptively large in its seating capacity and that actually there were already several hundred people there, mostly in the threepenny balconies. The bouts we saw were either between rather stringy lads, who arrived in the ring wearing overcoats, or between ugly lumpy pitmen with the blue coal-marks on their hairy bodies. Those ignorant persons who imagine that boxing contests reek of blood would here have been confirmed for once in their opinion. There was a lot of blood about, partly because most of the boxers were novices who hit out wildly and also bled easily. The flat-faced seconds seemed to be for ever sponging away the crimson stains. The crowd did not seem to mind this: they were a bloodthirsty lot. 'Go on, yer b——,' they seemed to be muttering all the time. This was not an evening when they were willing to concentrate on the finer points of the craft, which indeed were obviously absent. They wanted the rough stuff. 'Oo, yer b——!' they cried in delight when one of the stained gloves got home with a nasty thud. Some boxing matches are enchanting spectacles: the powerful lights above the ring cutting through the haze of smoke; the torsos of the pugilists; the quick ripple of muscle; the satiny bloom on their skins; the grace and speed and strength of those two figures in the brilliant little arena; the dim mounds of faces that can suddenly let out such a huge roar. This was not one of those boxing matches. It was uncompromisingly ugly. The naked arc lights, the empty rows of seats, the awkward blood-stained fighters, the jeering spectators, all helped to make the scene an unpleasant one. I looked about me and thought I had never seen a crowd of men whose looks pleased me less. There was not one intelligent sensitive face in sight. Or so it seemed, in that harsh setting. For a moment, I had a vision of a dark sub-humanity, like those underground creatures in Wells' *Time Machine*. 'Had enough?' asked my companion. I had. 'So have I,' he said. 'This stuff's no good. You ought to be here on one of the big nights, when Seaman Watson's fighting. He's a local lad, you know. Ay, he's a local lad. Let's go. I have to leave that message at the rehearsal.'

We went out. It was still raining. The lads who could not afford the three-pence for admission were still hanging about the entrance outside. The women were still trying to sell their peanuts. We rode in trams again, among a smell of wet clothes. In the shadow of an enormous ebony bridge, which looked as if it stretched into the outer spaces of the universe, we found a large but almost deserted pub. But vague noises came from upstairs, and I was steered in their direction. That was the rehearsal. It was being directed by a middle-aged man in a blue suit, who peered at his players through the smoke of his cigarette. When we crept in, a spectacled young man in a raincoat was de-claiming with passion some lines about Greek gods and Trojan heroes. 'Now then,' said the producer, when the spectacled youth had retired, gasping, 'now then, chorus.' Then, to my surprise, about a dozen women, mostly rather short women in coloured mackintoshes, who had been standing about in a slightly shame-faced fashion, like the mothers of children at a dancing class, suddenly grouped themselves, slowly moved forward, as if sowing imaginary seed or strewing invisible flowers, and in far-away voices began chanting verses that prophesied woe. A very tall girl, as if maddened by the sight of so many coloured mackintoshes, rushed out of a corner, flung up an arm, made her eyes flash away as if she were a human lighthouse, and angrily addressed the chorus, giving them three woes to their one. This roused another young man in a raincoat, who appeared to be in a towering rage and apparently did not care if he gave himself a sore throat. But the raincoats were not to have it all their own way. The mackintoshes grouped themselves again and returned to their chanting, conducted enthusiastically by the producer, who encouraged me to hope that he was about to throw away his cigarette and dance for us. Perhaps he might have done, but just then a rather shy and pretty tweed winter coat swam forward and told us softly that she was Argive Helen, and then delivered quite a long speech about herself, with coloured mackintoshes rustling all round her. Those who know *The Trojan Women* may search in vain for a scene in it resembling this, and possibly my memory may have failed me; but it was certainly *The Trojan Women* they were rehearsing. If you had been standing in the saloon bar downstairs and had heard them moving about on the floor above, how many guesses would you have had to make before you reached the right conclusion? You would have said they were playing snooker, or dancing, or having a whist drive, and might have gone on guessing for days before you had suggested that they might be rehearsing *The Trojan Women*. If you were writing a story about a large pub in Newcastle, you would never have the impudence to fill its first-floor front with people rehearsing Greek drama. But there is no end to the impudent surprises and odd twists of reality. My companion had now delivered his message, and at the end of Helen's speech and before the mackintoshes could get going, we sneaked down the stairs and I muttered: 'What's Hecuba to them, or they to Hecuba?'

Another tram and then a long walk in the rain—it never stopped raining all night—brought us into a basement where some people with painted faces and false whiskers were drinking coffee and eating buns. We were now, I was told, underneath the stage of the People's Theatre. This did not surprise me: I could not be surprised any more. But the theatre deserves a word. Its prices range from sixpence to a half-crown, and if you buy a serial ticket for five shillings you are admitted throughout the season for half-price. The productions that season included *Peer Gynt, Widowers' Houses, The Insect Play,*

Loyalties, and *The Trojan Women*: good fare, solid tack, value for money. The players are all amateurs. I met one of the theatre's most enthusiastic helpers, whom I will call Bob. We did not stay long, and Bob left with us. Once more we walked through the rain; we went to the Central Station and missed the train we wanted, went to a bus stop and found that we had missed the bus we wanted; walked through more rain, climbed on to a bus, got out and did more walking. We were now outside the city, high up somewhere, and in the comfortable little home of my friend, the bookseller. At least, that is where I think we were, for by this time the evening was becoming very unreal, a mad mixture of rain, grill-rooms, trams, rain, peanuts, boxers, trams, rain, Trojan women in coloured mackintoshes, buns in basements, theatricals, rain, buses, remote suburbs, and a never-ending stream of talk about books, plays, railways, shipbuilding, coal, the Means Test, Russia, Germany, politics, sport, life and death. But I remember walking with Bob to catch the last electric train back to Newcastle. We waited about a quarter of an hour in one of the wettest and most melancholy little stations I have ever seen. We might have been waiting for a ghost train. The metal rails went straight from one mysterious darkness to another. We were alone on that tiny platform. We sat in a dim shed of a waiting-room, with the rain dully drumming on the wooden roof. You could not have had a better opening scene for a sinister film. It was a grand little station for a murder. But though Bob and I did not always agree, we were far removed from thoughts of murder. Bob was busy, talking, and I was busy, listening. That murder was not mentioned will surprise some people when they learn that Bob was a militant communist.

Bob deserves some space to himself, not simply because I spent part of this evening and nearly all of the next evening in his company, but because he seems to me a figure of some significance. Though he is very much of an individual, he is also a distinct type too. There are a good many Bobs about—especially in the north—and before long there will probably be a great many more. Wipe out at once any mental sketch of a sullen, greasy, long-haired, blue-chinned 'comrade'. Bob is a strongly-built, alert working man in his thirties; with a good forceful face—eyes slightly aslant and wide apart, blunt nose, short moustache, square chin; and a clean neat appearance. He is married and has a fine little boy, of whom he is immensely proud. I do not think it would be fair to him to say here what his occupation is; but he is employed by a very large concern, works hard and for long hours, and his wages are just over two pounds a week. He has to be up before six in the morning, and as he lives some distance from his work, he is not back again until the early evening. He spends nearly all his leisure either helping at the Settlement for the unemployed or lending a hand with such activities as the People's Theatre. He admitted that this was hard on his wife, who saw so little of him, but told me that she understood and sympathised with him and made the best of it. In his amateur theatricals he is a promising comedian. When a bit of holiday comes his way, he likes to do a little careful water-colour sketching, and what he does is very creditable to an untrained man with not much time to spare. He is a kindly, lively but forceful sort of chap, who, if he were living in a pioneer society, where labour was in demand and ability soon rewarded, would quickly win promotion, be a foreman, a manager, and so forth; he is something of a natural leader. Having grown up in a very different kind of life, he has turned communist. He is not at all sentimental about his own class—except in its theoretical existence as 'the proletariat'—but quite sternly realistic in his attitude towards it (as we shall see, later.) He is not equally realistic, however, about other classes, with whom he hardly comes into contact. The world he lives in is not the sad muddle that most of us have begun to recognise, but is a mysterious and melodramatic place of vast sinister conspiracies, in which capitalists and bosses and officials plot together to trick him and his mates. Thus, he grumbled and sneered because the concern that employs him has lately been spending money on a certain extension of its premises. They could not spare money, he complained, to give their workpeople some decent wages, but they could throw it away—just to please a few officials—on these building operations. Now even I, who knew very little about the concern, did know that it was spending this money in a last desperate attempt to get more business, and that the process of finding the money for this extension must have been like wringing blood out of a stone. But this is typical of his attitude of mind. He did not make this an excuse to attack a muddled wasteful competitive system; which would have been legitimate enough. He saw it as one more example of the conspiracy of bosses and officials. He thinks that most people are poor because a few are rich. Any man receiving more than a few pounds per week automatically becomes one of the sinister conspiring class. The modern world is to him simply a wicked place, and not, as it seems to many of us, a stupid place. When he talks of his neighbours or the men he works with, he is a realist, quick to notice their many weaknesses; but when he argues, unconsciously he becomes an idealist and talks about 'the workers' as if they were a race of bright beautiful beings incapable of selfishness, indolence, corruption. On the other hand, men of the employing or managing classes are never to him men very much like himself who, though they may be the servants of a faulty and even cruel system, are honestly trying to do their duty and to be decent and kind and unselfish; they are always sneering cunning tyrants, to whom the very poverty and helplessness of the people are a source of deep satisfaction. And he is, I suspect, permanently trapped into this attitude, like thousands of other working men who have managed to raise themselves above the beer and betting mindlessness of their mates. I am not, of course, presenting my friend Bob as an example of a Marxian thinker. He is not really a thinker at all, except when he is shrewdly realistic about the life in his immediate neighbourhood. He made one great effort—an effort that not all of us would have been capable of making in his circumstances—to jump clear of this beer and betting jungle, this brutish fatalistic acceptance of the miserable muddle of our present society, and to arrive at the level of his own brand of communistic thought; and since then I suspect he has done no independent thinking at all but has simply applied a woefully rough-and-ready standard to everything. His communism is not a reasoned alternative to a social machine that is wobbling and running down, is not a transition from an obviously incompetent and unjust system to an order of society that embodies our ideas of competence and justice: it is the entrance into a Human Paradise and a new Golden Age, from which, by some mysterious means, all the selfish wickedness of the present world will be banished. Nobody could be more cynical than he is about elected persons and men in authority here and now, but he has no difficulty in persuading himself that in a communist England all elected persons and men in authority would acquire a new mystical virtue. This is Bob, and I have met scores like him. There must indeed be thousands like him in the making. And no picture of contemporary industrial England would be complete without a little portrait of him.

Nevertheless, in spite of much disagreement, I thought Bob himself a grand chap, and when he told me, on that deserted last train to Newcastle, that he would be spending the next night conducting a rehearsal of some unemployed young men, for a forthcoming pierrot show at the Unemployed Men's Settlement, I was only too glad to accept his invitation to call for him at his home. Then we parted outside the dark and dripping entrance to Newcastle's Central Station, where the newsboys, despairing of selling another paper, were begging for coppers. These lads looked the most miserable sodden bundles of old clothes. Bob told me, however, that they are great hands at betting. We are a nation of sportsmen.

[3]

It was a raw gloomy evening when I set out to find Bob's home. I think I shivered all the time from that internal cold, which was now beginning to make me feel miserable. In order to find Bob's little flat I had to explore a large part of Gateshead, and there was nothing in this exploration to raise my spirits. Once off the long dreary main road, there was nothing but their names, not always easily seen, to distinguish one street from another. There seemed a great deal of Gateshead and the whole town appeared to have been carefully planned by an enemy of the human race in its more exuberant aspects. Insects can do better than this: their habitations are equally monotonous but far more efficiently constructed. As the various industries of Gateshead are in a state of rapid decline, it is possible that very soon it will be in the position of the decayed mediæval towns, those ports that the sea has left, but unlike those mediæval towns it will not, I think, be often visited by tourists in search of the quaint and the picturesque. Ye Olde Gateshead Tea Rooms, I feel, will not do a brisk trade. The town was built to work in and to sleep in. You can still sleep in it, I suppose. When at last I found Bob, in a neat little sitting-room with a neat smiling little wife, I told him that I did not think much of his native town.

'Do you know what's the biggest town—either on the railway or on the direct road—between Newcastle and London? I'll bet you'll never guess. Well, this is it—Gateshead. You can catch a lot of people out with that. Gateshead's the biggest town between Newcastle and London. It's got more than a hundred and twenty-five thousand people in it, Gateshead has.'

And that, as he went on to admit, is about all Gateshead has in it. One hundred and twenty-five thousand people, but no real town. It has fewer public buildings of any importance than any town of its size in the country. If there is any town of like size on the continent of Europe that can show a similar lack of civic dignity and all the evidences of an urban civilisation, I should like to know its name and quality. No true civilisation could have produced such a town, which is nothing better than a huge dingy dormitory. I admit that it is only just across the river from Newcastle, which has some amenities. But Gateshead is an entirely separate borough. It has a member of Parliament, a mayor, nine aldermen, and twenty-seven councillors; and I hope they are all delighted with themselves. They used to build locomotives in Gateshead, very fine complicated powerful locomotives, but they never seem to have had time to build a town. A place like this belongs to the pioneer age of industrialism, and unfortunately the industry appears to be vanishing before the pioneers themselves have time to make themselves comfortable. It is a frontier camp of bricks and mortar, but no Golden West has been opened up by its activities. If anybody ever made money in Gateshead, they must have taken great care not to spend any of it in the town. And if nobody ever did make

money in the town, what is it there for? It cannot be there for fun. Gateshead
is not Somebody's Folly. How is it that a town can contain one hundred and
twenty-five thousand persons and yet look like a sprawling swollen industrial
village? The answer is that this is a dormitory for the working class. Perhaps
at first they wanted nothing better, and now, by the time that some of them
want something a great deal better, there is no money. Yet the town owes
its existence, on this scale, to Britain's famous industrial prosperity, to which
the town itself in turn contributed. The prosperity itself is now behind us,
like the Victorian age with which it is so closely associated, and now we may
ask what are the signs and marks of it left in Gateshead? To what must we
point, in admiration, when we stand here in Gateshead and think of that
vanished era? We can of course point to the hundred and twenty-five thousand
people, but there is nothing in their appearance or in their present situation
in life to suggest that they themselves are the finest legacies of that era. True,
some of them, like Bob, are fine sturdy fellows; but it is just those fellows
who condemn most thoroughly the whole dingy bag of tricks. Every future
historian of modern England should be compelled to take a good long slow
walk round Gateshead. After that he can at his leisure fit it into his interpre-
tation of our national growth and development.

   Bob had another visitor. He was a lad with a rather fixed smile, a gentle
face and voice, who sat up stiffly. He and I began arguing about Russia, and
though he did not convince me, I thought he made some good points and
talked well. During this argument I made one or two cheerfully outrageous
remarks, and as I brought them out I grinned across at him in a friendly fashion
to indicate that I did not expect to be taken too seriously. I thought at the
time that he did not appear to be responding too well to these grins, and put
this down to his earnest youthful enthusiasm, which forbade such trifling with
the sacred subject of communism. It was only afterwards that I learned, to
my horror, that the boy was blind. He was also semi-paralysed. Bob told me
that the boy is now able to take first-year classes in adult education. Up to
a year or two ago he learned nearly everything from his mother, a working-
class woman, who read to him hour after hour. Now, of course, he can read
Braille, and finds his way about, and is an active and very useful member
of that community. I still think he is wrong about Russia, but I wish so remarkable a lad could find it possible to be even half so enthusiastic and inspired
about England.

   Bob took me to the Bensham Grove Settlement. It is established—and has
been for a good many years—in a detached house, the only one of that size
I noticed in the neighbourhood. A little theatre has been built in the garden,

and there are one or two other small annexes. Conditions are probably worse on the Tyne than anywhere else in this country, but it is only fair to say that in no other district are more determined efforts being made, by means of these settlements and their various activities, to help the unemployed. (See the annual report of the *Tyneside Council of Social Service*.) Bob showed me round this settlement, which appeared to be very busy indeed. There was a play on in the theatre; there were classes being held in various parts of the house; the notice boards were covered with lists and programmes. Bob's embryo concert party was ready for him, and we all moved into a little hut where there was a piano and a tiny stage. The young men were a very mixed lot. Some looked very clean, neat and healthy; others were very grimy and seedy specimens. They were so mixed that it would be impossible to generalise about them. I spent so long in that hut that I can easily recall their faces, which ranged from a handsome ruddy youthfulness to dirty, young-old, toothless masks, and their voices, which included everything from a piercing tenor to a varied assortment of Tyneside grunts. One fellow—who afterwards laboriously went through a comic song, and appeared to be a most successful comic man except when it was his turn to be one—was specially noticeable, if only for his odd look and a hand that was nothing but a stump. I learned afterwards that he had been an epileptic, and that a few years ago, having been left alone (I believe in the place where he worked), he had fallen down in a fit and this hand had gone into the fire. When he was discovered the hand had been nearly burned off; and since then he has had no more fits. Of such stuff were the comedians made in this grim concert party. They were not good musical or dramatic material, but my friend Bob, who was an old hand as a producer, wrestled stubbornly with them, taking them through choruses, harmonised quartets, and concerted numbers in which unshaven Tyneside lads turned themselves into an agonising burlesque of coy fluttering maidens. Their best number—and I hope it went well on the night—was their opening chorus, in which, harried by the stamping, time-beating Bob, they thundered their conviction that happy days were here again. I can still hear them singing that chorus about the happy days, can still see their fixed anxious gaze, can feel the little hut shaking beneath the tramp of their heavy boots, and can recall the ironic sting of that roaring mock welcome. Most of them may have been poor creatures (and Bob had no illusions about them), but I should like to be there when they could sing that chorus in good earnest.

When the rehearsal was over Bob collected a friend or two from other parts of the Settlement, and we went back to his home, where his wife had coffee and sandwiches ready for us. We began talking about these young men who

'BUTTERFLY OF THE BACK STREETS', 1936 *Edwin Smith*

had grown up in a workless world. Bob explained that he had had great difficulty in persuading them to join his concert party, which was for their benefit
and not his own, as he had plenty of opportunities for his kind of work elsewhere; and that even when they had consented to join it was not easy to get
them to turn up punctually to rehearsals, to learn their songs and patter, and
to make them submit even to the easiest discipline. Sympathy, he declared,
was wasted on most of them, because, unlike older men, who had known what
steady employment and regular wages were, these youngsters did not 'fret'
because they had no work. There was no loss of self-respect, no anxiety, with
them. The others present agreed with him. Most of these young men, they
assured me, were undisciplined and carefree, the dingy butterflies of the back
streets. They had no sense whatever of waste and tragedy in themselves. They
were not at odds with their peculiar environment, which by this time had
moulded their characters and shaped their way of living. They had little or
no money, but never having had any, they did not miss it. They cadged cheerfully from relatives, and so managed to find a few coppers for cigarettes and
the pictures and a bit of betting. (Somebody recently had got up a free film

IDLE BY THE QUAY SIDE, 1936 *Humphrey Spender*

show for them, but hardly any of them had attended it, and they had been
seen, that very night, coming back from the ordinary cinema.) They lived below the level of worry. They were not citizens, though some of them soon
would be husbands and fathers. If the time ever came when they had to work
hard and to obey orders, it would find them resentful and untrustworthy. Having grown up in one kind of world they would be puzzled and probably annoyed by any other kind of world. They knew nothing about responsibility.
They are the new playboys of the western world. But of course they have to
play in Gateshead, which has obviously been designed only to work in. They
live, in short, in a workshop that has no work for them. They are the children
of an industrialism that has lost its industry, of a money-making machine that
has ceased to make money. If they live mean foolish little lives, whose fault
is that? Citizens must have a city. Seen at close quarters, as irresponsible corner
boys, they do not vanish as tragic figures. They are tragic to their parents,
and we can only hope that they may seem tragic, some day, to their children.

There was a railwayman present, and he told us that only that very day
he had been called upon to give an exact account of his duties. 'They thought

they might be able to give me the sack, man,' he explained, 'but when I told them all I did, they thought better of it. There used to be three different men—ay, man, three of 'em—doing what I have to do by myself now.' He went on to tell us, no doubt with some humorous exaggeration, that the company's policy of keeping on old employees as long as it could and of not taking on any young men had resulted in a droll state of affairs, in which you had to go round looking for a man strong enough to undertake anything that required a bit of muscle. If a heavy package arrived, the place had to be combed for a man still young enough to handle it without danger to himself. 'We've all got one foot in the grave, man,' he cried. His father and grandfather had been railwaymen before him, he said, but railways were railways in those days. Gateshead, of course, was a great railway town. We are all proud of our splendid railway systems, but I have never caught the wildest enthusiast among us beaming with pride at the thought of our railway towns. I left this specimen of them without regret, though I was sorry to see the last of Bob. When I got back home I sent him a copy of a book of mine, and at once he sent me the water-colour sketch of his, of one of the Tyne bridges, that I liked best, though I am sure it was his own favourite too. Of such stuff, it seems, are dangerous red agitators made, the fellows who ought to be locked up. I shall not join Bob's party yet; but I wish I had a party fit for him to join.

It was my bookseller friend who took me down the Tyne. The rain had gone but the morning was cold and rather misty. I had nothing to do most of the time but stare through the window of a saloon car, and I doubt if I was fit to do that, heavily dosed as I was with that belladonna mixture. I have no doubt that the subjective element, against which I warned you at the beginning of this chapter, now comes into play, blurring the scene; but I will at least make an honest attempt to put down what I thought I saw that day. We began by running along the old Quay Side as far as we could go. There I noticed nothing but a lot of miserable fellows hanging about, probably looking for the chance of a job. When we turned away from the water's edge, on our way to Wallsend, I found that the ebony dignity of central Newcastle had been left behind. These were all mean streets. Slatternly women stood at the doors of wretched little houses, gossiping with other slatterns or screeching for their small children, who were playing among the filth of the roadside. You would have thought that New Bridge Street was miles away, in another city altogether. Between Wallsend and North Shields the road was confusing, and the landscape more confusing still. It was strewn with broken-down pitmen's cottages and the ruins of higgledy-piggledy allotments. I never saw a bit of country that was in more urgent need of tidying up. If any decent woman had been shown a room half as bad as this, she would have itched to be at it. If T. S. Eliot ever wants to write a poem about a real wasteland instead of a metaphysical one, he should come here. We are all fond of saying that people 'get used to' things, but I do not believe that anybody can look complacently at a dirty mess of this kind. It must have been depressing folk for years. All round this hideous muddle, where industry had had a dirty black meal and had done no washing up, there must have been schools in which children were learning about Simon de Montfort and Keats and the properties of potassium. The fathers of many of these children were wondering how to get through another idle useless day. And here was this great mess waiting to be tidied up, and determined in the meantime to take the heart out of anybody who looked at it. I do not say that the scene as a whole was lacking in certain elements of the grim picturesque. On the right, there were sudden strange glimpses of the river far below; rather like a deep gulf in which a thicker mist moved sluggishly. The sight of it lifted the heart at once, probably because one accepted it as a symbol of escape. There was the estuary, water and air and light, and somewhere not far away was the wide sea itself, a window upon the world. There were glimpses too of the great cranes and the other paraphernalia of the yards, reminding you that these Geordies, stocky toothless fellows in caps and mufflers, cursing in their uncouth accent, could do a grand job of work whenever they were given a chance. I could not lend a hand with that work, but let nobody assume for a moment that I cannot appreciate its grim strength and mastery, its Promethean and Vulcanic grandeur, or that I moved through this setting for it like a flinching minor poet dreaming of roses. Labour of this kind, bending iron and riveting steel to steel, is the real thing, man's work. Grim and ugly as it might be, nevertheless if this riverside had been black and shattering with the smoke and din of tens of thousands of men hard at it, for the commonwealth and for their own decent comfort and self-respect, I think I would have found it wildly inspiring, a scene to overtop any poor praise of mine. There was, of course, some good work going on, but what chiefly caught the eye there were evidences of past greed, now satiated here and ravening elsewhere, and present indifference and neglect. Silent rusting shipyards are not an inspiring spectacle; neither are rows of broken-down cottages and forlorn allotments. If all these things are now as useless to the industrial and social body as nail-parings and hair-combings, they might at least be decently tidied away. They are, I gather, partly the result of severe surgical operations in our post-war economy. Neither the patient nor the operating theatre seems to have been cleaned up; and the resulting mess is not a pretty sight.

DOMESTIC STUDY, GATESHEAD, 1936   *Edwin Smith*

We crossed from North Shields to South Shields in a fat little ferry-boat, and on our way over my companion, whose father had been a marine engineer and who had been apprenticed to the trade himself, pointed this way and that up the raw gulf of the river and told me what a pitifully small tonnage of shipping there seemed to be about now. We ran up a sharp street into the main square of South Shields, which, I am delighted to add, seemed to me a pleasanter town now than I remembered it as being, from the war. But it has, I believe, a far larger middle-class population than most of the other neighbouring towns. We had lunch in a deserted and very warm hotel dining-room. The sunlight was struggling through to the square when we went back to the waiting car, and we were now ready to explore the towns on this south bank, between here and Gateshead. My companion was anxious that I should have a talk with one or two men of his acquaintance in Jarrow and Hebburn, and I might as well confess here that we never succeeded in finding any of those

men, though we spent most of the afternoon asking our way in a labyrinth of little streets trying to find them. But if we did not see the men, we certainly saw the towns, though we did not find our way into them without difficulty. They are plainly there, along the river bank, and I was with a Tyneside man who knew them, but nevertheless we had to ask our way several times and twist about and turn back before we contrived to reach Jarrow from South Shields. I suspect that devilish agencies were at work trying to prevent us from ever seeing Jarrow and Hebburn. They did not succeed. We managed at last to thread our way through a maze of monotonous streets, complicated by a spider's web of railway lines, and then went round and round Jarrow chasing two elusive officials. I will not add that these two officials had vanished into thin air because there is no thin air in Jarrow. It is thick air, heavy with enforced idleness, poverty and misery.

The most remarkable giant liner in the world is probably the *Mauretania*, for she is nearly thirty years old and is still one of the fastest vessels afloat. Her record, both for speed and safety, is superb. We are proud of her. Now the *Mauretania* was launched at Wallsend, just across the river from Jarrow; and she has lasted longer than Jarrow. She is still alive and throbbing, but Jarrow is dead. As a real town, a piece of urban civilisation, Jarrow can never have been alive. There is easily more comfort and luxury on one deck of the *Mauretania* than there can ever have been at any time in Jarrow, which even at its best, when everybody was working in it, must obviously have been a mean little conglomeration of narrow monotonous streets of stunted and ugly houses, a barracks cynically put together so that shipbuilding workers could get some food and sleep between shifts. Anything—strange as it may seem— appears to have been good enough for the men who could build ships like the *Mauretania*. But in those days, at least they were working. Now Jarrow is a derelict town. I had seen nothing like it since the war. I put a derelict shipbuilding town into *Wonder Hero* and called it Slakeby. Some people thought I overdid it a little in my Slakeby chapter. I assure those people that the reality of Jarrow is far worse than anything I imagined for Slakeby. It far outran any grim expectations of mine. My guide-book devotes one short sentence to Jarrow: 'A busy town (35,590 inhabitants), has large ironworks and ship-building yards.' It is time this was amended into 'An idle and ruined town (35,590 inhabitants, wondering what is to become of them), had large ironworks and can still show what is left of shipbuilding yards.' The Venerable

Opposite: **LADIES OF NORTH SHIELDS, 1936**   *Edwin Smith*

Bede spent part of his life in this neighbourhood. He would be astonished at the progress it has made since his time, when the river ran, a clear stream, through a green valley. There is no escape anywhere in Jarrow from its prevailing misery, for it is entirely a working-class town. One little street may be rather more wretched than another, but to the outsider they all look alike. One out of every two shops appeared to be permanently closed. Wherever we went there were men hanging about, not scores of them but hundreds and thousands of them. The whole town looked as if it had entered a perpetual penniless bleak Sabbath. The men wore the drawn masks of prisoners of war. A stranger from a distant civilisation, observing the condition of the place and its people, would have arrived at once at the conclusion that Jarrow had deeply offended some celestial emperor of the island and was now being punished. He would never believe us if we told him that in theory this town was as good as any other and that its inhabitants were not criminals but citizens with votes. The only cheerful sight I saw there was a game of Follow-my-leader that was being played by seven small children. But what leader can the rest of them follow?

After a glimpse of the river-front, that is, of tumble-down sheds, rotting piles, coal dust and mud, we landed in Hebburn, where we pursued, in vain, another man we wanted. Hebburn is another completely working-class town. It is built on the same mean proletarian scale as Jarrow. It appeared to be even poorer than its neighbour. You felt that there was nothing in the whole place worth a five-pound note. It looked as much like an ordinary town of that size as a dust-bin looks like a drawing-room. Here again, idle men—and not unemployable casual labourers but skilled men—hung about the streets, waiting for Doomsday. Nothing, it seemed, would ever happen here again. Yet oddly enough a great deal is happening here; more, in some directions, than has ever happened before. Its Council of Social Service possesses a particularly energetic secretary, and in this stranded hulk of a town there are courses on history and economics (an ironic course, this) and literature, an orchestra and ladies' and children's choirs, two girls' clubs for handicrafts, gymnasium classes, a camping and rambling club, and play centres for children. It is possible that Hebburn is coming nearer to civilisation in its poverty than it ever did in its prosperity. Probably these cultural activities are breeding a generation that would not tolerate the old Hebburn, even though it offered them work and wages again. If this should be true, then at least in one direction there has been a gain. But consider the gigantic loss. It is not merely that two-thirds of the town is living on the edge of destitution, tightening its belt another hole every month or two, but that its self-respect is vanishing—for

KEEPING UP STANDARDS IN JARROW, 1936   *Bill Brandt*

these are *working* towns and nothing else—and that it sees the sky for ever darkening over it. We went down to the social centre, which after some difficulty we found in a couple of huts by the side of a derelict shipyard. A little gnome-like man, grandly proud of everything, showed us round. There were places for carpentering and cobbling, a tattered library, and a newly-finished hut for their twopenny whist drives and dances. (I had an odd feeling all the time that I was looking at a camp just behind the front line in some strange new war.) This centre possesses a boat of its own that has already achieved some fame, and our gnome-like friend offered to go down to the water's edge, where it was moored, to show it to us. To get there we had to cross the derelict shipyard, which was a fantastic wilderness of decaying sheds, strange mounds and pits, rusted iron, old concrete and new grass. Both my companions knew about this yard, which had been a spectacular failure in which over a million of money had been lost. They had queer stories to tell of corruption in this and other yards, of lorry-loads of valuable material that were driven in at one gate and signed for, and then quietly driven out at another gate, of jobs so blatantly rushed, for show purposes, that in the last weeks wooden pegs were being used in place of steel rivets. As we came to the sullen water-front, we could hear the noise of the electric riveting from the few yards working across the river; but both of them agreed that it seemed quiet now compared with the deafening din of the riveters in the old days. There was one ship in the yards now where there used to be twenty. Down the Tyne we could see the idle ships lying up, a melancholy and familiar sight now in every estuary round the coast. There is hardly anything that brings you more sharply into line with the idiotic muddle of our times than the spectacle of these fine big steamers rusting away in rows. We have these vessels doing nothing; we have coal for their bunkers; our ports are filled with ships' officers and men out of work; we have goods that other people need, and across every stretch of ocean are goods that we need; and still the ships are there, chained and empty, rusting in the rain, groaning in idleness night and day. But one boat is not idle on that river. That is the one we looked at now, as she creaked at her moorings. She was an old ship's boat and as she was in a poor shape, she was bought for the social centre for four pounds. The men themselves patched her up. She carries a sail and ten men usually go out in her, working three lines. The fish they bring back—and they have had some good catches, though the Tyne estuary is no Dogger Bank—is not sold but distributed among the unemployed men's families. She is called the *Venture*, and a better name could not be found for her. I do not know that anywhere on this journey I saw anything more moving and more significant than that old patched boat, which hung for years from the davits of a liner but is now the workless men's *Venture*, creeping out with the tide to find a few fish. The effort she represents is something more than a brave gesture, though it is that all right. It means that these men, who were once part of our elaborate industrial machinery but have now been cast out by it, are starting all over again, far away from the great machine, at the very beginning, out at sea with a line and a hook. And it will not do. These are not simple fishermen any more than this island of ours is one of the South Sea islands. They are the skilled children of our industrial system, artisans and men with trades in their fingers, and every time they go out and fumble frozenly with their lines and hooks, they declare once again the miserable bankruptcy of that system. This *Venture* may be their pride, but it is our shame.

Chilled and aching, I stood by the side of the river and looked at the mud and coal dust below, at the slimy and decaying wood piles on either side, at the tumble-down sheds above, and across at the motionless cranes and idle ships now fading in the mist; and as I looked about me, I remembered the miserable huddles of mean streets and dirty little houses behind me, and the grimy wilderness we had passed through during the morning; and I asked myself, with failing courage and hope, whether the whole Tyneside had not taken a wrong turning. There was a time when this must have been one of the prettiest of our green estuaries. With a clear sky above him and clear water below, a man could have been happy here in the old days, content to live in peace without cinemas and newspapers and racing dogs and betting slips or even without rambling clubs and musical societies and gymnastics and lectures on the Economic History of England. (He would not have known—the lucky fellow—that it had an Economic History.) I am not given to sentimentalising the distant past, and have argued often and ferociously with those who do and have seemed to me to gloss over its ignorance and brutality and the narrow limits of its life. But I could see men reasonably content, if not happy, in this clean verdant river-sea country, with its fresh salt winds. Well, there is no more green estuary now. The whole riverside wears a black scarred face. It is not casually but ruthlessly ugly, as if every charm had been deliberately banished. But there was the new grimy fairy-tale of industry; there was work; there were rising wages. England would not be the England we know if the Tyneside were not the Tyneside we know. Coal, millions of tons of it, had been poured out down this channel; great ships had been built and repaired; engines had been constructed and sent away by the thousand; there had been enormous fortunes spent in wages and material, in profits and dividends. But still I wondered, as I stood there, shivering a little, whether it had all been worth while. Here was the pleasant green estuary, blackened and ruined, it seemed, for ever. Here was a warren of people living in wretched conditions, in a parody of either rural or urban life, many of them now without work or wages or hope, not half the men their peasant ancestors were. They seemed to have gained as little as the befouled river itself. And the fortunes, the piles of gold that the alchemy of industry had conjured from this steam and filth and din, where were they? What great work, I asked myself, owes its existence to those vast profits, those mounting dividends? What sciences and arts had they nourished? What new graces had they added to English life in return for what they had taken away from here? The ramshackle telephone exchange at the back of my mind put the call through, and I heard the bell ring and ring: but there was no reply.

On our way back from Hebburn to Gateshead, which was a journey among the very scrag-ends of industrial life, we passed no less than three funerals, each of them with a long black tail to it. Here, though you can no longer live well, you can still die and be buried in style. I had already noticed that although so many shops were closed in Jarrow and Hebburn, the shops that sold funeral wreaths were still open. True, the specimens they exhibited in their windows had a white waxiness that was now somewhat fly-blown, as if dissolution had anticipated their ultimate arrival at the grave or was becoming impatient and so setting its mark upon them. But there they were, and costing good money. It seemed as if Death provided the only possible spree left here. Once you had escaped from this narrow life your cold body was treated like an honoured guest and made a royal escape. There were flowers for the dead, if none for the living. All the neighbours turned out to witness this triumphant emigration. Here was something that asked for what was left of one's best clothes. Here was the remaining bit of pageantry. If you could no longer work and found it hard to play, you could still turn out and march to the cemetery. My companion told me that the district had always had a weakness for lavish funerals; its folk growing reckless and opulent in the presence of death. Years ago, he told me, his father, weary of seeing poor widows flinging their money away in this fashion, had had a few short sharp words with some of the local undertakers, who were not above encouraging the bewildered creatures to be lavish and outdo their recently bereaved neighbours. As we passed these long dragging funerals, I though how hideously we have bedizened the face and figure of Death. The major events of our lives are unfortunate for our dignity: we come into this world to the accompaniment of shrieks of pain and the reek of disinfectant; we are married among idiotic ceremonies, and silly whispers, giggles, nudges, stares and stale jokes; we leave

WAITING — FOR WHAT?, 1936   *Humphrey Spender*

this world in the company of wired flowers and dyed horses, commercial
gentlemen with professionally long faces, and greeny-black suits that do not
fit; and we can only say good-bye to the bodies we have loved in a monstrous
atmosphere of black bogy-men on parade. 'Thou thy worldly task has done,'
I muttered to the last and grimmest coach. 'Home art gone and ta'en thy
wages.' But there were probably no wages: home he had gone and taken his
dole. And where was this home? Where was the fellow whose cold carcase
had been screwed down inside that yellow tapering box? Was he in deep sleep
for ever, or was he watching in amazement this procession, or was he already
struggling into another life, perhaps not lacking so many elements of justice
as this one, somewhere beyond Sirius?

   In Gateshead, on our way back, we passed some little streets named after
the poets, Chaucer and Spenser and Tennyson Streets; and I wondered if any
poets were growing up in those streets. We could do with one from such streets;
not one of our frigid complicated sniggering rhymers, but a lad with such
a flame in his heart and mouth that at last he could set the Tyne on fire. Who
would rush to put it out? Not I, for one.

CHAPTER THIRTEEN

To East Durham

[1]

On a morning entangled in light mist, under a sullen sky, I left the Tyne by road for East Durham. Most of us have often crossed this county of Durham, to and from Scotland. We are well acquainted with the fine grim aspect of the city of Durham, with that baleful dark bulk of castle, which at a distance makes the city look like some place in a Gothic tale of blood and terror. The romantic traveller, impressed by the Macbeth-like look of the city, will be well advised not to get out of his train at Durham station. Some of us, wise or lucky, know West Durham, especially Weardale and Teesdale, which are very beautiful: rocks and heather, glens and streams flashing through golden woods. (As a woman might keep a wedding dress, so I keep the bright thought of that Northern countryside by me, occasionally taking it out to make sure that I still have it and that its enchantment has not faded.) But who knows East Durham? The answer is—nobody but the people who have to live and work there, and a few others who go there on business. It is, you see, a coal-mining district. Unless we happen to be connected in some way with a colliery, we do not know these districts. They are usually unpleasant and rather remote and so we leave them alone. Of the millions in London, how many have ever spent half an hour in a mining village? How many newspaper proprietors, newspaper editors, newspaper readers have ever had ten minutes' talk with a miner? How many Members of Parliament could give even the roughest description of the organisation and working of a coal-mine? How many voters could answer the simplest questions about the hours of work and average earnings of a miner? These are not idle queries. I wish they were. If they had been, England would have been much merrier than it is now.

Most English people know as little about coal-mining as they do about diamond-mining. Probably less, because they may have been sufficiently interested to learn a little about so romantic a trade as diamond-mining. Who wants to know about coal? Who wants to know anything about miners, except when an explosion kills or entombs a few of them and they become news? The railway and motor-coach companies do not run popular excursions to mining districts. Pitmen are not familiar figures in the streets of our large cities. The mining communities are remote, hidden away, mysterious. If there had been several working collieries in London itself, modern English history would have been quite different. (For example, we should not have had the General Strike of 1926.) But there are no collieries in London or very near it, and nobody goes to see—well, East Durham. I had never seen it before, though I had often been quite near to it. I did not really want to see it now, for I knew that it would be ugly and I had had enough of ugliness; but I felt that I should be a fraud, on this particular journey, if I went sneaking past East Durham. Several times before, during this journey, in Nottingham, Stafford, the West Riding and Lancashire, I had been on the edge of mining districts, but so far I had kept out of them. Here was my chance to visit an area that, so far as it was industrial at all, was a mining area and nothing else. I had to have one good stare at it. So there I was, on the Sunderland Road.

We passed over the high level bridge at Sunderland, and I caught a glimpse of the misty Wear, far below. It was not exactly crowded with shipping. Though there is, I believe, considerable unemployment and distress in the town, it looked fairly prosperous, clean and bright that morning. There are a lot of Jews in Sunderland and on the way we passed a large synagogue, which looked as strangely out of place there as a herd of camels would have done. Along the coast road between Sunderland and Seaham Harbour we came upon quite a number of men riding or wheeling bicycles loaded with two or three small sacks of coal. I heard afterwards that these men descend very steep and dangerous cliffs near Seaham Harbour and pick up coal from the shore. They were now going to Sunderland to sell the coal. Those people who still believe that the working folk of this country live in an enervating atmosphere of free bread and circuses might like to try this coal-picking enterprise for a day or two, just to discover if it is their idea of fun. To some of us it hints at desperation. When a drudging and chancy job of this kind is popular in a neighbourhood, it is reasonable to suppose that conditions are anything but easy in that part of the world.

Seaham Harbour itself is like no other town I have ever seen. It is a colliery town on the coast. It looks as weird as a cart-horse with scales and fins. Its position on the edge of the sea did not relieve it of any of the usual dreariness of colliery towns. In fact, to my eyes it seemed drearier than the ordinary inland mining towns, perhaps because the coast itself there has a dirty and depressing look. The sea was dingy and had somehow lost its usual adventurous escaping quality. You could not believe that by setting sail on that sea you could get anywhere in particular. It was not the kind of sea you wanted to bathe in. Perhaps in summer it looks different, altogether more inviting;

but I do not find it easy to imagine that district in sunshine and under a soft June sky. When I saw it winter had set in and apparently taken possession for ever. The town is almost entirely composed of miners' cottages, laid in dreary monotonous rows. They were all so small that they made the whole town look diminutive, as if it were only playing in a miserable fashion at being a town. You saw at a glance that there was very little money about. A couple of shillings here were obviously having to go a long way. Those persistent legends about miners who buy two pianos at once and insist upon drinking champagne would shrivel up and then utterly vanish within five seconds here. This was a place where an old mouth organ or concertina would have to do, and you would be lucky to get beer. Not that I have ever understood the wild indignation of those comfortable middle-class people who at one time went about telling us that miners had been seen drinking champagne. A man who has been working for seven hours at a coal face, crouching in a horribly cramped space about half a mile underground, has a right, if anyone has, to choose his own tipple; and I for one would be delighted if I knew that miners could afford to drink champagne and were drinking it. Horatio Bottomley and his friends, we are told, drank champagne all day for years and nobody protested, though Bottomley and his kind never filled anybody's coal scuttle, only emptied it, and probably never honestly earned for themselves a bottle of stout, let alone cases and cases of champagne. As for Seaham Harbour, it looked as if it could do with, and was not having, that bottle of stout. The town itself was under-nourished. There is no mystery about this. It is a mining town and its citizens are all being shockingly underpaid. They earn about two pounds a week—with luck. A great many of them find that their week's money is nearer thirty shillings than forty. A town on these wages is not a pretty sight.

I went first to Seaham Harbour chiefly because it has a particulary good Settlement, directed by Miss Jowitt. I heard a lot about Miss Jowitt when I was in Gateshead, where she was engaged in this work for about ten years. These settlements or Community Houses are not being run by people who are being elaborately good to the poor. There is about them no Fairchild Family atmosphere. Older readers of this book who do not happen to be acquainted with our distressed industrial areas will do well here if they recall the war years. In these unhappy districts there is a war on, and the allied enemies are poverty, idleness, ignorance, hopelessness and misery. East Durham, like the Tyne, is one of the liveliest fronts. The storm troops of decency and justice and knowledge and civilisation go up there. These settlement houses are their advance posts. The people who are attached to them receive very

EAST DURHAM LANDSCAPE, 1936   *Bill Brandt*

little money, live very frugally in the ugliest and most depressing surroundings, and work at least twelve hours a day. They are the people who know that there is a war on, a war that means something and that will not end in any Versailles treaties. Even yet England is a country that has far more than its share of persons who have regular incomes, people of independent and private means, men and women who more often than not live modestly in the country, and when they are not beagling or fishing, are probably yawning their heads off, wondering what to do with themselves and sometimes wishing they were something more than unknown second-class passengers in the ship of state. I suggest that if some of these people would also realise that there is a war on and that they too can do some bonny fighting in it, they would soon be busier and more useful and happier. And if any reader thinks that this is a priggish suggestion and that the writer of these chapters is rapidly turning himself into a prig as the book grows, I can only ask that reader, before finally passing judgment, to make the same journey that I have made. A few days in North-Eastern England will do the trick. After that, if there is any more talk from that reader about priggishness and sentimentality, he or she should go to Madame Tussaud's and ask to be given a permanent place and attitude there among the other wax dummies.

Once inside that advance post, the settlement house, I stayed on and on there, not taking note of what they were doing, for their activities were like others elsewhere, but listening and talking to the front-line troops there. It would be a poor return for their hospitality and good-natured acceptance of my intrusion into their busy lives if I began to sketch them here as if they were so many minor characters in a novel. I will only say that I was immensely impressed by them all, and especially by the wise and gracious woman who was their captain, by the fresh-faced young man who had come here from another part of the country to take classes in economics and history (though I told him that lectures on economics here seemed impudence), by the librarian who had been a miner himself for years and told me a great deal I did not know, by the German woman who had come to organise the music and to teach its rudiments (she solemnly declared, unless my memory is playing a trick, that these Durham folk were more musical by nature, if not by tradition, than the people in her German town), and by the enthusiastic young man who ran the dramatic side, though his enthusiasm for the drama in almost any decent form seemed to be shared by all the others, probably because it provided an escape from a dreary chaos into a tiny world where everything is artfully coloured, shaped and made significant. There was such a rushing stream of talk that it is difficult to remember a tenth of what was said, but much of what follows I gathered from them, though as my own impressions are by no means left out, I must take the responsibility. So protest, if you must, to me and do not disturb those busy folk in their advance post at Seaham Harbour.

The first impression of my own that was instantly confirmed was that of the strange isolation of this mining community. Nobody, as I observed earlier, goes to East Durham. The miner there lives in his own little world and hardly ever meets anybody coming from outside it. He sees far less of the ordinary citizen than a soldier or a sailor does. I have often heard people say that the miners are indifferent to the welfare of the country at large, caring for nobody but themselves. I doubt if this is any truer of them than it is of any other members of a trade or profession. (I have sometimes wondered if the legal profession could be said to think of the public before it thinks of itself. The monstrous cost of litigation, for example, does not suggest any marked altruism.) But even if the charge were true, there would be every excuse for the miner. Indeed, I could not blame him if he detested the whole coal-burning public. He is isolated geographically. More often than not he lives in a region so unlovely, so completely removed from either natural beauty or anything of grace or dignity contrived by man, that most of us take care never to go near a colliery area. The time he does not spend underground is spent in towns and villages that are monuments of mean ugliness. I shall be told by some people that this does not matter because miners, never having known anything else, are entirely indifferent and impervious to such ugliness. I believe this view to be as false as it is mean. Miners and their wives and children are not members of some troglodyte race but ordinary human beings, and as such are partly at the mercy of their surroundings. I do not want to pretend that they are wincing æsthetes, unnerved by certain shades of green and sent into ecstasies by one particular pink. But the channels of the senses are open to them just as they are to the rest of us. Their environment must either bring them to despair—as I know from my own experience that it frequently does—or in the end it must blunt their senses and taste, harden the feelings and cloud the mind. And the latter is a tragic process, which nothing that calls itself a democratic civilisation has any right to encourage. Let us rid ourselves once and for all of this still familiar, fallacious and despicable 'getting used to' argument, which even now some people use to preserve their own mental comfort at other people's expense. We know that man is one of the most adaptable of creatures. He can exist in deep caves, up in the tree-tops or in the snow and ice; by feeding on nothing but blubber or raw fish and coconut; by wandering naked in tropical jungles or sewing himself up in skins in the Arctic dark-

ness; he has been known to exist for years and years shut up in iron cages or perched on the top of pillars; he can make some sort of shift to live without eyes or legs or arms. No doubt man can 'get used to' almost anything. But what, in the name of Justice, has this to do with us? There have been civilisations of a kind that were deliberately planned so that a few persons could live like demi-gods while all the rest toiled as their slaves, with no rights as human beings. That is not our plan. It is to us an impossible civilisation, if only because our demi-gods would soon begin to think about the slaves; and the more they were worth working for, the more anxious they would be to associate themselves with their less fortunate fellow-creatures. We are on another and better road. We are not so far along it as we generally pretend to be, but there we are. And every time one of us complacently announces that people can 'get used to' notoriously bad conditions of work and living, he or she has taken a step back. Even if the people in question are adapting themselves to a dwarfing and distorting mode of life, it is our business to try and put a stop to the miserable process. If we do not choose to do this, then let us at least be honest and bold and instead of being smooth and glib about people 'getting used to' things, say boldly: 'Well, I don't care. Damn them, I'm all right.'

Your miner, then, is isolated, remote from the rest of the community, and generally in unpleasant surroundings, living in the beastliest towns and villages in the country. He sees little or nothing of you and me. On the other hand, he sees a great deal of his fellow-miners. They work together in an arduous and dangerous trade, in which they have to depend on one another for such safety as they have. The risks are still much greater than most people suppose, only the more spectacular tragedies taking up much space in the newspapers. During the five years ending with 1931 more than 5,000 people were killed in the coal-mining industry, and more than 800,000 were injured. It was estimated that in 1932 nearly one in every five persons employed underground was injured. The women in a mining village live for ever in the anxious atmosphere of the war years. At any moment they may find themselves running, half-demented, to the pithead. Every man or boy who goes underground knows only too well that he risks one of several peculiarly horrible deaths, from being roasted to being imprisoned in the rock and slowly suffocated. We must not make too much of this. Doing a grim, dangerous, necessary job frequently brings its own mental reward. You know, even if a lot of other

Opposite: OUT OF THE CAGE, 1936   *Edwin Smith*

people don't, that you are somebody. It is not a matter of swaggering. The deep satisfaction probably comes from being continually and severely tested and from being saved from the dull folly of taking existence itself for granted. Actually, miners in this country are not swaggerers: not, that is, *qua* miners. I have talked to dozens of them, and have heard them boast about beer, women, football, whippets, fighting, and various other things, but I never heard one of them so much as suggest that he was a fine brave fellow because he worked in a tiny dangerous place far underground. It would, I think, never occur to him that he was. He takes the risks and his own fortitude for granted. That, however, is no reason why we should. There are probably two reasons why we tend to do it. The first is that most of us never see anything of colliery life. The second is that there are so many miners. If there were only ten men in the country allowed to go down and work at the coal face, instead of thousands, those ten men would probably be regarded as national heroes and be given medals. As it is, the miner is one of the most overworked and deplorably underpaid men in the country. I call him overworked, although he may be spending two or three days a week in compulsory idleness, because the output of coal per shift expected of him is much larger than it used to be. And if he earned twice as much as he does now, he would still be underpaid. I know very well that if your supply of coal depended on my walking several miles to a pithead, descending in a cage for half a mile, walking again to the dwindling tunnel where I had to work, then slogging away for about seven hours in that hell, all for something like two pounds a week, your grates would be empty. People could preach economic necessity at me until they were blue in the face, I would not go down. Unless, of course, we all had to go down. Suppose we had a government that began announcing: 'Coal is a national necessity. But it is unjust that one class of men should do this hard, dangerous work at starvation wages. During the war we had conscription. We will now have conscription again, this time for the coalmines, where every able-bodied man shall take his turn, at the usual rates of pay. All men in the Mayfair, Belgravia, Bayswater and Kensington areas who have received Form 5673D will report themselves at King's Cross and St. Pancras stations on Tuesday next, for colliery duty.' What a glorious shindy there would be then! And if you could buy yourself out by subsidising a professional miner, how the wages in East Durham would rise!

Even in East Durham, however, the mining communities are not so completely isolated as they were. Road transport is breaking down that isolation. And so, I imagine, is the work of the settlements, where the intelligent pitman can now learn a great deal about the rest of the world. There is a widening

HOME FROM THE PIT, 1936   *Bill Brandt*

gulf between the sort of men who make use of the settlements and the various educational and cultural schemes and the men who are not interested, who try to carry on in the same old fashion, who more or less resemble the miner of the popular imagination. Betting is still one of the chief resources of this latter type of Durham pitman, as it is, of course, of a vast number of working men all over the country. Lack of money has reduced the size of the bets but not, I suspect, their frequency. It is a fact that men who are not working, and who sit indoors most of the day because a walk would make them hungry, men who are definitely under-nourished, will still make their bets, though only in coppers. We need not be surprised at this, any more than we need be surprised to learn that people who are short of food and clothes will yet spend money going to the cinema. It seems all wrong according to the scale of values of cheerful, well-nourished persons. But people who are feeling depressed, perhaps hopeless, have not the same scale of values. To them the cinema offers a few hours' escape from their lives, which have begun to look like prisons. I have never done much betting or gambling myself, not because I think it wrong, but because the excitement it offers is nothing new to me, for my whole life as an author is half a game of chance and every book or play I write is itself a gamble. But it does not require a great effort of the imagination to understand the attraction of betting for a man who is leading a miserably drab and confined existence. He can spare the sixpence; there is the fun of deciding on his horse, greyhound or football team; there is the excitement of the race or the match, even though he is not there himself; and then there is the possibility of winning ten or twenty sixpences. I think the man is a fool, simply because I know very well that he will lose far more than he will ever win, and that he is not really getting value for money for all the sixpences he has lost. But he is not a fool past my comprehension. I think every man on the dole or on short time and cut wages, and especially a man with a wife and children, should be told quite firmly that he cannot afford to make bets and that he is indulging his idiocy at the expense of the folk dependent upon him. The law, as we know, does everything to make his betting difficult for him. But probably the best method of curing him—for he is almost sure to be a childish fellow, nothing but an overgrown schoolboy—is to destroy this legend of sportsmanship that is still associated with the habit of losing your money to bookmakers. England is a country that officially discourages betting and gambling and at the same time socially encourages them with these popular ideas of a sporting life. A working class that takes its scale of values from that of eighteenth-century squires is obviously heading straight for the gutter. Somebody ought to write a book tracing in detail the workings of an aristocra-

PITHEAD CONVERSATION PIECE, 1936   *Edwin Smith*

tic land-owning tradition in present-day English social life. Even the Durham miner would be in that book. But not the miners who make use of the lecture courses and the books offered to them by the settlements and Community Houses. They are looking a lot further than the world in which the height of successful achievement is represented by a Derby winner.

I met some of their wives, sitting round a fire in a sewing circle. They were worn but neat and smiling women, mostly on the small side. Their frank talk about their men's wages was not pleasant to listen to. They were glad to see me and were neither resentful nor whining, but nevertheless they made me feel like a fat rich man. And I object to feeling like a fat rich man. That is yet another reason why we must clean up this horrible dingy muddle of life.

SEARCHING FOR COAL, EAST DURHAM, 1936   *Bill Brandt*

Nobody can be happy in it, for only an insensitive person can be oblivious to it, and I cannot see how anybody so thick and numbed can know real happiness. I will make this a personal protest. (After all, this is my journey and my book.) As an unusually hard-working, anxious author, heavily loaded with responsibilities, an Atlas of a scribbler, I object to a state of things that can make me feel, even for a moment, like a fat rich man. I ought to have had more sense and kept away from the place, from that circle of women sewing on the razor-edge of life. Most of my fellow-authors do not go blundering in like that; they never go near these uncomfortable places; they continue writing their charming stories about love affairs that begin in nice country houses and then flare up into purple passages in large hotels in Cannes; they have some sense and so never feel like fat rich men. The younger women among those miners' wives were emphatic on one subject. *Their* sons were not going into the pits. No more coal-mining in the family for them. And when a North-country woman begins a statement with '*My lad*' in that tone of voice, you may depend upon it that unless her lad is peculiarly obstinate he will not do what she says he must not do. In these parts the women have far more influence than they would appear to have at first. There is a matriarchal principle at work up there. It is generally assumed among them that although men have the muscle and perhaps, for contriving, arguing, book-learning purposes, the brains, women have the *sense*, the *gumption*. (I take this to be Shakespeare's view of the sexes, and the best one going.) If these women have definitely decided against the mines, thereby probably breaking a family tradition, there will soon be a lot of young men in East Durham looking for other kinds of work. It is not because a pitman's life is hard and dangerous. These women, the wives and daughters of pitmen (and perhaps I ought to explain here that in Durham collieries are always 'pits' and miners 'pitmen'), know all about that, and are ready to take the chances their mothers took. But they see no reason why their lads should work in the pits for wages that look more like pocket-money than real pay. Can you blame them? For my part I did not find them resentful enough, though no doubt the less resigned spirits among them do not favour sewing circles. I am always hearing middle-class women in London saying that they could do with a change. They should try being a miner's wife in East Durham.

[2]

One of the young men who had come from another county, to earn a bare living among this ugliness, in order that he might take part in the adult edu-

cational movement here, was my companion and guide during a short exploration of the district. We went by car. On the way he told me that the local
miners have a curious lingo of their own, which they call 'pitmatik'. It is, you
might say, a dialect within a dialect, for it is only used by the pitmen when
they are talking among themselves. The women do not talk it. When the pitmen
are exchanging stories of colliery life, usually very grim stories, they do it in
'pitmatik', which is Scandinavian in origin, far nearer to the Norse than the
ordinary Durham dialect. It should be an excellent medium for grim tales of
accidents far underground, the sagas of the deep pits. One characteristic of
the local life that astonished this young lecturer was the people's passion for
jazz bands, their own bands and not merely those heard on the wireless. Even
the children have rudimentary jazz bands of their own, and they have parades
in fancy costume. This I take to be a desperate attempt to bring some colour
into the life of the place. After a week or two there, I think I should be blowing
through a paper-covered comb with the noisiest of them. You must make
something happen in that dreary landscape.

The country itself was very queer. Running across it, like great cracks, were
the narrow valleys called 'denes', where there was usually a rushing stream,
and perhaps some trees. These were pleasant enough, often quite picturesque.
But as their charms were hidden away, well below most of the road levels,
you did not see them but only saw what looked like a featureless and desolate
plain, darkly studded here and there with pitheads and 'tips'. It did not seem
an English landscape at all. You could easily imagine that a piece had been
lifted out of the dreary central region of some vast territory like Russia or
America, then dropped on to this corner of our island. True, I saw it on a
dull November day, when nearly all the colour had been drained out of the
world. The scene, as I remember it, was a brown monochrome, except where
an occasional pithead brought a black stain into it, or a cloud of steam showed
a distant little curl or two of white. I must go and look at that landscape
again in a different light, in May or June; though it is hard to believe that
the calendar up there ever reaches May or June. We passed through several
villages that looked hardly more than slums that had been scattered along
the road. This odd ribbon development is fairly common in colliery areas.
The last village we visited, however, had been built on another plan. If there
is a queerer village in all England than this, I have never seen it, and I do
not know that I want to see it. Even in East Durham, this village of Shotton
is notorious. It is not very long since I was standing in its one street; I have
before me, as I write this, a sketch of it, now sadly smudged, that I did in
my notebook, together with some notes that I made on the spot; but even

so it seems incredible. I cannot help feeling that I shall be told that there is no such place, that I have invented my Shotton; and already I have examined no less than three good maps and have failed to find it. If I had been completely alone when I saw it I think that now I should be accusing myself of creating a weird Shotton fantasy, as a symbol of greedy, careless, cynical, barbaric industrialism. But my friend the lecturer was there, I know, and I can remember talking to several people; so some of it must be true. Imagine then a village consisting of a few shops, a public-house, and a clutter of dirty little houses, all at the base of what looked at first like an active volcano. This volcano was the notorious Shotton 'tip', literally a man-made smoking hill. From its peak ran a colossal aerial flight to the pithead far below. It had a few satellite pyramids, mere dwarfs compared with this giant; and down one of them a very dirty little boy was tobogganing. The 'tip' itself towered to the sky and its vast dark bulk, steaming and smoking at various levels, blotted out all the landscape at the back of the village. Its lowest slope was only a few yards from the miserable cluster of houses. One seemed to be looking at a Gibraltar made of coal dust and slag. But it was not merely a matter of sight. That monster was not smoking there for nothing. The atmosphere was thickened with ashes and sulphuric fumes: like that of Pompeii, as we are told, on the eve of its destruction. I do not mean that by standing in one particular place you could find traces of ash in the air and could detect a whiff of sulphur. I mean that the whole village and everybody in it was buried in this thick reek, was smothered in ashes and sulphuric fumes. Wherever I stood they made me gasp and cough. Out of one of the hovels there a queer toothless mumbling old fellow came pointing and peering and leering, first at the 'tip' and then at us, but neither of us could understand what he was saying. Perhaps he was the high priest or prophet of the belching black god up there. We retreated a few yards, into the roadway, where we found the landlord of the inn standing at his door. He did not know the height of the giant 'tip', but said that the atmosphere was always as bad as it was then and that sometimes it was a lot worse. And it had always been like that in his time. So it must have been, for a pile of smoking refuse as big as a hill cannot have grown in a year or two. There must have been a lot of labour put into the ground and a lot of wealth taken out of it before the 'tip' began to darken the sky and poison the air. I stared at the monster, my head tilted back, and thought of all the fine things that had been conjured out of it in its time, the country houses and town houses, the drawing-rooms and dining-rooms, the carriages and pairs, the trips to Paris, the silks and the jewels, the peaches and iced puddings, the cigars and old brandies; I thought I saw them all tumbling and streaming out, hurrying away from Shotton—oh, a long way from Shotton—as fast as they could go. But I did not stay long, staring, with my head tilted back. The giant 'tip' saw to that. I began coughing again, not being eruption-proof. 'Let's get out of this horror,' I said hastily, and out we got. In two or three minutes the wretched village had disappeared, but the 'tip' was still there, the hill that had come out of the deep earth. I hope it will always be there, not as a smoking 'tip', but as a monument to remind happier and healthier men of England's old industrial greatness and the brave days of Queen Victoria.

Any other place in the neighbourhood would, I hoped then and still hope, have seemed an anti-climax after Shotton. So I asked to see no more. I went off thinking how fantastic it was that in our political theory the folk who live in Shotton, at the foot of that steaming hill and smothered with ashes and fumes, are as good as anybody else, and have votes. Votes! You would think that they were not supposed to have even noses and lungs. You would imagine that they were held to be members of a special race, born tip-dwellers. It was hard to believe that Shotton and, let us say, Chipping Campden in the Cotswolds were both in the southern half of this island of ours, not more than a good day's motor journey from one another, both under the same government. No doubt it was fortunate for England that you could dig down at Shotton and find coal. But it did not seem to have been very fortunate for Shotton. The Cotswolds were to be congratulated, it seems, on their lack of coal deposits. All this part of Durham, I reflected, had done very well in its time for somebody, but not, somehow, for itself. There had been a nasty catch in this digging-for-coal business. Not for everybody, of course: the ground landlords and royalty owners had not done badly out of it, and I did not notice anybody resembling one of them hanging about Shotton. I fancy they take their sulphur elsewhere and in another form. 'Is there anything else you'd like to see?' my companion asked. I thanked him. 'No,' I continued, 'there's nothing more I want to see here. Not for a few more years, I think.' You will notice that I expressed no wish to go down a mine. I had been down a mine before, and as everybody at some time or other must have read a detailed account of a coal-mine, there is no need for me to describe one. Since I was buried during the war I have taken a dislike to narrow little passages half a mile underground. I am heartily glad that I have not to go down a mine. I can think of fifty different reasons why I am delighted not to be a miner. Many of those reasons have already been advanced in this chapter, but I can immediately think of many others. For example, miners are always being abused by the over-ground people. If miners go on strike they are told they are unpatriotic scoundrels, because a large supply of coal is an urgent

PITMEN'S SUNDAY MORNING, 1936 *Edwin Smith*

national necessity. But if miners suggest that the supply of coal, being an urgent national necessity, should be entirely controlled by the state and not left to a chaotic private enterprise that is no longer either private or enterprising, they are told once more that they are unpatriotic scoundrels, the bought spokesmen of Red Russia. Their wives are no better off. While they are wondering where the next day's dinner is coming from, a few million people in London are still enjoying fanciful mental pictures of miners' wives dropping empty champagne bottles into the works of their beautiful pianos. And perhaps their children are the worst off of all, for they grow up in the ugliest possible surroundings, with not a garden in sight, and no nice little visits to the seaside, live in houses not big enough even for one coal-blackened man and his anxious woman, know that they must not follow their fathers and grandfathers into the pit, and cannot see, as they grow older, the ghost of another sort of job in sight. When I was a boy there was a popular sentimental ballad, which we used to burlesque heartily, called, 'Don't go down the mine, Daddy'. We did not know then that we were joining in a prophetic chorus, roaring out the profoundest wisdom.

BEVERLEY MINSTER, 1938   *Val Doone*

CHAPTER FOURTEEN

To Lincoln and Norfolk

[1]

Two mornings later it seemed as if I awoke in another England. The northern desolation had been banished. My face was turned away from the Tyne and from the East Durham coalfields. Even the weather temporarily conspired to persuade me that I was now looking towards another England. There was neither fog nor heavy rain. From my bedroom window I could see, across gardens of freshening green, the towers of York Minster, only a shade more substantial than the smoky pearl of the sky, ready to float away at a sign, like Aladdin's palace. The trees in the gardens were bare and black so that their branches made a pretty tracery against the green. The morning itself, at that hour and for two or three hours more, was clean out of season. It

was April or a most lamb-like March. I took the road to Barmby Moor like
a man reprieved. That road, through Barmby Moor to Beverley, seemed to
me to cut through a most delicious landscape, at once homely and remote.
The land rose in shallow terraces, all charmingly laced with those black
branches I had noticed in the gardens at York. These, I suppose, were the
wolds. But you had the huge sky of flat countries, and on this sky the morning
worked furiously, as if it were one of our old landscape painters. It suddenly
swept curtains of cloud across the sky, pulled down showers of rain, poked
a little hole here and there into the clearest azure, and for a long time hung
out a gigantic rainbow in the most shamelessly romantic fashion. Old Turner
himself might have been up there, pulling the strings. Below this fine extravagance of lighting, the flat levels of land, the fields and hedgerows and farm
buildings, were never the same for two moments together but were unfailingly
appealing. It was Arcadia with a faint Dutch flavour. Durham might have
been a thousand miles away, or lost in another age. This south-east corner
of Yorkshire, which is not on the way to anywhere but Hull, has a curiously
pleasant remoteness of its own. You feel there that you are a long way from
anywhere but you also feel, for once, that it is a good thing to be a long way
from anywhere. There is none of that awful homelessness, that little lost-dog
feeling: you do not know where you are but it is all as good as bread. There
are some charming villages on the way. One of them—I think its name was
Bishop Burton—gave me the most entrancing glimpse of a pond, old walls
and red roofs. Within a second, I had settled there and was done with the
world: the bookish hermit of Bishop Burton. It was that kind of place, one
of our ten thousand might-be homes. I was expecting Beverley, and yet when
it came, suddenly towering in that pretty rustic flatness, it was, as these things
always are, an overwhelming surprise. To see Beverly Minster suddenly hanging in the sky is as astonishing as hearing a great voice intoning some noble
line of verse. I am no Catholic, no mediævalist, no Merrie Englander—though
I have seen things on this journey that have come nearer to converting me
than all their books—but I cannot help asking myself and you why our own
age, which boasts of its conquest of material things, never seems to offer us
here any of these superb æsthetic surprises. You go up and down this country
and what makes you jump with astonishment and delight is something that
has been there for at least five hundred years. And it is not its age but its
mere presence that does the trick. If you want to know the difference between
working for the glory of God and working for the benefit of debenture-holders,
simply take a journey and keep your eyes open. I find it difficult to believe
in the God who inspired the creators of Beverley Minster. But I am beginning

to find it even more difficult to believe in the debenture-holders who inspired the creators of the Black Country slag-heaps and the Durham 'tips'. If it has to be a choice between Beverley and Jarrow, write me down a mediævalist.

So I came again to Hull, after many years. I found I could not remember anything about the city except that it has a railway station called Paragon, from which I took a train home, twenty years ago, when I landed there from the Continent. I had never been to Hull since. Unless you should happen to be going to one of the Baltic countries, Hull is out of your way. You cannot pass through it to anywhere. The long wide estuary of the Humber cuts it off from the south. It is not really in Yorkshire, but by itself, somewhere in the remote east where England is nearly turning into Holland or Denmark. It is a large and growing city, with a fine trade of its own in timber, grain, oil-seed, fruit and fish; but nevertheless it is one of those places you must determinedly visit and not one of those places you are always arriving at by accident. I went to the hotel at the station and found myself for once in a brand-new bedroom, for a whole floor had just been opened. As I have complained about hotel bedrooms more than once in this chronicle, I must put on record that this was a reasonable approximation to what an hotel bedroom should be: it had running water, of course; good lighting; an amusing little electric fire set about two feet from the floor; and a comfortable armchair. I soon needed that electric fire, for the almost April morning had gone and in its place was a cruel sleety day that might have been brought over in the last ship from Finland. But even the weather—and I never knew such a place for icy rain—could not make Hull look as cheerless as most big ports. It had an air of prosperity. The actual figures for local trade have not actually been very brilliant these last few years, and you could easily prove from them that it has suffered as much from the depression as most of the other larger ports. But if atmosphere is more truthful than statistics—and I believe it is—then Hull has been fortunate. It has not the usual down-and-out look, nor any suggestion of stagnation in the docks. Something of the outward character of the Scandinavian and Baltic countries with which it trades has crept into the appearance of Hull. It has a cleanish, red-brick look. Go to big ports like London and Liverpool and you find the docks themselves and all the roads leading to and from them buried in a thick gloomy atmosphere, as if they were the last places the daylight found and the first it left. They are regions of huge dark walls, mud and smoke and perpetual winter dusk. Hull has none of this terrifying murk. Its docks have daylight in them. The roads leading to them are honest roads and not Stygian avenues in warrens of darkness. Hull is the third port in the country. All the figures known to the Board of

Trade will not convince me that it is not relatively well off. It certainly has the air of having escaped the depression, or at least the lower depths that the Mersey and the Tyne have known. Even with icy rain flaying the streets, there were plenty of people about, and not out-of-works but brisk shoppers and spenders. These people are pleasant but queer. They are queer because they are not quite Yorkshire and yet not quite anything else. They are, in fact, citizens of Hull, like their fathers and grandfathers before them. Unlike many ports, Hull has not a population that has drifted there from all over the place; partly because it is not one of these cities that have grown very rapidly and have about them a faint fungus odour. It was founded by Edward the First, and it has been growing steadily ever since. It is still growing.

The docks now belong to the London and North-Eastern Railway Company, and one of its officials, a Hull man, showed me round. I saw more timber than I have ever seen in my life before; there seemed to be miles of it. I may have seen some of that very timber being loaded in Vancouver Harbour when I was there two years ago. But the great King George Dock does not handle timber but grain. At the end of the long row of electric elevators is the enormous Silo, into which you can pour 40,000 tons of grain. We climbed to the top of this strange monster, with its elaborate internal organisation of conveyor belts and giant bins, and found ourselves on what must have been the coldest and slipperiest roof in England. From there, however, we had a noble view of the Humber, with the whole seven miles of Hull's dock-front below us on one side and across at the other side the mysterious smudge that was New Holland. It was good, even though one's eyes were watering, to see an estuary that had ships on business in it and not merely rows of ships lying up. Hull is the great port for lighters and barges, because an unusually big proportion of the cargoes arriving there is carried on by water, after being transhipped. You could, in fact, go to almost any large town in England from here and never set foot on shore, by using the Ouse, the Trent, or the canals. I was shown one tidy-sized vessel, in dock not far away, that has a very odd routine of her own. She is a small old liner that has been converted into a fish-carrier. Early every spring she sets out for Iceland and Greenland with a skeleton crew, picks up Icelanders, and then goes fishing in Arctic waters, until her refrigerator holds are crammed full with halibut and cod. Then she returns and docks, selling her two thousand-odd tons of fish, not in a lump, but day by day, not, I take it, without some consideration of the prevailing market prices. There are two of these Arctic fishing liners.

Hull has an enormous trawling fleet, and I was taken to see a new trawler being completed in the old Prince's Dock, which is in the centre of the town,

HULL HERRING DRIFTER, 1935   *Hull Daily Mail*

where you can have trawlers and trams almost running into one another. (You have the same odd mixture in Bristol.) There were riveters, engineers, carpenters, and painters at work on her, so that it was hard to move about, but I managed to see about half of her with the prospective skipper, who proudly showed his chart-room and told me that the vessel would do over eleven knots and carry, in the best season, about eighteen men. These Hull trawlers do not fish the North Sea but sail up to the Arctic and may be away for three weeks. I liked the look of this new one, but I can think of many things I would rather do than go plunging about in the northern seas, somewhere between North Cape and Spitzbergen, in such a craft, with seventeen other fellows and a great deal of ice and fish. But the skipper's face, a young and clean-shaven one, lit up every time he mentioned her. He was the bridegroom, and there, in Prince's Dock, noisy with hammerings and smelling of paint and varnish but his own and beautiful, was the bride. And to understand how far he would probably take her on their honeymoon trip, you should get a big atlas and turn to the North Polar Chart.

Later in the day, with sheets of rain still falling outside, I smoked a pipe or two in the private office of one of the oldest firms of shipping agents, and talked to its senior director. He was, as they all are, a Hull man, and began by talking about the changes he had known. Among other things, he told me that in his youth the smaller coasting ports really had an authentic W. W. Jacobs flavour. Although no enemy of the railway company and appreciative of its enterprise, he disliked its possession of the docks, which should, he declared, be under the control of a Harbour Board, as in London. Also he condemned the recent developments in town-planning that had resulted, here as elsewhere, in the creation of new workmen's quarters outside the town. The men, especially the dockers, should have been re-housed in their old districts, within a stone's throw of their work. Most of the dockers have no regular employment; they have 'to stand a ship', which means going down to the docks to see if they are wanted, early in the morning and then again in the afternoon. If there is no work for them on the morning shift, they can do nothing until the afternoon. When they lived close at hand, they could 'stand the ship' on a cold winter's morning and return at once to their firesides, if not wanted, and keep warm and dry until they tried again in the afternoon. But now that they live a bus or tram ride away, they do not want to make the long journey back home if there is nothing for them in the morning, and so they hang about—or alternatively spend money they can ill afford on shelter and hot food and drink—until the afternoon. Thus they are worse off than they were before, simply because they have been removed so far from their work. Their womenfolk especially grumble about it. All this seems sound reasoning as far as it goes; though it is rather pitiful that, first, dockers cannot be paid enough to make a twopenny bus-fare no great matter, and that, secondly, in these days of telephones, it should be necessary that they should have to travel several miles without knowing whether they are required or not. I would have thought, in my ignorance, that if a fairly large number of dockers have been re-housed together outside the city, a little elementary organisation at both ends, a telephone message or two from the docks to some little office near where the men live, could soon put an end to these futile journeys and this waiting about in the cold and wet. But there may, of course, be difficulties I do not understand. In any event, there is a good deal to be said in favour of building on the old sites, instead of going outside, a long way from places of work, and there destroying a good piece of country. We ought to make up our minds to use all the space inside our towns, without overcrowding, of course, and then to keep as much as possible of the surrounding countryside unspoilt. For my part, I would much rather live in the centre of a town and have quick access to unspoilt country, than live in a wide wilderness of little bungalows, in neither honest town nor country.

My acquaintance, the shipping agent, went on to say that a foreign friend of his had just been criticising our habit of living well outside the cities in which we work. 'You people,' said this foreigner, 'should have bungalows and cottages in the country where you could spend two or three months in summer—as we do. But then the rest of the time, especially in winter, you should live here in Hull. You could then have a good social life.' My acquaintance, who lives in the country himself, confessed that there was something in this criticism, and admitted that he and his wife knew little of the social life they had once known. As there were a great many others, substantial citizens, who also lived a long way out of the city, the social life of the place was not what it had been. And this habit, he pointed out, had a bad effect on many things, notably, the theatre. He himself had been a constant playgoer in the old days, but now that he lived so far away he rarely stayed in the city to visit a theatre. And there were dozens like him, all of them men of standing and comfortably off. It was he himself who pointed out how bad this was, but I was quick to agree with him. I think the foreign critic was right. It would be much better if our provincial citizens lived in their cities, except during the summer months, instead of merely working in them. This habit of living outside, which owes much of its growth to the increased use of motors, explains in part the social disintegration that one notices in so many provincial cities. The very people who, at one time, would have been the chief supporters of local music and drama and so forth now spend their evenings with bridge and the wireless twenty-five miles away. That is one reason why the provincial theatre is not what it was. The competition of the cinema has of course done something, and so have the cheap bad touring companies, but the fact that the richer citizens no longer live in the city partly explains the decline. (There is an excellent little repertory theatre in Hull, but it has a hard struggle to keep going.) In spite of so many prophecies to the contrary, we are now less urban than our fathers and grandfathers were; the country-gentleman tradition is livelier to-day than it was twenty-five years ago; and I understand there are far more people hunting now than there were before the war. Men of the director or manager kind have moved, or are moving, out of the city, and tend to be interested in it only as a place in which to earn money. I have noticed in more than one big provincial town that the old residential districts, where once the solid citizens lived in comfortable rows, have fallen from majesty and grace, and are given up to dentistry, corsets, boarders, and estate agents' boards. The result is that the various social and artistic activities of these towns are

now chiefly organised by people who belong to the employed and not the
employing class, people who cannot afford to live miles away and who also
cannot afford to spend much money on these activities. A further result is
that these activities themselves are taking on a new character. For example,
the only theatre that is really alive in many of these towns is one in which
speeches that challenge the existing order of things receive the loudest applause. Thus I suspect that this retreat of the wealthier and more conservative
classes from a full urban life in the provinces may produce—probably is
already producing—some curious results, which will ultimately be more dis-
tressing to those classes than to the rest of us.

Next morning I was up in good time, for I had arranged to go round the
Fish Market. They claim there that it is the finest in the world. Most of us
still think of Grimsby as pre-eminently the fishy place, but now Hull beats
Grimsby—for sheer quantity, if not for quality. Last year's catch approxima-
tely weighed 215,000 tons and was sold for over two and a half million pounds
sterling. Fishing is the biggest industry of the city. Its fleet of trawlers are
very up-to-date, long-distance craft, which use wireless, direction-finders,
depth-sounding apparatus, and every other scientific device that can possibly
help them to reap the deep seas. So off we went, through a raw morning, to
St. Andrew's Docks. It was cold on the way, and it seemed colder still when
we arrived there and found ourselves surrounded by dead fish, ice, and blue-
handed porters. It was not, I was promptly told, a good morning. It looked
good enough to me, for it did not look as if there could be a cod left in the
Northern seas. On one side was a misty and pleasing confusion of masts and
funnels, finely tangled in the silvery mesh of the morning; and on the other,
where we were standing, was a tremendous perspective of 'kits', the open wood-
en barrels, about three feet deep, in which the fish is packed after it has been
sorted. We looked down on an apparent infinity of cod and codlings. But
before making their nearer acquaintance, I was taken round the central building of the Market. Hull is very proud of this building. It contains the merchants' offices, banks, railway offices, and a post office. I had to inspect all
these, which were not very different from the various offices one sees anywhere,
except that they were surrounded by leagues of dead fish and that their hours
are not the same. They must open in the small hours— and a very cold dark
business it must be too—and I suppose when I looked in upon them, it was
well past their noon. Fantastic working hours of this kind have an atmosphere
of their own. I believe that if I were a clerk, I would prefer them to the ordinary
hours. To set out for work in the very black of the night, to see the dawn
break over the cash-book, to be finishing when other fellows are just settling

down to the day's grind; all this would please me, give the job an urgency and romantic flavour; you would always feel you were working somewhere between Christmas Eve and a declaration of war; and, not least, these must be jobs at which you have to be sustained by frequent cups of tea. The room I liked best, however, was the trawler owners' and merchants' club, which smelled cosily of sausages and cigars and had a chart in it showing the position of all the trawlers still out. After eating your sausage, which you have earned, having been up since before dawn, you light your cigar and stand in front of that chart, wondering how the *Annie Brown* is getting on somewhere off the Murman Coast. I remember reading a novel in with the hero, in the very first chapter, rebelled against being a wholesale fish merchant, like his uncle, on the ground that such a career was too painfully prosaic. That novelist can never have known anything about fish merchants. He ought to visit Hull. You can justly object to this fishy life because it is too wildly romantic and speculative and keeps such queer hours; but it is monstrous to suggest that it is prosaic. It offers you a better gamble than Monte Carlo, and a more poetic atmosphere.

We descended into the actual Market, among the ranged kits. It was very raw down there, among the cod and codling and the ice and salt. The breath of the Arctic was stinging our cheeks. We too might have been just off the Murman Coast. Cod, of every possible size, easily dominated the morning's catch. I saw only a few halibut, but these were of gigantic size, lying there like murdered Roman emperors. What a pity it is that this generous fish is not so exciting to taste as it is to look at, blanched in death. I had a talk with one of the trawler owners, who told me among other things that the trawler crews were still a race apart, perhaps the last of the wild men in this tamed island of ours, fellows capable of working day and night without food and sleep, when the occasion demanded it, and then also capable of going on the booze with equal energy and enthusiasm. They are intensely loyal to their skippers, he told me, but do not give a damn for anybody or anything else. I could not help thinking it a shame that somebody does not give us a film about these men, slaving and roaring away just round the corner, as a change from anachronistic Wild West heroes or gangster gutter rats. The existence of such fellows, not yet forced into the dreary pattern of cockney clerks and shop-walkers, is yet one more reason for preserving our fishing industry. Let us—for sanity's sake—keep some variety in our manhood. We could also do with more variety in our menus. I was shown several varieties of fish here that were quite useless for the home market because the English, even the poorest, will not touch them. They are re-shipped to the Continent, where folk are either wiser or less fastidious. One of these rejected fish was

FISH IN ST. ANDREW'S DOCK, c.1935 *Hull Daily Mail*

that horny pink fellow known to the trade as 'the swaddy', which is, of course, old-fashioned slang for 'soldier'. I heard a story of one trawler skipper hailing another in the Northern Seas and asking from where he had come. 'From Aldershot,' was the reply, in deepest disgust. 'I've got nothing so far but a load of so-and-so swaddies.' Kits of these fish had been sold that morning at three shillings each, and there would be easily enough in each kit to feed a large family for a week. I am not suggesting that any family should try to feed itself for a week on this fish; but there is nothing wrong with it—the French, whose palate is at least as good as ours, make great use of it, and I fancy I have eaten it myself in France—and it seems strange that this and a few other perfectly edible fish should still be totally rejected in a country where so many people are living miserably on bread and margarine. All the time I was being shown the huge Ice Factory and the Fish Meal and Oil Factories I was wondering whether it would not be possible for an enterprising Ministry of Health to tackle this problem of diet, not in order to bully a lot of poor folk into eating things they do not want to eat, but in order to give the more enterprising housewives among them an opportunity of getting clear of the wretched tea and bread and margarine and fried potato fare without spending any more money. It seems ridiculous that, every day, tons and tons of quite edible and wholesome fish should be brought here and then exported at a cheap rate, simply because there is against such fish a popular prejudice, dating probably from the good old give-me-a-thick-beefsteak days, when we were all hard at work and could live like lords.

I was glad to have had the chance of exploring Hull, even if only in the most perfunctory fashion. It remains in my memory as a sound and sensible city, not at all glamorous in itself yet never far from romance, with Hanseatic League towns and icebergs and the Northern Lights only just round the corner. I do not know if they have much music there, but if they do, they should insist upon hearing the symphonies and tone-poems of Sibelius. If these were played long and loudly enough, I can imagine the stacked timber creaking and stirring and perhaps suddenly putting out a green shoot, and the seemingly dead halibut raising their vast heads. That this paragraph will annoy the typical citizen of Hull, who prides himself upon being a plain and downright fellow, I have no doubt whatever; but he should give it a chance, for he is not so plain and downright as he would have us believe, and neither is that city of his.

[2]

A short but somewhat complicated train journey took me to Lincoln. Fog descended upon the brief afternoon; and there were patterns of frost everywhere. I stamped my feet on deserted station platforms, under dim lights; I travelled in old and empty carriages, which rumbled into the dark plain of Lincolnshire; and I peered through the misted windows at mysterious little stations. It was not a journey in this year, this life. I felt like a family solicitor in a mid-Victorian novel, something by Wilkie Collins or Charles Reade; probably going to some remote Grange to read a tortuous and sinister will. It was quite dark when I arrived at Lincoln itself, so there was no chance of seeing once again from the train that splendid apparition of the cathedral on the hill. There was a strange taxi on duty at the station. It was very tall and very old, furnished inside in red leather, with red leather tassels too; and the general effect was that of a club library. In this queer apartment, perfect for a visiting dean, I climbed the steep hill to the top, for my hotel was near the cathedral. This hotel was a surprise. It was comfortable and civilised. Once inside it, I became myself again. After settling in and indulging in that preliminary prowl familiar to all travellers, I enquired for the proprietor to congratu-

THE JEW'S HOUSE, LINCOLN, 1938   *A. F. Kersting*

late him on his hotel, only to learn that he was away. He is, it seems, a Jew, and I was told that this was not his only hotel in the city. A very smart man, they all said. I could not help reflecting on the odd prominence of Jews in the history of Lincoln. The oldest house in the place is the Jew's House, and in the Middle Ages the Jews of Lincoln were notorious for their supposedly gruesome pastimes. And now, in the twentieth century, it is a Jew who controls the hotel business here, and makes his money looking after the tourists who come to see the Cathedral and the Jew's House. I should like to read a history of the Jews in Lincoln. As this was not the tourist season, there were very few other guests in the hotel. Most of them, I gathered, were there on educational business; and I was delighted to see a couple of examiners cracking a bottle instead of cracking my own poor husk of knowledge.

Before the fire in the lounge, I struck up an acquaintance with an engineer

LINCOLN CATHEDRAL, WEST FRONT, 1938   *A. F. Kersting*

of about my own age, who was having a drink there. It appeared that we had a common friend. He invited me to call at his house, which was only a few hundred yards away, later in the evening; and there I went. Once outside the hotel, you were walking in a mediæval city, and might have been in the twisted, dark, and icy old Paris of Villon that lives for ever in the imagination. It was bitterly cold and the steep streets as slippery as glass. The house I was bound for was on the very edge of the hill, and at that hour, in that light, it might have been clinging to the frozen face of an Alp. We had some good talk. Both of the men present were much-travelled engineers. One knew the East very well; the other knew North America and Russia. 'I remember a party we had in Kharkov,' the latter began one reminiscence by saying, and it seemed to me a perfect opening phrase. Neither was a Lincoln man, but they had been there some years. I was laughed at for assuming, on the word of the guide-books, that Lincoln made agricultural implements. This, it seems, is a standing joke, for the fact is that the city has long ceased to make agricultural implements on any scale worth mentioning, but on the other hand does manufacture things like big excavators, pumps, and oil engines. The tanks used in the war were made here. But not near where we were sitting, at the top of the hill, which is the ancient city, dominated by the Cathedral. The manufacturing Lincoln lies at the bottom of the hill, by the side of the railway. It appears that there is great local snobbery about this hill. To be anybody in Lincoln you must live 'uphill', like my host and his friend, who nearly sent themselves to social oblivion, in their innocence, by first considering residence on the mere plain. Maids wanting a job point out that they have 'uphill experience' and so demand 'uphill' mistresses. In short, a successful social life in Lincoln is essentially uphill work. You labour down below, in the clanging twentieth century, and spend your leisure by the side of the Cathedral, in the twelfth century. I was astonished to learn that the local council had recently pulled down some ancient buildings there and were contemplating further destruction, much to the indignation of my companions, although they were not natives themselves and neither antiquaries nor æsthetes. They grumbled a good deal about the stupidity of the municipal authorities, but were rather surprised when I suggested that they should try to get on the council themselves. I have noticed this before, that there exists everywhere a large class of these sensible grumbling citizens, fully aware of what a town council should do or not do, who never think of offering themselves as prospective councillors.

Next morning I set out early to explore the old town. There was a wind straight from Siberia stinging this summit. Not another tourist in sight; and the inevitable shops filled with brass door-knockers and toasting-forks looked very forlorn. (Who are the people who load themselves with this trumpery brass in every cathedral city?) There were very few citizens about either. There were men with little zinc baths suspended round their necks, all busy throwing sand on the glassy slopes, down which you lean rather than walk. It is odd that in the middle of this immense flatness, we should have a town with streets that seem steeper than any we have elsewhere. A good deal of the exterior of the Cathedral has been restored, and it is nothing like so impressive close to as it is at the right distance, a mile or two away on the plain. But that is not so damaging a statement as might first appear, for few things in this island are so breathlessly impressive as Lincoln Cathedral, nobly crowning its hill, seen from below. It offers one of the Pisgah sights of England. There, it seems, gleaming in the sun, are the very ramparts of Heaven.

That east wind, however, blew all thoughts of idling in the Minster Yard out of my mind. I was not sorry to join my engineer acquaintance of the previous evening, who had promised to take me into the other Lincoln, smoking and spluttering below, and there show me the big excavators his firm was making. We dropped out of the Middle Ages and ran into a little industrial area as typical of our own time as anything that could be imagined. These giant excavators, which sink their great steel teeth into the earth and bite away tons and tons of it in a few minutes, are brutal fellows, and making them is a brutal job. Massive chunks of solid steel have to be planed and drilled to provide parts of these machines. There is about such processes, to a mere ignorant onlooker, a controlled ferocity that is rather frightening. We make a metal harder than any of our ancestors ever knew, and then we proceed to cut and shape it as if it were so much pinewood. You feel in places like these that we have harnessed devils and demons that might break loose at any moment, and begin planning and drilling everything within sight, ourselves included. I saw one machine that was cutting out the teeth in a large cog-wheel, and this machine required no supervision whatever, but once set in motion, quietly went on cutting out teeth until the wheel was finished. There is no need to describe the excavators themselves, as most people, by this time, must have seen them at work. But here there were bigger ones than I had ever seen before, and I was shown a few giants. One monster I examined at some length, and went into the steel cab to see the controls, which were so ingenious that the enormous brute could easily be handled by one man, and not necessarily, I imagine, a very intelligent or experienced man. Yet this one machine could do the work of 800 navvies. This is a small fact that throws a sharply focused light on the industrial world of to-day. At one stroke, 800 manual labourers are obliterated. I do not protest against the fact. What little navvying I did, during the war, I heartily disliked. Let the steel monsters do it, by all means. But I cannot believe that an industrial and economic system, which assumes that 800 men are shovelling away, are drawing wages, are buying food and clothing, can possibly continue functioning properly when the 800 men have been dismissed and in their place is a solitary machine that only asks for one man and a regular feed of heavy engine oil. In other words machines of this kind are obviously revolutionising industry, and if we want to avoid a complete breakdown, it seems to me our economics will have to be revolutionised too. The trouble is, it would appear, that our engineers are miles ahead of us, are already living, professionally, in one world while the rest of us are living, or trying to live, in another world. Either they must stop inventing, or, what is more sensible, the rest of us must begin thinking very hard.

Some of these machines have been adapted for trench-digging, and I was told that a number of them have been sold to at least two foreign governments for that purpose. This is not quite as bad as the armament ramp, in which the very people who tell you that your country is in danger are also busy selling the other folk the very stuff that constitutes the danger, but nevertheless it made me think a bit. There is something peculiarly idiotic about the present state of things. If there is always a real danger of war, then why do governments allow implements of war to be exported, possibly to be used against us? If there is no real danger of war, then why do governments allow such implements to be imported or spend a penny on them? As it is now, we seem to regard armaments or machinery with a military use as so many toys or sporting goods, as if they were of no graver importance than tennis rackets or golf balls. And yet most of us know very well that there are serious differences between Wimbledon and modern warfare. But the nations go on playing a sort of lunatic game, cosily exchanging and accumulating weapons of dreadful destruction. I do not include excavators among these, though, as I suggested to my guide, they could be very damaging weapons of offence on occasion. He agreed, and told me how one of their men, who had taken a machine somewhere out East, discovering that the corrupt native police had arrested his native assistants in order that they should buy themselves out again, promptly moved his great excavator over to the police station and threatened to set it going if the men were not released. The police, rightly jumping to the conclusion that this terrible machine would utterly destroy their station in about four bites, gave way at once. It would be a bad day for Lincoln if all these excavators suddenly went mad, for they would tear up the lower town in an hour or two.

[3]

From Lincoln to Boston is no great distance, but the train makes a leisurely journey of it, lounging along by the side of the river, the Witham, like an angler. I noticed a lot of wild birds, but I cannot tell you what they were because I do not know anything about wild birds. I call them 'wild birds' not because you might expect to see clouds of tame birds in these parts, but because these birds seemed to me quite unusual and exotic. They were an essential part of the remoteness of the district; and I have never been in any corner of this country that felt more remote. That is rather odd, because, after all, I was sitting in a train, and not wandering about moors and fells, miles and miles from a railway and perhaps from a house. This South Lincolnshire country, first Kesteven and then Holland, is no dreary uninhabited waste; it is for the most part good settled land; and civilised long before my own West Riding. The sense of remoteness comes partly from its geographical situation, for it is tucked away in an odd corner; and partly from a certain foreign quality in it. They do not call this district Holland for nothing. This is Dutch

England. The very train was ambling along in the Dutch manner. The morning was cold but very bright and clear. There were blue reflections in the ice on the river bank. The farmsteads were cosy red places. Nearer Boston there were windmills, real windmills, hard at work, and not merely sheltering tea-room patrons. Every minute it was all becoming more Dutch and less English. The train curved round and then I saw, for the first time, that astonishing church tower known as the 'Boston Stump'. This tower is not quite three hundred feet high; but nevertheless, situated as it is, it looked to me more impressive, not as a piece of architecture but simply as a skyscraper, than the Empire State Building in New York, with its eleven hundred feet. It is all a matter of contrast. Here the country is flat; you have seen nothing raised more than twenty or thirty feet from the ground, for miles and miles; and then suddenly this tower shoots up to nearly three hundred feet. The result is that at first it looks as high as a mountain. Your heart goes out to those old Bostonians who, weary of the Lincolnshire levels and the flat ocean, made up their minds to build and build into the blue. If God could not give them height, they would give it to Him. And of course, although this tower looks blunt enough from a distance to be called a stump, it is actually a fine piece of architecture, like the grand old church from which it spouts. When Boston was a port of some importance—and at one time, in the thirteenth century, it was the second port in the country—the tower was put to many uses, notably as a lighthouse and a watch-tower. But its chief use, then and now, is as a magnificent means of escape from mere flatness. It lifts the eyes and the heart.

It was market day in Boston. The square was filled with stalls, and any remaining space in the centre of the town was occupied by either broad-faced beefy farmers and their men or enormous bullocks. If there were any marked signs of an agricultural depression in these parts, I missed them. My hotel was in the market square, and it was so crowded with farmers and farm-hands, clamouring for beer, that it was not easy to get in at all. It was now early afternoon and I suppose that business was over for the day. This was the hour when bargains were sealed with a pot or two of ale. Never have I seen more broad red faces in a given cubic capacity. Two more farmers and another seed merchant, and the hotel would have burst. If Boston is like this when agriculture is under a cloud, what is it like when farmers are making money? The very Stump must be splashed with beer and decorated with froth. But this, of course, was their one great lively day in the week; and in an hour or two they would all return to those cosy red farmsteads surrounded by immense fields and probably not see anybody but a neighbour or two until next market day. Moreover, this is not a typical agricultural region. Boston is the market

THE BOSTON STUMP, c.1938 *Herbert Felton*

town of a district of large farms, of 500 acres or so, and these farms are on rich silty lands that are admirable for a great variety of crops. The very process that destroyed Boston's importance as a seaport, pushing it further and further inland, enriched the whole farming community. Now they grow wheat, sugar beet, potatoes, and various garden produce. Though one local cynic said to me: 'Potatoes? Ay, we grow a lot round here. But some of 'em bought a lot o' cheap German potatoes, covered 'em up for a year, and now sells 'em as home-grown. Smartish chaps round here, I can tell you—ay.'

It was not very pleasant exploring the town because the wind was icy and curiously gritty, so that when your eyes were not watering from the cold, they watered to get rid of the grit. There was nothing remarkable about the stalls in the square, for you could have matched them in almost any market town. I looked inside the church, which was empty of visitors. Then I paid my sixpence and began to climb the tower. It was a very long and steep climb, up a staircase that got narrower and narrower and darker and darker until one was threatened with claustrophobia. At last, aching and exhausted, I tottered out on to the tiny platform at the top, where a fiendishly cold wind was raging, making my eyes smart. Through a blur of protective tears I stared down at the curiously Dutch landscape. The little old town was huddled at my feet. It was plain to be seen from here how the centuries had quietly ruined the place as a seaport, for there was the river, which had once found the open sea here, now wandering several miles beyond the town, through green pastures, in search of the receding Wash. But there was no staying long up there, at the mercy of that wind. I went clattering down the long dark steps, accompanied by an ache in both legs that did not completely leave me for several hours. There was still some daylight left at the bottom, and though the sun had gone and it was colder than ever, I decided to walk some way along the river bank.

Much of the old town must have been destroyed, but what remains has a very pleasant quality. Thus, the pantiles everywhere pleased the eye and the mind, as they always do. There were some fishing boats moored along the river bank, and just by the bridge a tramp was sitting warming himself at a fire he had made. He was the only tramp I saw in this part of the world, which is perhaps too cold in winter and not populous enough for them. The distribution of tramps about the country is a subject I should like to see handled by a competent authority. What determines their migrations? Here, for example, they were almost non-existent, so that the sight of one, sitting at his own fireside, called for some comment, whereas in other districts you are never out of sight of them. At one time I lived in the country just north of Oxford, and there, along the Oxford–Woodstock road I saw more tramps than I have ever seen before or since. Winter and summer, in all weathers, there were dozens of them lining that road. I cannot understand why there were more there than anywhere else, though I can understand why they keep clear of this eastern England, with its bleak winds and weary long roads between villages. I might have questioned this tramp outside Boston, but having got thoroughly warm, perhaps for the first time for days, he looked more than half asleep, so I left him alone, to drowse and dream by his fire. Fortunately, it is not an offence to make a bit of a fire for yourself in the open, as it is to sleep in the open when you have nowhere else to sleep. It is worth remembering that the whole twelve apostles would have been liable to summary arrest in this Christian community, simply as vagrants, and quite apart from their subversive doctrines.

Turning at the bridge, I walked back to the town along the other bank of the river, past some little chandlers' shops that appeared to specialise in vast jars of piccalilli, evidently a favourite pickle with the nautical, probably because it offers a closer approximation to a hot meal than anything else you can get out of a cold jar. It was dusk and tea time when I found myself back in the square, where the stall-holders were packing up their unsold toilet sets, linoleum squares, blankets, and chocolate. I went into the cinema café for tea. There were some rural folk in there and, as I waited for tea, I wondered why countrymen should so often have such high-pitched voices. Two tables near me were occupied by girls, and it was curious to see how carefully they had modelled their appearances on those of certain film stars. Even twenty years ago girls of this kind would have looked quite different even from girls in the nearest large town; they would have had an unmistakable small town or rustic air; but now they are almost indistinguishable from girls in a dozen different capitals, for they all have the same models, from Hollywood. It was only the girls here, however, who had this cosmopolitan appearance; the young men looked their honest, broad, red-faced East Anglian selves. Having nothing better to do, I attended the 'first house' of the cinema, which was showing a film version of Maugham's *Our Betters*. It was a poor film, but what interested me was the attitude of the small audience towards it. Either they were very bored or puzzled—or possibly both—but certainly they hardly ever laughed, never applauded, and gave no signs of taking any interest in the picture. You cannot blame them. What have the antics of a tiny remote smart set to do with them? When Mr. Maugham sat down to be adroitly cynical about the marriages of American heiresses—a theme that is more Edwardian than strictly contemporary—he was not thinking about the householders of Boston, Lincs. We talk about the cinema giving the people what they want, but really I am not sure that it does not do less of that than the older forms of popular entertainment. If a little fit-up theatrical company came to this place, they would give their audiences melodrama, broad farce, pantomime; and they would certainly never dream of offering them anything that resembled *Our Betters*. But the cinema is always offering them such things. What pleases Hollywood has to please South Lincolnshire. That week Hollywood was clearly not winning, but as it has already changed the faces of the more enterprising young women of the district, it has some considerable victories to its credit. What a mad mixture it all is, even here, in this remote and decayed little town! The tremendous church tower, the seaport no longer on the sea, the English town that looks Dutch, the chandlers and corn merchants, the farmers and bullocks, the floods of beer, the imitation Greta Garbos and Constance Bennetts alongside the time-old rural figures, the tramp crouching over his fire, *Our Betters*—what a crazy muddle! I brooded over it, a trifle glumly, as I ate my dinner in the hot little grill-room beneath my hotel. And a very bad dinner it was too.

[4]

The next stage of this journey, from Boston to Norwich, I did by road. It was not quite so cold as it had been during the last few days, but there was still plenty of ice about. Nearly all the morning the sky was a uniform darkish grey except in the east, where there was a low band of pale gilt; so that it looked all the time as if dawn were just breaking. Not far out of the town we passed several huge farm waggons, the largest I have ever seen; they were drawn by three horses, two in front, one behind. No farming community that wants to suggest it is not prosperous should use such waggons, which looked like the very symbols of fat harvests and a teeming earth. The road, going to King's Lynn, passed through country as solidly rural as any I ever remember. It was almost as if they were all doing it on purpose, like the manufacturers of children's toy farms. Nearly all the faces we saw were very Flemish: long noses and long upper lips and small eyes, and a self-contained, almost secretive look; you could match them by the dozen in any gallery of early Flemish portraits. I did not stay in King's Lynn, but merely walked round the centre of it. A companion town to Boston, obviously; containing far more impressive old buildings, but lacking that superb tower and, perhaps, that air of being the most remote town in England. It is rather larger, more dignified, and more sombre, though, oddly enough, one of its remaining industries is the manufacture—or is it the creation?—of merry-go-rounds for fairs. This part of Norfolk, I was told, is a great centre for your sporting gentleman farmer, who likes being in the neighbourhood of Sandringham.

Between King's Lynn and Norwich the country lost its distinctive flavour. We were no longer in Dutch England, but solidly in Norfolk, though that, of course, can be Dutch enough in places. I was not paying my first visit to Norwich, though I had never stayed there before. But I must have lunched several times at the Maid's Head, and then spent an hour looking at the antique shops in Tombland. The last time we were there, I remembered, we had bought a John Sell Cotman and a pretty set of syllabub glasses. Now I drove straight to the Maid's Head, a fantastically rambling but comfortable old place, and they gave me one of those Queen Elizabeth bedrooms you find in such hotels. It would have served as an excellent background in an illustration for *Barnaby Rudge*. But then, to my mind, Norwich has the most Dickensian atmosphere of any city I know, except perhaps Canterbury. And this is simply due to the look of the place and not to any strong associations with Dickens. It was dusk before I was able to go out, this afternoon, and I walked into a very gloomy old city—for this was half-day closing—the shops were shut, and Norwich is not brilliantly illuminated at any time. There were very few people about. Tombland was shuttered and deserted. In the narrow old streets running out of it, where the feeble light of occasional street lamps showed you ancient, gnarled and gnome-like houses and little shops, you expected to run into characters from *Edwin Drood* going muffled through the chill gloom. It was difficult to believe that behind those bowed and twisted fronts there did not live an assortment of misers, mad spinsters, saintly clergymen, eccentric comic clerks, and lunatic sextons. Impossible to believe that the telephone could find its way into this rather theatrical antiquity. You peered, in passing, through the lighted window of an estate office, where an elderly clerk was at work so true to type that he looked like a good character actor, and you felt that in there you could buy or rent nothing but remote crazy manors. In Tombland the trams and buses came and went incredibly, like lumbering time machines. Between the Cathedral and the Castle, both hearts of darkness, I spent a spectral hour, roaming about somewhere on the boundaries of dissolution. I had only to stand a moment too long at one of those dim street corners and my car and wireless set and typewriter would be whisked away from me and I would be lost and gone in some dusty limbo. I bought a local evening newspaper and held on to it, to keep myself in present time. I managed to get back to the Maid's Head, though this was a doubtful harbourage in such an hour, for it was so quiet and ancient and mazy, with not a Morris stirring in the interior yard. Undoubtedly I was still in Norwich; but was I in the right one?

TOMBLAND ALLEY, NORWICH, 1938 *A. F. Kersting*

I dined that night with a friend, a Norwich man of some fame and one very knowledgeable about the city and the surrounding district. He lives cosily and conveniently on the outskirts, with a tram terminus at his left hand and a neat little potato crop, of his own growing, at his right. I always find myself happy and at home—though, alas, always far from home—in the cities where I am asked at once, confidently and proudly, what I think of the place. They do it in Bristol and they do it in San Francisco. And of course Norwich is one of these cities. As soon as I had been given my glass of sherry I had to tell them what I thought of Norwich. I answered truthfully that I knew little about it, but that I had always liked what I had seen of it. Like Bristol, it is no mere provincial town; it is not simply an old cathedral city; it is something more—an antique metropolis, the capital of East Anglia. In a very large slice of England, to thousands and thousands of good sensible folk who live and work there, Norwich is the big city, the centre, and has been these hundreds of years. My own native town is more than twice the size of Norwich, but somehow it does not seem half the size. This is not merely because Norwich has its cathedral and castle and the rest, but also because it has flourished as the big city in the minds of men for generations. It is no mere jumped-up conglomeration of factories, warehouses and dormitories. It may be minute compared with London, Paris, Rome, but nevertheless it lives its life as a city on the same level of dignity. It is not a place in which to make money quickly and then to plan a sudden exit. It is not filled with people who are there because they have never been offered a job elsewhere. No, Norwich is really a capital, the capital of East Anglia. I wish it were bigger and more important than it is. Perhaps it ought to be turned into a real capital of East Anglia.

A great many people are coming to believe that government in this country is now far too centralised. Too much work has to be done in Westminster. There is too wide a gap between the local councils and Parliament. These people suggest that England should be divided into four, five or six provinces, and that these provinces should to some extent govern themselves. Their representatives would be able to settle among themselves the merits of a large number of questions. Business in the House of Commons would not be so congested and unwieldy, and Parliament would be able to give its undivided attention to broadly national affairs. Moreover, regional self-government of this kind would do something to revive the spirit of democracy. Under a democratic system politics should be local, so that you can keep an eye on them. Indeed, in a large modern state you need a very elaborately constructed pyramid of representational government, with parochial councils for the base and a national assembly at the apex, in order that the democratic system can work properly. It cannot work properly if legislature is something that is happening, under a cloud of mysterious etiquette, in a distant capital It is a system that assumes that nearly everybody is taking an interest in government. The more difficult it is for anybody to concern himself in political matters, the worse it is for democracy. Centralisation is one of the deadliest enemies of the system. For this reason alone there is much to be said in favour of regional government in England. But I also suggest that such government would bring a new dignity to provincial life, just as it would increase the importance of the various new provincial capital cities, where the deputies or senators would meet. And on any such division of the country into provinces Norwich would be capital of its own region, as it has been, for nearly all practical purposes, these last three hundred years. That, however, is what I meant by wishing, above, that it were bigger and more important than it is. I should like to see it nobly housing the East Anglian senators, who would be as sagacious and weighty a body of legislators as you could wish to find. I heard that the local constabulary are rarely less than ten to a ton, and I believe that the senators would be equally massive, in mind as in body.

The East Anglian is, of course, a solid man. Lots of beef and beer, tempered with east wind, have gone to the making of him. Once he is sure you are not going to cheat him or be very grand and affected, he is a friendly chap; but if you want the other thing, you can have it. The Ironsides were recruited from these parts, which has produced a great many fighting men of all kinds, from pugilists to admirals. Perhaps we of the West Riding brought some of our aggressive qualities from Norfolk. My host reminded me of the connection between the two districts. The worsted trade of Bradford originally came from Norfolk, where Worsted is a village. Up to the Industrial Revolution Norwich had a fine trade in worsteds, but lost it to the West Riding, which had the coal and better communications. And when its textile trade dwindled, Norwich turned to the manufacturing of fancy boots and shoes, chiefly women's, and has continued in that trade to this day. But many of her textile workers migrated to the West Riding; and my host told me that he remembered an old bank cashier saying that in his youth more money orders came to Norwich from Bradford than from any other place. But Norwich was concerned in much more important migrations than these. It was here that so many of the Flemish and Huguenot weavers came; solid and sober families of workers, escaping from persecution. It was intolerance that made us a present of them,

Opposite: AN EAST ANGLIAN, 1934   *Humphrey Spender*

and robbed France of their solid services. The Dutch came here in considerable numbers too, and my friend remembered hearing a sermon in Dutch in the city. Norwich is also the city of Quaker bankers, who were very prominent in the life of the place during the latter half of the eighteenth century and the first half of the nineteenth, during which period the city was a literary and publishing centre and had its own famous school of landscape painters. It was the fact that the Quaker was a man of his word that made him so acceptable as a banker or trader in the eighteenth century, when the junketing squires had to look somewhere for money. You have then a very rich mixture in the city, equally famous for its old churches and its sturdy dissenters. And like all cities with mixed trades—here they are shoes, mustard and starch, ironware, beer—it has escaped the full weight of the industrial depression. Its citizens are proud of the old place. They have a right to be, and I, for one, wish there was more of it. Home Rule for East Anglia!

We had had some talk at dinner about the villages and the local farmers, and the next morning, which was fine and not too cold, we went out exploring the countryside in a small car. It does not take you long to lose Norwich. A few turns down side-roads, once you are past the tram terminus, and you are soon in the true country. We stopped at a village grocer's and general store, known to my friend, and found the proprietor and his son busy setting out their stock, which was beginning to wear a Christmassy look. The little shop was very clean and bright, quite different from the nasty little shops that ask to be swept out of existence in all the larger towns. They were a busy, canny pair, cautious in their statements and given to rubbing their long chins. They had known better times, they admitted, but 'couldn't grumble'. The small farmers in these parts—and they are nearly all small farmers—had, I knew, been having a bad time, and my friend, who is a trustee administering an estate and has had to do business with a lot of them, confirmed this. But he also showed the usual scepticism of those who have to deal with the farming community but do not belong to it. The East Anglian farmer, he declared, is a very stubbornly conservative fellow, who will often insist upon raising a certain crop simply because his father and his grandfather before him always raised that crop, without reference to the needs and conditions of the time. This is the way to be a character, but not the way to make money. He was doubtful, however, about their losses. We called on one acquaintance of his, a middle-aged man farming about a hundred acres, and not, according to report, making them pay. He was a shabby and muddy little man, with carroty curls and stubble, and bright blue eyes. He did not look very intelligent and, for all I know to the contrary, may be a very unintelligent farmer; but truth compels me to say that he talked about his farm and his work quite intelligently; and listening to him, you felt that with so much sense and energy he deserved to make a decent living for himself out of his hundred acres. We wandered about, looking at his beasts, which were in good condition, and at his fields, which were scattered about not very conveniently for him. He told us, among other things, that he listened regularly to the agricultural talks on the wireless. He belonged to old farming stock, and a very bewildered look crept into his honest face when he spoke of the difficulty of making his farm pay. It must be difficult for a farmer, and one of generations of farmers, to understand that his slow traffic with the land and the familiar beasts is a business like manufacturing and selling pins or boots and that the strange antics of men in offices, thousands of miles away, and the weather on the other side of the world, and the rumours of wars, the negotiations of diplomats, the suspicions and panics of fantastic foreigners, the mysterious ebb and flow of credit, can all combine quietly to take his living away from him and finally steal the very acres from under his nose. What is so difficult for an urban outsider to understand, on his part, is how farmers work out their budgets. Clearly their position is quite different from that of the townsman, or the ordinary wage-earner anywhere. To begin with, the farm itself is where he and his family live, so that its rent—or purchase price—includes that of his dwelling-house. Then again, unlike the ironmonger or the bookseller, he can often make his breakfast and dinner off what he is not selling. A farm that contains within itself cattle, sheep, pigs, poultry, potatoes and vegetables, is nothing less than a vast larder, out of which the farmer and his family are taking liberal supplies. Does he credit himself with the value of these supplies in his budget? The point is, he may not make much, but does he need to spend much? Nobody insists upon a farmer dressing neatly in a black coat, striped trousers, shiny boots and spats. He has not to travel every day. He is not compelled to provide his children with expensive holidays, to give them some fresh air. He has not to do any window-dressing of any kind to attract custom or to keep up appearances. He has, I imagine, nothing like the social and charitable demands on his pocket that an urban employer has. If he is regularly attending to his work, then he need not spend a penny getting exercise, as most sedentary workers have to do. He can be in a bad way of business, but it will be a long time before he and his family go hungry. Ultimately, if things go from bad to worse, he can starve, like other men. But does he starve? I ask out of my ignorance. I have met starving engineers and schoolmasters and casual labourers and clerks and miners and sailors, but I have yet to meet a starving farmer. Is this still my ignorance?

We discussed these and similar topics all the way back from the farm to the outskirts of Norwich, where we stopped to have a look at Earlham, the charming old house that appears in Mr. Lubbock's volume of that name; once the home of a fine old banking family, and now the proud possession of the city itself. This is an admirable example of the public spirit of the Norwich citizens. An even better example is found in the city's purchase of land all round the edge of the town, which is now enclosed in a green ring about two miles wide. This is what every city should do. It ought to have been done in London years ago. Not only is the open space valuable in itself, but it also sets a boundary to the city. It is time we discouraged this sprawling practice of our cities, which, instead of spoiling more and more of the surrounding countryside, would be compelled to rebuild their worst districts and to make the best of the area they already occupy. They have played the octopus long enough.

Coming away from Earlham, we began to talk about the literary figures of Norwich, chief of whom are Sir Thomas Browne and Borrow. The house once occupied by the delectable Sir Thomas has been marked by a tablet, to the confusion of a certain well-known directory, which in its 1929 edition included Sir Thomas Browne among the medical practitioners of Norwich. (There is a good short story to be written about some innocent who sent for him—not in vain.) On the edge of the city we met an old nursery gardener well known to my companion. He was the true, old-fashioned Dissenting type: cropped whiskers, shaven chin, and a mouth that turned down at each end; black suit and 'a dicky'; a wooden look that suddenly twinkled; a passion for imparting information. I knew plenty of them when I was a boy—stiff, creaking figures they seemed too, these ancients of days, more like mechanisms, to my young mind, than like flesh-and-blood men; but I doubt if any of them are still living. You would, I imagine, find more of them alive and kicking here in Norwich than anywhere else. Our man was certainly alive and he might be said to have been kicking one of his assistants, who had forgotten to carry out some order. 'And just yew go down to Bewts Chemists,' the old man concluded, 'and ask 'em to put yew up one o' their little bo'l's o' their Memory Mixture—that's what yew go an' dew.' Then he turned to us, with a face made of wood but with a twinkle in his little deep-set eyes. I knew that either he would utter the least possible number of words or, if we found favour in his sight, would immediately impart some information to us and instruct us. We found favour. He began to tell us how to grow roses, and as he, like a superb conjurer, knows the trick of bringing the most extravagantly lovely roses out of the sullen ground, we listened to him with respect. He then told us what sort of winter it would be and from what quarter the prevailing wind would blow. He spoke with far more certainty than the young men who report on the air pressures in Iceland and off the Azores. He knew, he explained, because he had examined the holes made by the tiny shrew-mice, which have information about the coming winter denied to us, and always make their holes away from the direction of what will be the prevailing wind, and dig deep if a hard winter is before them. You cannot, he told us emphatically, just as if we were two small boys he had caught trying to build a planet or two, improve on Nature. And he spoke of Nature—as such people always do—as if he had been a member of the small committee that had first appointed her. He put me back thirty years, into Sunday School. I was delighted to have met him; a good, if narrow man, and a character. How odd that roses, the lovely wantons, should bloom so profusely for him, that he should know far, far more about them than ever the smiling drunken Omar did.

After lunch—and the dining-room of the Maid's Head is the perfect place in which to eat boiled beef, carrots and dumplings—I joined the crowd that was shopping in Queen Street and London Street. It was a fine afternoon; the shops were already stocked for Christmas (which seems to be inalienably associated now, in the commercial mind, with dabs of cotton wool); there were a great many people, both men and women, staring and chattering and popping in and buying; and the city looked very different from what it had done the day before. It had, in fact, a solidly prosperous appearance; and was at once gay and weighty, not unlike one of those cheeses decorated with coloured paper that were now appearing in the grocers' windows. I went into several of the antique furniture shops—Norwich is filled with them—rather in the hope of picking up a good early water-colour drawing than of finding a piece of furniture I wanted; but I was unlucky this time and there was nothing remarkable on view. In one strange old shop I found a long thin man who specialises in making reproductions of old pieces, which reproductions are honestly sold for what they are. (Though what happens to them afterwards may be a different story.) Some of them had taken a good craftsman a year or eighteen months to make, and the workmanship was often better in the reproduction than in the original piece. The value, of course, was nothing like the same. It seems queer that we should take such pains to copy exactly what our forefathers made. They did not copy what their forefathers made, but preferred their own contemporary styles, which matched the age. We have our own styles, of course; I am writing this on a desk that was made this year to my order, a desk that is just as twentieth century in its style as a Chippendale or a Sheraton is eighteenth century; and, moreover, is twentieth century—or, if you like, nineteen-thirty-three-ish—without looking like a fitting in a cocktail bar. And in this same room are two chairs, a desk chair and an armchair, that are as contemporary in design as a Rolls-Royce. At last we are beginning to achieve our own characteristic furniture, good solid furniture too and not merely stunt pieces made of metal tubing; but so far these things are a tremendous extravagance, and to acquire one or two specimens you have to be determinedly self-indulgent. What happened in the reigns of Queen Anne and George the Third? Had you to be extravagant then to acquire those pieces of furniture we now covet? Or did you merely go out and buy a few chairs, a table and a bureau, and find that, without being self-indulgent, you had acquired some delightful pieces? The question is not one of the larger problems of our time, but neither is it entirely trivial.

Back in the hotel, after tea, I met a free-lance journalist with whom I had several friends in common. We had the big fireplace in the smoke-room to ourselves, and over a drink we talked about our trade of writing. He had spent some years as a journalist in America, and put forward the view that our law of libel, which is very much stricter than the American one, gagged the enterprising journalist and favoured corruption in public affairs. He declared that you dare not tell the truth about municipal matters in any English provincial newspaper, whereas in America, if you nosed out some corrupt job—and there were always plenty to nose out—you could put your discoveries into print. Many people will say at once, in reply to this, that public life is not so corrupt here as it is in America; and neither is it, but on the other hand, especially in municipal affairs, it is a great deal more corrupt than such people imagine. During my travels this autumn I have heard a good many stories in proof of this. But until the people concerned are actually in the dock nothing gets into print. Our hush-hush atmosphere is perfect for a cool rascal who is pocketing public money. So long as he looks respectable, does not get drunk in broad daylight, lives with his own wife, he is probably safe. There is something to be said for this journalist's argument. We do not want here the gutter-raking that frequently passes in America as the protestations of a reforming spirit. But on the other hand we need a great deal more freedom than we have at present. Editors and publishers in this country are terrified—and rightly terrified—of the crushing law of libel, which works so badly now that it is actually creating a new branch of blackmail. And it is an ironical circumstance that there are several books on American public affairs, books containing attacks on various American public figures, that are openly sold and read and commented on over there but that have not been published at all in England, because, if the books did appear here, the persons attacked in them would instantly take advantage of our law of libel. This is not a very serious deprivation. It is much more serious that our Press, especially our provincial Press, should be gagged. What with the necessity of pleasing advertisers and the further necessity of escaping libel actions, our editors hardly dare open their mouths. I should like to be in some of our provincial cities for a day or two if some American methods in journalism were applied, and the truth about Councillor What's-His Name and Alderman Such-and-Such was splashed in the headlines. It is easy to imagine a quick descent into muck-slinging, if all restrictions were removed; but surely there is a sensible half-way position, between being gagged and gutter-raking, that the Law could allow us to occupy. Please note the ignominy of that last phrase—'could allow us to occupy.' As if laws were not created for our benefit but were the arbitrary dictates of some capricious monster! How well-drilled we are, and yet how we give ourselves away in these casual phrases!

My Norwich friend dined with me that night at the hotel, where our small table was anchored not far from an enormous one, set out for a fine dinner party. Indeed, it seemed that some local professional man was giving a party there, and just as we were finishing they all came in, splendid in full evening dress but all very jolly. There is no reason why I should mention this, except that to me, obscurely I admit, that solid, civilised and jovial dinner party at the old inn was somehow typical of the city. We left them their dining-room, and went to see *The School for Scandal* at the Maddermarket Theatre. I had heard a lot about this little amateur repertory theatre, with its apron stage and Elizabethan interior. It has done some very good work, especially with miracle plays and the Elizabethan drama; and I knew it was entirely the creation of one enthusiast, Mr. Nugent Monck, who made this very charming little theatre out of an old warehouse. It is a lovely toy; not too comfortable, and rather too dimly lit for my taste, but nevertheless a delicious place. The familiar old comedy was not brilliantly acted, for the company is an amateur one and eighteenth-century comedy needs great polish; but it was pretty to look at, and, by an ingenious use of curtains as scenes, it moved at a great pace; so that one sat there, in that dim little theatre, staring at a flickering dream of brocaded wits and beaux. And how delightful to turn in from dusky old St. Andrew Street and St. John's Alley and find oneself at Lady Sneerwell's. How delightful when the piece was done and Mr. Monck had been congratulated, to wander out again into the ancient streets, where at every corner that held a bit of lamplight you saw a perfect stage set, one after another, with century after century caught and held, in a gable, a bit of heavily shadowed timbering, a fat bulging bay window, a fanlight all Georgian elegance, in tiny spaces of yellow light and with a frosty glitter of stars above the sleeping city.

ELM HILL, NORWICH, 1938 *A. F. Kersting*

Delightful too to have a last drink, sprawling in front of the fire at the Maid's Head, and to hear the honest roars of a Norfolk man as he describes to you his bemused adventures in certain artistic quarters of that remote and fantastic fellow capital city, London. If this same friend of mine had been a Manchester or a Newcastle or a Birmingham or a Leeds man, he would have done what hundreds of us have done and removed to London; but he is not, he is a Norwich man, and there he stays, coming to London as a London man might go to Berlin or Rome, and not hesitating to let out a good East Anglian bellow of laughter when he remembers Bloomsbury and Chelsea and the doings there. One of the last things he told me was that he might be compelled, being a dutiful fellow, to stand for the city council. For my part, I hope to see him Mayor before I die; and promise now to go and see him in the part, peep at him in whatever glorious old mullioned, timbered or bulging bay-windowed parlour the city gives its chief citizen. What a grand, higgledy-piggledy, sensible old place Norwich is! May it become once more a literary and publishing centre, the seat of a fine school of painters, a city in which foreigners exiled by intolerance may seek refuge and turn their sons into sturdy and cheerful East Anglians; and may I live to see the senators of the Eastern Province, stout men who take mustard with their beef and beer with their mustard, march through Tombland to assemble in their capital.

CHAPTER FIFTEEN

To the End

[1]

It is no use pretending that there is not a good fat slice of England between Norwich and old Highgate Village in the borough of St. Pancras. A hundred miles of solid England lie between the two. There are several counties. There are towns, whichever route you try, plenty of towns, all ancient and of good report. At the beginning of this journey, if I had come this way, I would have looked at every one of them and made notes in a little black notebook. But this was the end and not the beginning; I did not even know where the little black notebook was; I had long ceased to consult my guide-book and my economic geography; and being a vain, idle and weak mortal (and if I hadn't been, I should not have been the man for this job), I said that though we were now in Norwich we must be in Highgate Village and home before the day was out. When you consider those hundred miles, those counties, those ancient towns through which we should have to rush, doing nothing but 'making time', as the chauffeurs say, you can see that I was not really completing the journey but suddenly abandoning it, giving it up as a bad job. In the original itinerary I sketched for myself—in that first idiotic flush, when you plan things for a self that is not you at all but somebody three times as strong, energetic, conscientious, determined—there were hopeful references to places like Newmarket, Cambridge, Bury St. Edmunds, Ipswich, Colchester. No doubt I could have produced some pretty paragraphs on Newmarket, which is perhaps more like a place conjured out of an old sporting print than any other in England. Even I, who dislike racing and horsy people, have been enchanted by Newmarket before to-day; by the wide green ribbons of the gallops on the heath, the nodding glossy processions of racers, the old-fashioned monkey-like stable hands, and the equestrian clatter and breeziness of the town itself, which does not really belong to this century at all. A luxury town, if there ever was one. Then, Cambridge. I know Cambridge well enough, having spent three years there, and many an odd day or two since. A lovely old place, far lovelier now than Oxford. But either you are completely and happily at home there or are always faintly uncomfortable, longing to escape from King's Parade and the Trumpington Road. I was always faintly uncom-

fortable, being compelled to feel—and quite rightly too—a bit of a lout and
a bit of a mountebank. No, it was too late to bring Cambridge into this book.
As for returning the other way, and finding Bury St. Edmunds, Ipswich, Colchester, all good bustling market towns that I had seen before and lunched
and dined in, it was too late for that too. I would not set foot in Essex. Because
Essex begins somewhere among back streets in London's eastern suburbs,
some people think it has no mystery, but I know that Essex is a huge mysterious
county, with God knows what going on in its remoter valleys. No Essex for
me. I was going home, and by the shortest route. We would 'make time'. At
this piece of news my driver's face lost that mixed look of distrust, contempt
and irony which it always wears when he is anywhere not within three miles
of High Street, Camden Town. I have seen whole regions of well-advertised
loveliness dwindle and blanch before that look. The further we are from High
Street, Camden Town, the more sardonic it appears. I have never commanded
its owner to drive me into Westmorland and Cumberland, out of sheer com-
passion for those counties. But now, it seemed, sense was returning to the
world; we were to go no more a-roving and asking silly questions, but were
to move steadily at fifty-odd miles an hour in the direction of Gamage's and
the Holborn Empire, without another senseless halt, real travellers 'making
time.' He declared, happily, that we should be home for early tea.

He was wrong. We did not make time. This was to be no journey worth
talking about—except as an ordeal—where cars are washed and greased. Time,
swiftly conspiring with the elements, showed us a thing or two. The first part
of the journey was all right. We went rushing through an empty sunlit East
Anglia, through Thetford, Newmarket and Royston. We reached Baldock and
went roaring down the Great North Road. But then the sun went out. Then
the surrounding country disappeared. Then the top of the road in front
vanished. We had stopped rushing and roaring now. For some time we travelled on twenty yards of road, and it looked always the same twenty yards.
After that the twenty yards were reduced to ten, then five. The cars coming
in the opposite direction, from London, approached us very cautiously in a
haze of orange light. There was, we were told, a fog in London. It seemed
to me that there was also a fog where we were too, and by this time I did
not know where we were. The five yards were further reduced to about two.
The far side of the road soon went, and the near side was uncertain. Sometimes
it was there, and sometimes we lost it altogether. Our view now was restricted
to a large wobbling green rectangle, on which were painted some words on
the subject of furniture removal to all parts of the country. But even between
us and this rectangle the fog was being pumped in all the time. Somebody

might have been squeezing a gigantic tube of shaving cream at us. The woolly
air was loud with the complaints of a long line of cars not allowed to make
time. If the green rectangle went fuzzy and its words disappeared, we crawled
after it. If it stopped, then we stopped. Sometimes figures miraculously
appeared, even faces; mysterious beings who pointed and shouted before being
pulled back into the mountainside of cotton wool. Then the green rectangle
disappeared for ever, and we had to be content with a smaller greeny-yellow
horizon that had a large battered cabin trunk fastened to it with rope. We
watched the cabin trunk: it was all we had. It seemed to be even less certain
of itself than the green rectangle, for it stopped and hesitated far more. Once
it took a turn and we followed it, only to stop again and find that a figure
in brown overalls was outside our window, telling us that this was not the
road at all but the entrance to a garage; and as there appeared to be hundreds
of cars hooting behind, all the traffic of the Great North Road must have
been diverted into his garage entrance for the next half-hour. Sometimes the
fog thinned a trifle, and I remember seeing a vague pricking of red light that
for one second resolved itself into the word *Service*. But service for what or
whom, I never knew. The yellowing thickness closed over us again. Up to
now I had stared, until my eyes ached, either at the faint scribble of a kerb
below or at the jelly-like cabin trunk in front. But I was doing no good.
Whether we stopped or went groaning on into nothing out of nothing, no
staring of mine could help; and so I lit a pipe and huddled down, dismissed
this England that was only blinding vapour for the England that I had already
seen on my journey.

[2]

Southampton to Newcastle, Newcastle to Norwich: memories rose like milk
coming to the boil. I had seen England. I had seen a lot of Englands. How
many? At once, three disengaged themselves from the shifting mass. There
was, first, Old England, the country of the cathedrals and minsters and manor
houses and inns, of Parson and Squire; guide-book and quaint highways and
byways England. We all know this England, which at its best cannot be
improved upon in this world. That is, as a country to lounge about in; for
a tourist who can afford to pay a fairly stiff price for a poorish dinner, an
inconvenient bedroom and lukewarm water in a small brass jug. It has few
luxuries, but nevertheless it is a luxury country. It has long ceased to earn
its own living. I am for scrupulously preserving the most enchanting bits of
it, such as the cathedrals and the colleges and the Cotswolds, and for letting

the rest take its chance. There are people who believe that in some mysterious way we can all return to this Old England; though nothing is said about killing off nine-tenths of our present population, which would have to be the first step. The same people might consider competing in a race at Brooklands with a horse and trap. The chances are about the same. And the right course of conduct, I reflected, was not, unless you happen to be a professional custodian, to go and brood and dream over these almost heart-breaking pieces of natural or architectural loveliness, doing it all at the expense of a lot of poor devils toiling in the muck, but to have an occasional peep at them, thus to steel your determination that sooner or later the rest of English life, even where the muck is now, shall have as good a quality as those things.

Then, I decided, there is the nineteenth-century England, the industrial England of coal, iron, steel, cotton, wool, railways; of thousands of rows of little houses all alike, sham Gothic churches, square-faced chapels, Town Halls, Mechanics' Institutes, mills, foundries, warehouses, refined watering-places, Pier Pavilions, Family and Commercial Hotels, Literary and Philosophical Societies, back-to-back houses, detached villas with monkey-trees, Grill Rooms, railway stations, slag-heaps and 'tips', dock roads, Refreshment Rooms, doss-houses, Unionist or Liberal Clubs, cindery waste ground, mill chimneys, slums, fried-fish shops, public-houses with red blinds, bethels in corrugated iron, good-class drapers' and confectioners' shops, a cynically devastated countryside, sooty dismal little towns, and still sootier grim fortress-like cities. This England makes up the larger part of the Midlands and the North and exists everywhere; but it is not being added to and has no new life poured into it. To the more fortunate people it was not a bad England at all, very solid and comfortable. A great deal of very good literature has come out of it, though most of that literature never accepted it but looked either backward or forward. It provided a good parade ground for tough, enterprising men, who could build their factories in the knowledge that the world was waiting for their products, and who also knew that once they had accumulated a tidy fortune they could slip out of this mucky England of their making into the older, charming one, where their children, well schooled, groomed and finished, were almost indistinguishable, in their various uniforms, pink hunting coats to white ties and shiny pumps, from the old inhabitants, the land-owning aristocrats. But at first you had to be tough. I reminded myself how more than once I had thought that the Victorians liked to weep over their novels and plays, not because they were more sensitive and softer than we are but because they were much tougher and further removed from emotion, so that they needed good strong doses of pathos to move them at all. The less fortunate

THE BACK-SIDE OF BOLTON, 1937   *Humphrey Spender*

classes were very unlucky indeed in that England. They had some sort of security, which is more than many of them have now, but it was a security of monstrously long hours of work, miserable wages, and surroundings in which they lived like black-beetles at the back of a disused kitchen stove. Many of their descendants are still living in those surroundings, but a few people now have the impudence to tell them to be resigned and even thankful there, to toil in humble diligence before their Maker and for His chosen children, the debenture-holders. Whether they were better off in this England than in the one before, the pre-industrial one, is a question that I admitted I could not answer. They all rushed into the towns and the mills as soon as they could, as we know, which suggests that the dear old quaint England they were escaping from could not have been very satisfying. You do not hurry out of Arcadia to work in a factory twelve hours a day for about eighteen-pence. Moreover, why did the population increase so rapidly after the Industrial Revolution? What was it about Merrie England that kept the numbers down?

One thing, I told myself, I was certain of and it was this, that whether the people were better or worse off in this nineteenth-century England, it had done more harm than good to the real enduring England. It had found a green and pleasant land and had left a wilderness of dirty bricks. It had blackened fields, poisoned rivers, ravaged the earth, and sown filth and ugliness with a lavish hand. You cannot make omelettes without breaking eggs, and you cannot become rich by selling the world your coal and iron and cotton goods and chemicals without some dirt and disorder. So much is admitted. But there are far too many eggshells and too few omelettes about this nineteenth-century England. What you see looks like a debauchery of cynical greed. As I thought of some of the places I had seen, Wolverhampton and St. Helens and Bolton and Gateshead and Jarrow and Shotton, I remembered a book I had just read, in which we are told to return as soon as possible to the sturdy Victorian individualism. But for my part I felt like calling back a few of these sturdy individualists simply to rub their noses in the nasty mess they had made. Who gave them leave to turn this island into their ashpit? They may or may not have left us their money, but they have certainly left us their muck. If every penny of that money had been spent on England herself, the balance would still be miles on the wrong side. It is as if the country had devoted a hundred years of its life to keeping gigantic sooty pigs. And the people who were choked by the reek of the sties did not get the bacon. The more I thought about it, the more this period of England's industrial supremacy began to look like a gigantic dirty trick. At one end of this commercial greatness were a lot of half-starved, bleary-eyed children crawling about among machinery and at the other end were the traders getting natives boozed up with bad gin. Cynical greed—*Damn you, I'm all right:* you can see as much written in black letters across half England. Had I not just spent days moving glumly in the shadow of their downstrokes?

The third England, belonged far more to the age itself than to this particular island. America, I supposed, was its real birthplace. This is the England of arterial and by-pass roads, of filling stations and factories that look like exhibition buildings, of giant cinemas and dance-halls and cafés, bungalows with tiny garages, cocktail bars, Woolworths, motor-coaches, wireless, hiking, factory girls looking like actresses, greyhound racing and dirt tracks, swimming pools, and everything given away for cigarette coupons. If the fog had lifted I knew that I should have seen this England all round me at that northern entrance to London, where the smooth wide road passes between miles of semi-detached bungalows, all with their little garages, their wireless sets, their periodicals about film stars, their swimming costumes and tennis rackets and dancing shoes. The fog did not lift for an instant, however; we crawled, stopped, crawled again; and I had ample time to consider carefully this newest England, from my richly confused memory of it. Care is necessary too, for you can easily approve or disapprove of it too hastily. It is, of course, essentially democratic. After a social revolution there would, with any luck, be more and not less of it. You need money in this England, but you do not need much money. It is a large-scale, mass-production job, with cut prices. You could almost accept Woolworths as its symbol. Its cheapness is both its strength and its weakness. It is its strength because being cheap it is accessible; it nearly achieves the famous equality of opportunity. In this England, for the first time in history, Jack and Jill are nearly as good as their master and mistress; they may have always been as good in their own way, but now they are nearly as good in the *same way*. Jack, like his master, is rapidly transported to some place of rather mechanical amusement. Jill beautifies herself exactly as her mistress does. It is an England, at last, without privilege. Years and years ago the democratic and enterprising Blackpool, by declaring that you were all as good as one another so long as you had the necessary sixpence, began all this. Modern England is rapidly Blackpooling itself. Notice how the very modern things, like the films and wireless and sixpenny stores, are absolutely democratic, making no distinction whatever between their patrons: if you are in a position to accept what they give—and very few people are not in that position—then you get neither more nor less than what anybody else gets, just as in the popular restaurants there are no special helpings for favoured patrons but mathematical portions for everybody. There is almost every luxury in this world except the luxury of power or the luxury of privacy.

The young people of this new England do not play chorus in an opera in which their social superiors are the principals; they do not live vicariously, enjoy life at second-hand, by telling one another what a wonderful time the young earl is having or how beautiful Lady Mary looked in her court dress; they get on with their own lives. If they must have heroes and heroines, they choose them themselves, from the ranks of film stars and sportsmen and the like. This may not seem important, but nevertheless it is quite new in English life, where formerly, as we may see from memoirs and old novels, people lived in an elaborate network of relations up and down the social scale, despising or pitying their inferiors, admiring or hating their superiors. You see this still in the country and small towns, but not in this new England, which is as near to a classless society as we have got yet.

Unfortunately, it is a bit too cheap. That is, it is also cheap in the other sense of the term. Too much of it is simply a trumpery imitation of something

not very good even in the original. There is about it a rather depressing monotony. Too much of this life is being stamped on from outside, probably by
astute financial gentlemen, backed by the Press and their publicity services.
You feel that too many of the people in this new England are doing not what
they like but what they have been told they would like. (Here is the American
influence at work.) When I was a boy in Yorkshire the men there who used
to meet and sing part-songs in the upper rooms of taverns (they called themselves Glee Unions) were not being humbugged by any elaborate publicity
scheme on the part of either music publishers or brewers, were not falling
in with any general movement or fashion; they were singing glees over their
beer because they liked to sing glees over their beer; it was their own idea
of the way to spend an evening and they did not care tuppence whether it
was anybody else's idea or not; they drank and yarned and roared away, happy
in the spontaneous expression of themselves. I do not feel that any of the activities in this new England have that spontaneity. Even that push towards the
open which we have now decided to call 'hiking' has something regimented
about it. Most of the work, as we have already seen, is rapidly becoming standardised in this new England, and its leisure is being handed over to standardis-
ation too. It is a cleaner, tidier, healthier, saner world than that of nineteenth-
century industrialism. The difference between the two Englands is well
expressed by the difference between a typical nineteenth-century factory, a
huge dark brick box, and a modern factory, all glass and white tiles and chromium plate. If you remember the old factories at closing time, go and see
the workpeople coming out of one of these new factories. The change is startling. Nevertheless, I cannot rid myself of a suspicion that the old brick boxes
had more solid lumps of character inside them than the new places have. It
is possible that, being a literary man, I attach too much importance to 'character', preferring a dirty diseased eccentric to a lean healthy but rather dull
citizen. Unconsciously I may see people as so much possible raw material for
novels and plays. England of the eighteenth and nineteenth centuries was a
wonderfully rich country for a novelist because it was full of odd characters.
(Like the old Russia. The new Russia, on the other hand, seems to be giving
its novelists a lot of trouble.) I must guard against this, the bias of my trade.
You cannot estimate the life of a people by the wealth of dramatic material
it offers you. We all know that you can make a novel or a play out of an
unhappy marriage, whereas a happy marriage is a tedious theme. Dickens protested violently against the bad conditions of his time, but if he had been born
into a neat clean world, where little boys were never sent to work in blacking
factories, where there were no overworked half-starved clerks crouching like

gnomes in gloomy little offices, he would not have been the grandly fantastic Dickens we know. Probably we authors are busy cutting the ground from under our feet, a not ignoble occupation. After all, the world does not exist simply for creative writers who happen to like strong effects. It is better that people should be leading decent useful contented lives than that they should be asking to be immortalised in their misery. But even after making all allowance for this professional bias, I cannot help feeling that this new England is lacking in character, in zest, gusto, flavour, bite, drive, originality, and that this is a serious weakness. Monotonous but easy work and a liberal supply of cheap luxuries might between them create a set of people entirely without ambition or any real desire to think and act for themselves, the perfect subjects for an iron autocracy.

Then I remembered younger folk here and there, all products of this newest England, and I saw that there is a section of people who have its strength but are untouched by its weakness. I met them all over the country, not many at a time, for there are not enough of them to make a crowd in any one place. There would have been a great many more if the finest members of my own generation had not been slaughtered in the war. Most of these people of course are younger. They are not prigs, though being young and earnest they are inclined at times to be a shade too solemn. They are not saving their souls or going about doing good. But they have a social consciousness; their imagination is not blunted; they know that we are interdependent and that bluffing and cheating are useless. There are several of them, without names, in this book. I usually found them doing a not very pleasant job of work for the benefit of people worse off than themselves. They are good citizens and as yet we have no city worthy of them. Perhaps they are building it themselves now. These people were very nice to me, but I did not always like meeting them. It is not pleasant suddenly seeing yourself as impatient and weak, greedy and egoistical.

Here then were the three Englands I had seen, the Old, the Nineteenth Century and the New; and as I looked back on my journey I saw how these three were variously and most fascinatingly mingled in every part of the country I had visited. It would be possible, though not easy, to make a coloured map of them. There was one already in my mind, bewilderingly coloured and crowded with living people. It made me feel dizzy. I returned to the fog-bound car, which was now crawling and halting in a world of sepia vapour, in which lost cars, making no time at all, hooted their despair. There was nothing I could do.

[3]

My hands and feet were cold, and I thought longingly of the cup of tea that I ought to have been enjoying at home by this time, and would have been enjoying at home if the Thames valley and the London smoke had not been up to their old tricks. We were all very clever people nowadays, I said to myself, but we still allowed the fog to smother us and the 'flu to lay us out. We were brilliant, I decided, only in patches. Our civilisation was rather like the stock comic figure of the professor who knows all about electrons but does not know how to boil an egg or tie his bootlaces. Our knowledge begins anywhere but at home. We would understand anything so long as it did not immediately concern us. Aldebaran or Betelgeuse, I told myself, stood a better chance with us than the North of England. That brought me, sharply, back to the England of the dole. This word dole has two meanings. It means a charitable distribution, especially a rather niggardly one. It also means, or did mean in its archaic use, a man's lot or destiny. We have contrived most artfully to combine these two meanings. As I looked back on it, the England of the dole did not seem to me a pleasant place. We could not be proud of its creation. We could not really afford to be complacent about it, although we often are. It is a poor shuffling job, and one of our worst compromises. When I began to ask myself exactly what was wrong with it, faces and voices from that unhappy world returned to my memory. I saw again the older men who, though they knew they were idle and useless through no fault of their own, felt defeated and somewhat tainted. Their self-respect was shredding away. Their very manhood was going. Even in England, which is no South Sea Island, there are places where a man feels he can do nothing cheerfully, where gay idling is not impossible. But the ironist in charge of our affairs has seen to it that the maximum of unemployment shall be in those very districts that have a tradition of hard work and of very little else. Life on the dole in South Devon, let us say, may be bad enough, but life on the dole on the Tyneside is a great deal worse. I saw these older workless men as a series of personal tragedies. The young men, who have grown up in the shadow of the Labour Exchange, are not so much personal tragedies, I decided, as collectively a national tragedy. I do not believe that people are entirely at the mercy of their environment. Exceptional persons not only refuse to be moulded by their environment but actually set about changing environments themselves. But they have to be exceptional. Average people are largely products of a temporary set of conditions. The atmosphere in which these young unemployed men have grown up is poisoned. It is that of a workaday world

WAITING AT THE CORNER . . . 1936 *Humphrey Spender*

that has no work, of a money-ridden world that has lost its money. They are playboys who cannot really play. Nobody says to them: 'Look here, you have arrived at manhood in a time so bewildering that we don't know where we are. The old rules aren't working. We haven't made any new ones yet. There's a dreadful lag between man the inventor and producer and man the organiser and distributor. We haven't caught up with the machines yet. It's all a transition. The world's going under a new management. The present muddle has put you fellows out, and at the moment you can't settle down to work as your father and grandfather did at your age. Perhaps you never will. Probably we're going to change all our ideas about work. Meanwhile, get on with your lives. There's plenty to do. The town you live in is a disgrace to any civilised community. Clean up the miserable hole. And remember you're not waifs and strays and corner boys, you're citizens of a new world. Keep yourselves in good shape. Learn something worth knowing. This is your chance.' We do not say that, but if we do not mean that, then what do we mean? Are we really saying: 'Here, you nuisances, take this. It isn't much—just enough to keep you alive. A little more or a little less and you'd start kicking. With this you'll be alive but not kicking. And now get out, and let us forget about you.'

I asked myself what this game was that we were playing. It cannot be every man for himself and the devil take the hindmost. It cannot be that or we should not have unemployment and health insurance and old age pensions and the rest, on the one hand and, on the other hand, I should not be paying more than a third of my income away in taxes. These suggest a real corporate life. But it cannot be very real or we should all be showing, roughly, the same kind of face. I remembered then how, just after the Armistice, I had been sent to look after some German prisoners of war. They had a certain look, these prisoners of war, most of whom had been captured two or three years before. It was a strained, greyish, faintly decomposed look. I did not expect to see that kind of face again for a long time; but I was wrong. I had seen a lot of those faces on this journey. They belonged to unemployed men.

I reminded myself firmly that I was no economist, that I had not that sort of mind, moving easily among abstractions. My childlike literary mind always fastens upon concrete details. Thus, when the newspapers tell me that there is yet another financial crisis and that gold is being rushed from one country to another and I see photographs of excited City men jostling and scrambling and of bank porters and sailors carrying boxes of bullion, I always feel that some idiotic game is going on and that it is as preposterous that the welfare of millions of real people should depend on the fortunes of this game as it would be if our happiness hung upon the results of the Stock Exchange golfing tournament. This spectacle of sailors carrying gold seems to me to belong to the pantomime of *Ali Baba and the Forty Thieves;* and not to anything more serious. A fellow literary man, another simpleton, once told me an idea of his for a film, which would show men searching for gold in hellish deserts and among icy peaks, making feverish discoveries, then toiling away mining the precious stuff, until at last, after the most colossal sequences of adventure and slavery, you would see the bars of metal being carefully taken down into the vaults of banks, underground once more. That seemed to me, I remember, an excellent idea, in which I took a possibly childish delight. That is the kind of mind I have, not quite fully adult. On the rare occasions when really grown-up persons, such as economists and bankers and City men, condescend to mention their mysteries to me, I show a lack of comprehension and seriousness that brings a smile to these solemn faces. So I told myself, as I stared at the fog, that even in trying to think about these things, I was foolishly floundering out of my depth. But I risked it. Perhaps the enveloping fog gave me courage. I thought then how this City, which is always referred to with such tremendous respect, which is treated as if it were the very beating red heart of England, must have got its money from somewhere, that it could not have conjured gold out of Threadneedle Street, and that a great deal of this money must have poured into it at one time—and a good long time too—from that part of England which is much dearer to me than the City, namely, the industrial North. For generations this blackened North toiled and moiled so that England should be rich and the City of London be a great power in the world. But now this North is half derelict, and its people, living on in the queer ugly places, are shabby, bewildered, unhappy. And I told myself that I would prefer—if somebody must be miserable—to see the people in the City all shabby, bewildered, unhappy. I was prejudiced, of course; simply because I belong to the North myself, and perhaps too because I like people who make things better than I like people who only deal in money. And then again, I reflected, it is much pleasanter either working or idling in the City, a charming old place, than it is in Bolton or Jarrow or Middlesbrough; so that the people there could stand a little more worry. Perhaps I would not have dragged the City into this meditation at all if I had not always been told, every time the nation made an important move, went on the Gold Standard or went off it, that the City had so ordered it. The City then, I thought, must accept the responsibility. Either it is bossing us about or it isn't. If it is, then it must take the blame if there is any blame to be taken. And there seemed to me a great deal of blame to be taken. What had the City done for its old ally, the industrial North? It seemed to have done what the black-moustached glossy gentleman in the old melodramas always did to the inno-cent village maiden.

It was all very puzzling. Was Jarrow still in England or not? Had we exiled Lancashire and the North-east coast? Were we no longer on speaking terms with cotton weavers and miners and platers and riveters? Why had nothing been done about these decaying towns and their workless people? Was every-body waiting for a miracle to happen? I knew that doles had been given out, Means Tests applied, training places opened, socks and shirts and old books distributed by the Personal Service League and the like; but I was not thinking of feeble gestures of that kind, of the sort of charity you might extend to a drunken old ruffian begging at the back door. I meant something constructive and creative. If Germans had been threatening these towns instead of Want, Disease, Hopelessness, Misery, something would have been done quickly enough. Yet Jarrow and Hebburn looked much worse to me than some of the French towns I saw at the end of the war, towns that had been occupied by the enemy for four years. Why has there been no plan for these areas, these people? The dole is part of no plan; it is a mere declaration of intellectual bankruptcy. You have only to spend a morning in the dole country to see that it is all wrong. Nobody is getting any substantial benefit, any reasonable satisfaction out of it. Nothing is encouraged by it except a shambling dull-eyed poor imitation of life. The Labour Exchanges stink of defeated humanity. The whole thing is unworthy of a great country that in its time has given the world some nobly creative ideas. We ought to be ashamed of ourselves. Anybody who imagines that this is a time for self-congratulation has never poked his nose outside Westminster, the City and Fleet Street. And, I concluded, he has not used his eyes and ears much even in Westminster and Fleet Street.

[4]

Having thus decided that any praise of ourselves at this time was not decent, I immediately changed my own tune, suddenly remembering many things. I had travelled almost the length of the country and had talked to scores of people. True, I had had no talk with the sort of dangerous lunatic who believes that he can bring the Golden Age nearer by derailing express trains and blowing up bridges. But I had listened to almost every other kind of political and social theorist. They had always talked quite freely. They never suddenly looked over their shoulders or suggested that we should whisper in a corner. I had heard people say in a loud cheerful tone that they thought Soviet Russia a much better country than England. I had heard Jews denounce Fascists, and Fascists denounce Jews. I was not met in any town by the local representatives of the secret police. All over the world the shutters are being closed, the blue pencils are being sharpened, the gags and seals and chains and warrants for summary arrest are being brought out. Yet there is some liberty still in England. Milton could be living at this hour. A good many of my fellow-authors who are for ever sneering at liberal democracy have still sense enough to keep within its tolerant boundaries, and do not venture into those admired territories where they would soon find themselves kicked about by uniformed hooligans or shoved into a gaol that knew nothing of *Habeas Corpus*. I know that things happen in England, chiefly behind the scenes. No doubt letters are opened, persons are followed, 'pressure is brought to bear' here and there. I am not fool enough to think that a travelling novelist has seen it all. It is a pity that we spoil a fine record by allowing a few contemptible moves of this kind to be made. We are told—sometimes when one of these dirty little bits of business is being put through—that at all costs we must keep our England, but the England to keep is the England worth keeping, the country of the free and generous temper.

Even people who are supposed to know what intellectual liberty means seem to make a sad hash of applying its standards nowadays. What is protested against as a crushing tyranny in one country is tolerated as a necessity in another. Some of my friends rage against the absence of liberty in Italy and Germany but quite overlook its absence in Russia. We English frequently do not let our imaginations travel as far as India. The Americans who know all about India seem curiously ignorant about what happens in their own states. The Irish, who must have done more talking about freedom than any other people, are now busy putting themselves into prison. Milton would not admire our post-war European statesmen-rulers, for they prefer what he could not praise, that 'fugitive and cloistered virtue, unexercised and unbreathed, that never sallies out and sees her adversary, but slinks out of the race.' There is no race now, and secret police, storm troops and machine-guns are at the competitors' entrance, and the great man has the track to himself and is always busy declaring himself the winner. So far we have been free from this miserable nonsense in England. We can criticise the government without looking over our shoulders. There is no penalty as yet for using your reason. During the course of this journey, I reflected, I had seen a good many fellows standing on boxes at street corners, and nearly all of them were heartily damning the government. They were not always a pleasant spectacle, but I was glad to see them. It meant that England was still out of fashion. I think I should have been even better pleased if I had seen more people listening to them. We shall of course never work up the enormous excitement over comparatively small political issues that there was fifty years ago. I suspect that if there had been more popular amusements, those meetings in Free Trade Halls and the like would not have been so densely packed. Gladstone and Dizzy had not to face the competition of Laurel and Hardy and Clapham and Dwyer. A great proportion of the English electorate is probably becoming less and less politically-minded. (And if being politically-minded only meant taking a passionate interest in House of Commons intrigue, I should not blame them. I never meet members of that House without feeling that they simply belong to a rather amusing, rowdy club in Westminster. I have dined at the same table with prominent Tory and Labour politicians, and found that they had far, far more in common with one another than they had with me, being members of the same club. This is only natural *under the circumstances*. But they do not look very hopeful circumstances.) People are beginning to believe that government is a mysterious process with which they have no real concern. This is the soil in which autocracies flourish and liberty dies. Alongside that apathetic majority there will soon be a minority that is tired of seeing nothing vital happen and that will adopt any cause that promises decisive action. There are signs of this about already. If that majority does not waken up, it may find, too late, that it has taken too many good things in English life for granted.

I could think, and did, of many good things I had found in the course of this journey. For example, the natural kindness and courtesy of the ordinary English people. I have noticed more downright rudeness and selfishness in one night in the stalls of a West End theatre than I have observed for days in the streets of some dirty little manufacturing town, where you would have thought everybody would have been hopelessly brutalised. And how often did I hear some wretched unemployed man and his wife say, 'Ay, but there's lots worse off than us.' What a desperate battle these people fight, especially the brave and stubborn North-country women, to preserve all the little decencies of life! Sometimes I feel like opposing the dictatorship of the proletariat simply because the proletarians I know are too good to be dictators. But then I do not like dictators. I came to the conclusion, however, that I should like to be dictator myself long enough to sweep away once and for all the notion that for the people who do the hard monotonous physical work any dirty little hole is good enough. As I thought of what the nineteenth century has left us in every industrial area, I felt at once angry and ashamed. What right had we to go strutting about, talking of our greatness, when all the time we were living on the proceeds of these muck-heaps? If we lived on some God-forsaken prairie, dusty in summer, frozen in winter, it might not matter, but we have ravished for unjustly distributed profit the most enchanting country-side in the world, out of which lyrics and lovely water-colours have come flowering like the hawthorn. And I saw again, clean through the fog that was imprisoning me, the exquisite hazy green landscape. I remembered the German in my hotel in Italy last year. He had lived and travelled all over the world; and I asked him which country he thought the most beautiful. He told me, England.

I thought about patriotism. I wished I had been born early enough to have been called a Little Englander. It was a term of sneering abuse, but I should be delighted to accept it as a description of myself. That *little* sounds the right note of affection. It is little England I love. And I considered how much I disliked Big Englanders, whom I saw as red-faced, staring, loud-voiced fellows, wanting to go and boss everybody about all over the world, and being surprised and pained and saying, 'Bad show!' if some blighters refused to fag for them. They are patriots to a man. I wish their patriotism began at home, so that they would say—as I believe most of them would, if they only took the trouble to go and look—'Bad show!' to Jarrow and Hebburn. After all, I thought, I am a bit of a patriot too. I shall never be one of those grand cosmopolitan authors who have to do three chapters in a special village in

Southern Spain and then the next three in another special place in the neighbourhood of Vienna. Not until I am safely back in England do I ever feel
that the world is quite sane. (Though I am not always sure even then.) Never
once have I arrived in a foreign country and cried, 'This is the place for me.'
I would rather spend a holiday in Tuscany than in the Black Country, but
if I were compelled to chose between living in West Bromwich or Florence,
I should make straight for West Bromwich. One of my small daughters, bewildered, once said to us: 'But French people aren't *true*, are they?' I knew exactly
how she felt. It is incredible that all this foreign-ness should be true. I am
probably bursting with blatant patriotism. It does not prevent me from behav-
ing to foreigners as if they felt perfectly real to themselves, as I suspect they
do, just like us. And my patriotism, I assured myself, does begin at home.
There is a lot of pride in it. Ours is a country that has given the world something
more than millions of yards of calico and thousands of steam engines. If we
are a nation of shopkeepers, then what a shop! There is Shakespeare in the
window, to begin with; and the whole establishment is blazing with geniuses.
Why, these little countries of ours have known so many great men and great
ideas that one's mind is dazzled by their riches. We stagger beneath our inheri-
tance. But let us burn every book, tear down every memorial, turn every cathedral and college into an engineering shop, rather than grow cold and petrify,
rather than forget that inner glowing tradition of the English spirit. Make
it, if you like, a matter of pride. Let us be too proud, my mind shouted, to
refuse shelter to exiled foreigners, too proud to do dirty little tricks because
other people can stoop to them, too proud to lose an inch of our freedom,
too proud, even if it beggars us, to tolerate social injustice here, too proud
to suffer anywhere in this country an ugly mean way of living. We have led
the world, many a time before to-day, on good expeditions and bad ones,
on piratical raids and on quests for the Hesperides. We can lead it again. We
headed the procession when it took what we see now to be the wrong turning,
down into the dark bog of greedy industrialism, where money and machines
are of more importance than men and women. It is for us to find the way
out again, into the sunlight. We may have to risk a great deal, perhaps our
very existence. But rather than live on meanly and savagely, I concluded, it
would be better to perish as the last of the civilised peoples.

Warmed a little by my peroration, I noticed that a lamp was cutting the
fog away from a charming white gate. Doors were opened. Even the very fire-
light was familiar. I was home.

Notes on the Illustrations

Frontispiece. Six-Foot Road, Netherton, Dudley, c.1930. *Photographer Unknown.* Dudley Libraries, Local History Department. The name of the road precisely described its width. The area was demolished in 1956.

Page 8   The Great West Road, 1933. *Topical Press.* BBC Hulton Picture Library. The photograph was taken at Boston Manor Road.

11   The Factory Face of the 'Thirties, 1933. *Herbert Felton.* National Monuments Record. The Pyrene factory was built in 1930 in the Great West Road.

16   High Street, Southampton, c.1935. *Photographer Unknown.* Southampton University Library, Cope Collection. A view from the top of the Bargate, looking south. Almost all this street was flattened by air raids during the Second World War.

19   The *Aquitania* off the Royal Pier, 1935. *Ruskin Graphics.* Southampton University Library, Cope Collection.

20   The *Mauretania's* Last Voyage, 1934. *Ruskin Graphics.* Southampton University Library, Cope Collection.

25   Salisbury Cathedral, 1935. *A. F. Kersting.*

28   The Chatterton Memorial, 1935. *Reece Winstone.* Erected beside St. Mary Redcliffe (in unconsecrated ground) about 1840, the statue was demolished in the late 1960s and replaced with a plaque inside the church.

31   Bristol Sherry in Transit, 1938. *Reece Winstone.*

35   The Swan Inn, Mary-le-Port Street, 1934. *Reece Winstone.* Built in 1434, this building was demolished in 1936 to make way for a shoe shop.

37   The City Docks, Bristol, seen from the site of the future Redcliffe Bridge, 1935. *Reece Winstone.*

38   College Green, 1934. *Reece Winstone.* The raised College Green and the 1850 High Cross have now been replaced by a new Council House.

40   Lower Slaughter, Glos., c.1931. *G. F. Allen.* J. Allan Cash Photo Library.

Page 43   The Wool Hall, Chipping Campden, c.1940. *E. W. Tattersall*. J. Allan Cash Photo Library.

48   Snowshill Manor, Glos., c.1930. *Photographer Unknown*. National Trust. This is the manor house described, but not named, in the book, pp. 48–52

51   Snowshill's Owner, c.1930. *Photographer Unknown*. National Trust. The late Charles Paget Wade, whose name is not mentioned in the book, took possession of Snowshill Manor in 1919, restored the house and formed there his museum of bygones and his model village. He gave Snowshill to the National Trust in 1951, and it is now open to the public.

55   The Cathedral Church of St. Michael, Coventry, c.1933. *Photographer Unknown*. City of Coventry Archives. Almost all of this building was destroyed by an air-raid in November 1940.

56   Bablake Hospital, Coventry, 1937. *Sir John Summerson*. National Monuments Record.

59   Butcher Row, Coventry, c.1933. *F. Smyth*. City of Coventry Archives.

60   Assembling Daimler Cars, c.1933. *Photographer Unknown*. Jaguar Cars.

71   Victoria Square, Birmingham, at night, 1931. *George Bott*. John Whybrow Collection.

74   Witherford Way, Bournville, 1933. *Roy Dixon*. Bournville Village Trust.

76   Decorating Easter Eggs, c.1930. *Photographer Unknown*. Cadbury Ltd.

84   Tramscape, Corporation Street, Birmingham, c.1930. *H. J. Whitlock*. John Whybrow Collection.

86   Gas Works, Tipton, c.1931. *Photographer Unknown*. Black Country Society. The Mond gas works is probably the one which the author saw in the distance from Dudley Castle.

88   Phoenix Passage, Dudley, c.1930. *Photographer Unknown*. Archives and Local History Department, Dudley Libraries. Phoenix Passage was demolished under a slum clearance order in 1935.

90   Black Country Vista, c.1934. *Photographer Unknown*. Black Country Society. The street is Brick Kiln Street, Tipton.

96   'Good Companion' Portables, 1936. *Photographer Unknown*. Imperial Business Equipment, Ltd. The 'Good Companion' portable came into manufacture in July 1932, a year before the author's visit to Leicester.

Page 107 Harry Hughes' Boxing Booth, Goose Fair, c.1930. *Photographer Unknown*. Local Studies Library, Nottingham County Library.

108 Goose Fair at Night, c. 1930. *Photographer Unknown*. Local Studies Library, Nottingham County Library.

111 Notts Forest v. Notts County, 1931. *Nottingham Guardian* photograph.

113 Goose Fair Helter-Skelter, 1933. *Photographer Unknown*. Local Studies Library, Nottingham County Library.

116 Chesterfield, the Twisted Spire, 1935. *Reece Winstone*.

119 Dry-Walling near Haworth, c.1937. *E. W. Tattersall*. J. Allan Cash Photo Library.

122 Wool Room at Drummond's Mill, c.1930. *Photographer Unknown*. Stroud Riley Drummond Group.

134 Kilnsey Crag, Wharfedale, 1935. *W. A. Poucher*.

137 A Corner of Kettlewell, 1933, *Walter Scott, Bradford*.

138 Hubberholme c.1937. *E. W. Tattersall*. J. Allan Cash Photo Library.

141 Grassington Square, 1933. *Walter Scott, Bradford*

147 Halifax Townscape, 1936. *Bill Brandt*.

159 Market Street, Bradford, 1930. *Walter Scott, Bradford*.

163 Bottle Kilns at Etruria, c.1935. *Harold White*. Wedgwood Museum, Barlaston.

166 The Art of Throwing, c.1934. *Photographer Unknown*. Wedgwood Museum, Barlaston.

169 Turning and Decorating, c.1934. *Photographer Unknown*. Wedgwood Museum, Barlaston. The craftsman is at work on the original engine turning lathe introduced by Josiah Wedgwood in 1763.

171 Oven-Firing at Etruria, c.1934. *Photographer Unknown*. Wedgwood Museum, Barlaston.

176 Etruria, c.1931. *Harold White*. Wedgwood Museum, Barlaston. The Etruria factory was built for Josiah Wedgwood, 1768–69.

Page 181   Pitt Street, Liverpool, 1937. *L. J. D'Andria.* Liverpool City Library. A view of the east side of Pitt Street from Dickenson Street, taken by the Roman Catholic priest at St. Peter's in Seel Street, who was possibly the priest who showed the author round Liverpool's Chinese quarter in 1933.

183   Liverpool's Chinatown, Pitt Street, 1937. *H. A. Smith. Liverpool Daily Post* photograph.

185   Salthouse Dock by Night, c.1933. *S. Charles Dietterle. Liverpool Daily Post* photograph.

188   Repairing Nets in Canning Dock, 1936. *J. E. Marsh.* Liverpool City Library.

195   Palace Theatre, Manchester, 1938. *Photographer Unknown.* Manchester City Library.

197   Lancashire Funeral, 1937. *Humphrey Spender.*

198   Washday, Bolton, 1937. *Humphrey Spender.*

201   No Frivolity on the Pier, 1937. *Humphrey Spender.*

205   Blackpool Lit-up, 1937. *Humphrey Spender.*

211   Lancashire Mill-Girl, 1937. *Humphrey Spender.* She is adding lead weights to harness cords for a Jacquard machine.

216   Collapse of the Cotton Trade, 1932. *T. C. Egan.* Lancashire Library, Blackburn District. The chimney being felled is that of the Duke Street mill, Blackburn.

221   Train Leaving Newcastle, 1936. *Bill Brandt.*

231   'Butterfly of the Back Streets', 1936. *Edwin Smith.*

232   Idle by the Quay Side, 1936. *Humphrey Spender.*

235   Domestic Study, Gateshead, 1936. *Edwin Smith.*

236   Ladies of North Shields, 1936. *Edwin Smith.*

239   Keeping up Standards in Jarrow, 1936. *Bill Brandt.*

243   Waiting—for What?, 1936. *Humphrey Spender.*

Page 247   East Durham Landscape, 1936. *Bill Brandt.*

250   Out of the Cage, 1936. *Edwin Smith.*

253   Home from the Pit, 1936. *Bill Brandt.*

255   Pithead Conversation Piece, 1936. *Edwin Smith.*

256   Searching for Coal, East Durham, 1936. *Bill Brandt.*

261   Pitmen's Sunday Morning, 1936. *Edwin Smith.*

262   Beverley Minster, 1938. *Val Doone.* BBC Hulton Picture Library.

266   Hull Herring Drifter, 1935. *Hull Daily Mail* photograph.

271   Fish in St. Andrew's Dock, c.1935. *Hull Daily Mail* photograph.

273   The Jew's House, Lincoln, 1938. *A. F. Kersting.*

274   Lincoln Cathedral, West Front, 1938. *A. F. Kersting.*

279   The Boston Stump, St. Botolph's, c.1938. *Herbert Felton.* National Monuments Record.

284   Tombland Alley, Norwich, 1938. *A. F. Kersting.*

287   An East Anglian, 1934. *Humphrey Spender.*

294   Elm Hill, Norwich, 1938. *A. F. Kersting.*

299   The Back-side of Bolton, 1937. *Humphrey Spender.*

305   Waiting at the Corner . . ., 1936. *Humphrey Spender.*

Front Endpaper. Hubberholme Church and George Inn, 1933. *Walter Scott, Bradford*

Back Endpaper. Colliery Country, 1936. *Edwin Smith.*

The photographs by Humphrey Spender reproduced on pages 197, 198, 201 and 205 first appeared in his book *Worktown People*, published in 1982 by the Falling Wall Press. The copyright is vested in the photographer in association with the Mass-Observation Archive.

EDITOR'S AFTERWORD

The decision having been made to illustrate this book with photographs taken during the decade in which it was written, my problem was not merely to find appropriate photographs but also to establish the dates when they were taken. Many of the photographers of the 'thirties had died, and it is surprising how few of them had recorded the precise dates when their work was done.

Fortunately two of the outstanding photographers of the period, Bill Brandt and Humphrey Spender, are still with us, and, as it happened, much of their early work was done in Lancashire and the North-East under the immediate stimulus of the publication of Mr Priestley's book. Another, the late Edwin Smith, happened to develop his special skills as a visual historian on Tyneside in the mid-'thirties, and he always meticulously recorded the dates of his photographs. The archive of his magnificent work has been scrupulously preserved and made available for research by his widow.

A fourth photographer of the period, still active, is Reece Winstone, not only a photographer of exceptional talent but a man who has visually recorded and dated the social and architectural history of his native Bristol throughout the past fifty years.

For the rest, I visited almost all the places on Mr Priestley's itinerary and relied largely on the help given to me by public librarians, custodians of museums, and the picture libraries of local newspapers. The resources available, however, were slightly limited by the fact that the 'thirties are not quite far enough away to be regarded as history, and photographs of that decade are not yet considered to be as picturesque, amusing and collectable as those of, say, the Edwardian period. However, I found sufficient visual treasure trove, especially in the Black Country, Liverpool and the Wedgwood Museum at Barlaston.

One of the most delightful rewards of my investigations was the identification of the unnamed Cotswold manor house and its eccentric owner, described on pages 48 to 52 of this book, whose names the author himself had completely forgotten.

In addition to the photographers and picture libraries mentioned in the notes above I have been helped in the search for illustrations by Mrs. Atkins of the Dudley Leisure and Recreation Services; Mr. G. Philip Brown, of the East Yorkshire Local History Society; Mr. Stephen Croad, of the National Monuments Record; Mr. Howard Davis, of the *Liverpool Post and Echo*; Miss Naomi Evetts, of the Liverpool Record Office; Mr. Ted Gower; Mr. G. Hampson, of the Southampton University Library; Sir Tom Hopkinson; Mr. A. J. Mealey, of Coventry City Library; Mrs. Lynn Miller, of the Wedgwood Museum; Miss E. M. Willmott, of the Bradford Central Library; Mr. William Mitchell, of the Dalesman Publishing Company; Mr. W. Muirhead of the Bournville Village Trust; Miss Dorothy Ritchie, of the Nottingham County Library; Mr. M. Shepley, of the *Hull Daily Mail*; Sir John Summerson; Mr. David Verey; Mr. E. J. D. Warrilow; Mr. John Whybrow; and Mr. David Whyley, of the Black Country Society.

I am also grateful to my friends, John and Griselda Lewis, for guidance in the selection of illustrations and advice on the design and make-up of the book.

JOHN HADFIELD

Index to Names and Places

Adelphi Hotel, Liverpool, 178
Aquitania, 19, 312
Armstrong, William, 177
Austen, Jane, 26

Baildon, 140
Bablake Hospital, Coventry, 56, 57, 313
Bargate, Southampton, 16, 17
Barmby Moor, 263
Barnaby Rudge (Dickens), 283
Barnsley, 119, 120
Baskerville, John, 69
Bath, 26
Bennett, Arnold, 160–165
Bennett, Constance, 93, 282
Bensham Grove Settlement, 229, 230
Bentley, Phyllis, 146
Berengaria, 17
Beverley, 262–264, 316
Birkenhead, 178
Birmingham, 13, 15, 64–84
Birmingham Art Gallery, 66–68
Bishop Burton, 263
Black Country, 85–90
Blackburn, 204–217, 315
Blackpool, 10, 198–204, 301, 315
Blubberhouses, 139
Bolton, 198, 299, 300, 307, 315, 316
Bolton Woods, 135
Bonington, R. P., 67
Boot's, Chemists, 103
Borrow, George, 290
Boston, 277–282, 316
Boston Stump, 278–279
Boulton, Matthew, 65
Bournville, 72–80, 313
Bourton-on-the-Water, 39
Bradford, 26, 120–159
Bradford-on-Avon, 26
Breughel, 117

Brighton, 201
Bristol, 23–38
Broadway, 47
Brown, Ford Madox, 67
Browne, Sir Thomas, 290
Buckden, 136
Bunyan, John, 92
Burford, 39, 41
Burne-Jones, Sir E., 67
Burns, Charlie, 129
Burnsall, 135
Burslem, 160
Bury St. Edmunds, 295, 296
Butcher Row, Coventry, 57, 59, 313

Cadbury Bros., 72–80, 313
California, 9
Camberley, 10, 12
Cambridge, 27, 295, 296
Camden Town, 296
Canning Dock, Liverpool, 188, 315
Canterbury, 12, 27
Chamberlain family, 65
Chatterton, T., 27, 28, 312
Chesterfield, 116, 118, 314
Chipping Campden, 42–45, 260, 313
Cirencester, 43
'City, The', 217, 306, 307, 308
Civic Theatre, Bradford, 154–156
Clifton, 29, 33
Coketown, 85
Colchester, 295, 296
Coleridge, 27
Collings, Jesse, 32
Collins, Wilkie, 272
Colmore Row, Birmingham, 65, 68, 71
Community House, Blackburn, 214
Constable, John, 25
Corporation Street, Birmingham, 68, 84
Cook, Thomas, 92

Cotman, J. S., 67
Cotswolds, 39–54
Coventry, 55–63
Cowes, 23, 24
Cox, David, 67

Daimler Cars, 58–62, 313
Darlington, 218, 219
Darwin, Erasmus, 65
David Lewis Club and Hostel, 186, 187
de Montfort, Simon, 91, 234
de Morgan, William, 175
De Wint, P., 67, 68
Dickens, C., 207, 283
Dovers Hill, 54
Drummond's Mill, 122, 314
Dudley, 85–88, 313

Earlham, 290
East Durham, 244–261, 316
Edwin Drood (Dickens), 283
Eliot, T. S., 234
Ellis, Irving, 129
Elm Hill, Norwich, 294, 316
Empress of Britain, 17
Etruria, 163, 170–176, 314, 315
Evesham, 43

Farringford, 23
Fenton, 160
Fields, Gracie, 191
Fleetwood, 200
Ford's Hospital, Coventry, 57
Fry's chocolate, 29

Gandhi, 209
Gateshead, 219, 228–235, 242, 243, 300, 315
Girtin, T., 67
Gloucester, 43
Goose Fair (Nottingham), 104–109, 111–15, 314
Gornal, 89
Grassington, 135, 140, 141, 153, 314

Great North Road, 296, 297
Great West Road, 8–11, 312
Grevel, William, 44
Griggs, F. L., 44
Grimsby, 269

Hakluyt, R., 27
Halifax, 131, 146, 147, 314
Hallé Orchestra, 190
Hall of Memory,
    Birmingham, 69
Hampshire, 14, 17, 24
Hanley, 160
Harrogate, 139, 140, 153
Harry Hughes' Boxing
    Booth, 107, 314
Harvey's Sherry, 29, 31, 312
Hawes, 136
Haworth, 119, 314
Hebburn, 238, 242, 307, 310
Herschel, Sir William, 65
Highgate Village, 295
Holland, Lincs, 277
Hubberholme, 138, 314
Huddersfield, 120
Hull, 264–272

Ilkley, 135, 140, 153
Imperial Typewriter Co.,
    94–97, 313
Independent Labour Party,
    124
Ipswich, 295, 296
Irving, Sir H., 153
Isle of Wight, 23–24

Jacobs, W. W., 267
Jarrow, 237–239, 300, 307,
    310, 315
Jesmond Dene, 219
Jew's House, Lincoln, 277,
    316
Jowitt, Miss, 246–248

Keighley, 87, 131
Kesteven, 277
Kettlewell, 136, 137, 314
Kilnsey Crag, 134, 314
King George Dock, Hull,
    265
King Lear (Shakespeare), 91
King's Lynn, 282

Lady Godiva, 57, 58
Langstrothdale, 136
Leeds, 145, 146

Leicester, 91–102
Lenin, 125
Lewis, David, Club and
    Hostel, 186
Lincoln, 272–277, 316
Lincoln Cathedral, 274,
    275, 316
Liverpool, 177–189
Liverpool Cathedral, 178
Longton, 160
Lubbock, Percy, 290
Luddenden Foot, 106

Macleay, Mr., 178
Maddermarket Theatre, 293
Maid's Head, Norwich, 283,
    291
Manchester, 190–199
Manchester City Art
    Gallery, 192
Manchester Guardian, 190
Margate, 200
Market Harborough, 91
Market Hall, Hull, 269
Market Street, Bradford,
    159, 234, 314
Mary Rose (Barrie), 33
Marx, 125
Mazzini, 125
Maugham, W. S., 281
Mauretania, 20, 237, 312
Menston, 140
Middlesbrough, 121, 307
Midland Hotel,
    Manchester, 192, 196
Monck, Nugent, 293
More, Hannah, 27
Morris Works, 63
Muirhead, Blue Guide to
    England, 9

National Trust, 54
Nelson, 87
Netherton, 312
New Forest, 17, 24
Newcastle-on-Tyne, 13, 15,
    219, 221, 228, 315
Newmarket, 295, 296
New Street, Birmingham, 68
Nikisch, 153
North Shields, 233, 236, 315
Norwich, 283–294
Nottingham, 102–115
Notts Forest v. Notts
    County Football Match,
    109–111, 314

Oakroyd, Jess, 151
Oldbury, 85
Osbaldeston, John, 207
Osborne, 23
Otley, 140
Oxford, 27
Oxford Book of English
    Prose, 9

Palace Theatre,
    Manchester, 192–195, 315
Palace Yard, Coventry, 57
Parr, Samuel, 65
Paradise Street,
    Birmingham, 69
People's Theatre
    (Newcastle), 223–225
Pitt Street, Liverpool,
    181–184, 315
Player's Tobacco Co., 103
Playhouse, Liverpool, 177
Portland Bill, 19
Potteries, The, 155–174
Pre-Raphaelites, 67
Preston, 198, 199
Priestley, Joseph, 65
Prince's Dock, Hull, 265,
    266
Pyrene Factory, 11, 312

Quebec, 15

Raleigh Cycle Co., 103
Reade, Charles, 272
Richter, 153, 190
Ripon, 219
Rochdale, 87
Rodney Street, Liverpool,
    178
Romsey, 24
Royston, 296
Rugeley, 89
Russia, 302, 309
Ryde, 23

St. Andrew's Docks, Hull,
    269, 271, 316
St. George's Hall, Bradford,
    153
St. Helens, 30
St. James's Hall, Newcastle,
    222
St. Mary's Hall, Coventry, 57
St. Michael's Cathedral
    Church, Coventry, 55,
    313

Salisbury, 24, 25
Salthouse Dock, Liverpool, 185, 315
Savage, R., 27
Schillerverein Club, Bradford, 124
School for Scandal, The, Sheridan, 293
Seaham Harbour, 245, 246
Shakespeare, W., 46, 91, 118
Shallow, Justice, 46
Shaw, Bernard, 10, 151
Sheffield, 118, 119
Shelf, 120
Sheridan, R. B., 26, 293
Sherwood Foresters, 53
Shotton, 258–261, 300
Silver Box, The (Galsworthy), 155
Slakeby, 237
Slaughter, Lower and Upper, 39, 40, 312
Slender, 46
Smethwick, 85
Snowshill Manor, 48–52, 312
Southampton, 1–22, 312
South Devon, 304
South Shields, 235, 237
Sowerby Bridge, 146
Stafford, 89

Stamp and Beaver's *Geographic and Economic Survey*, 9
Stoke-on-Trent, 160–176
Sunderland, 208

Teesdale, 244
Temple Meads Station, Bristol, 27
Tennyson, Lord, 23, 58
Theatre Royal, Bradford, 153
Thetford, 296
Thornton, 146
Tipton, 86, 313
Tombland, Norwich, 283, 284, 316
Tomlinson, H. M., 153
Thompson, T., 208
Tunstall, 160
Turner, J. M. W., 67
Tynemouth, 219
Tyneside, 218–243, 304

Varley, J., 67
Venture, 240, 241
Victoria Square, Birmingham, 66, 71, 313
Vimy Ridge, 132

Wade, Charles Paget, 49–51, 313

Waddington, Herbert, 129
Walsall, 87
Wallsend, 233, 237
Watt, James, 65
Weardale, 244
Wedgwood, Josiah, 65, 169
Wedgwood's pottery works, 170–176, 314
Wednesbury, 87
Wednesfield, 87
Wells, H. G., 106
Wensleydale, 133–135
West Bromwich, 89–90, 311
West Riding, 10, 118–159
Wharfedale, 133–139
Whitman, Walt, 140
Willenhall, 87
Wills family, 34
Winchester, 15, 16
Withens, 106, 147
Witney, 42
Wolfe, Humbert, 124
Wolsey, Cardinal, 91
Wolsey Company, 99–102
Wolverhampton, 87, 300
Wonder Hero (Priestley), 237
Woodstock, 280
Wuthering Heights, 124

Yarmouth, 200
York, 27, 262